The
HARLEY-DAVIDSON
Century

Edited by Darwin Holmstrom

MBI Publishing Company

First published in 2002 by MBI Publishing Company, Galtier Plaza,
Suite 200, 380 Jackson Street, St. Paul, MN 55101-3885 USA

The information in this book is true and complete to the best of our
knowledge. All recommendations are made without any guarantee on the
part of the author or Publisher, who also disclaim any liability incurred in
connection with the use of this data or specific details.

We recognize that some words, model names and designations,
for example, mentioned herein are the property of the trademark holder.
We use them for identification purposes only. This is not
an official publication.

MBI Publishing Company books are also available at discounts in bulk
quantity for industrial or sales-promotional use. For details write to Special
Sales Manager at Motorbooks International Wholesalers & Distributors,
Galtier Plaza, Suite 200, 380 Jackson Street,
St. Paul, MN 55101-3885 USA.

Library of Congress Cataloging-in-Publication Data Available

ISBN 0-7603-1155-2

Edited by Darwin Holmstrom

Designed by Tom Heffron

Printed in Hong Kong

Contents

THE *A PRIORI* MOTORCYCLE

By Darwin Holmstrom

"We have in our minds an a priori motorcycle which has continuity in time and space."

—Robert M. Pirsig,
Zen and the Art of Motorcycle Maintenance

When most people close their eyes and imagine a motorcycle, chances are that motorcycle looks very much like a Harley-Davidson. That happens not just because Harleys are the most popular bikes in America, or because the H-D marketing folks are geniuses at what they do. That happens because Harley-Davidson builds the archetypal motorcycle, the mythic bike that exists beyond the input provided by our traditional senses.

The philosopher Kant called such mythic archetypes *a priori* knowledge, knowledge we can't learn, but only intuit. This knowledge speaks to us in feeling, not words, just like Harley-Davidson motorcycles. The Motor Company builds motorcycles that look the way the primordial biker inside each of us feels motorcycles should look.

When I close my eyes, my inner biker flashes an image of a 1965 XLCH Sportster through my mind, and damned if I don't lust after a mid-1960s XLCH Sportster. This desire makes little sense from any logical standpoint, and people often try to talk me out of buying such a beast. They regale me with cautionary tales of magneto ignitions gone awry. They fill my head with horror stories of the shattered ankles that can result from poorly timed kick starts. They warn me of rear cylinders blown apart so hard that shrapnel explodes from the cases with enough force to lacerate the toughest engineer's boot.

In truth, a 1965 XLCH Sportster would not meet my present needs very well. I use a motorcycle for three primary purposes: commuting, touring, and sport riding. For commuting, a modern Evolution Sportster would prove much more practical than a temperamental classic like the XLCH. For touring I'd be better off with any version of the Twin Cam Electra Glide. And for spirited riding I tend to prefer high-performance sportbikes like the motorcycles Erik Buell builds, bikes capable of arcing through corners at three times the posted speed limit. All these motorcycles would be more logical choices than a mid-1960s Sportster, but when I close my eyes,

it is not the latest Buell XB9R Firebolt, Electra Glide Ultra Classic, or even current Sportster that pops up on my internal radar. It's a 1965 XLCH.

There is, I think, a reason Harley-Davidson motorcycles define the very word *motorcycle* for so many people. The primordial biker inside of us doesn't think about things like torsional stiffness, mass centralization, or maximum power-to-weight ratios. The primordial biker thinks about motorcycles at a much more elemental level. And what could be more elemental than a Harley-Davidson motorcycle? A big, powerful engine (V-twin, of course), a couple of wheels, a place to put some fuel, a place to sit, a simple frame to tie it all together: You put those basic pieces together, you come up with a Sportster. What more do you need?

We all receive slightly different mythic input on what constitutes the archetypal motorcycle. Peter Egan's inner biker may tell him the XLCR Café Racer is the *a priori* motorcycle. Mike Seate might picture the elemental choppers built by Jesse James and Bill Dodge at West Coast Choppers. Allan Girdler may envision an XR750 dirt tracker, and Greg Field would almost certainly conjure up a 1936 Knucklehead. Others may see a Heritage Softail, a Road King, or a Dyna Wide Glide as displaying the essence of the motorcycle. They may even consider the current XL 883 Sportster the *a priori* motorcycle, and when you think of it, that makes good sense. There's not a whole heap of difference between the current 883 and the 1965 XLCH Sportster that defines the notion of *motorcycle* deep within my own reptilian brain stem.

Perhaps therein lies the reason that Harley-Davidson motorcycles continue to dominate our very perceptions of what a motorcycle is—they have a continuity in time and space that locates us. That continuity anchors us, provides some stability in this ever-changing, chaotic world. That continuity is, after all, what Robert M. Pirsig described as the very definition of the *a priori* motorcycle.

Behold: the *a priori* motorcycle.

MORE THAN A MACHINE

By Brock Yates

At some weird moment in the late 1980s every hotshot 40-year-old advertising executive, stockbroker, and upwardly mobile professional in America woke up and decided the one thing he needed in his life was a Harley-Davidson. Here was this collection of straights suddenly trading their three-piece Armanis and their Guccis for black leather jackets and motorcycles so down-scale, so déclassé, so hokey that two years earlier they would have sooner hung a velvet Elvis or a cornball Thomas Kincaid original in their living rooms than own a goober bike like a Harley.

What the hell was going on here? What was it about this particular motorcycle that almost overnight made it the darling of the boy-boomers and an unprecedented sales bonanza? How come a machine best known for oil leaks, roadside breakdowns, and an exhaust note better suited to a flathead Ford with a blown head gasket suddenly rivaled Lamborghinis in terms of raw status? How could a company stuck in the backwater, beer-swilling burg of Milwaukee only a few hours shy of bankruptcy turn itself around by making a machine essentially unchanged for almost the entire twentieth century?

As we plunge into the uncertain waters of the new millennium, nobody has a really sensible answer as to why the Harley-Davidson Motor Company has transformed itself from the manufacturer of bad mechanical jokes with all the cache of chain saws into one of the most respected businesses in America. Yes, the firm has excellent management and brilliant marketing. Yes, within the past few years Harley-Davidson has vastly improved its product line in terms of quality and reliability. Yes, Harley-Davidsons are legitimate motorcycles, although techno-snobs will still tell you that the high-revving crotch-rockets from Japan make Harleys look like flintlocks in an arsenal of M16s.

So what makes a Harley so desirable that an otherwise rational man will consider bagging his wife, burning down his big house in the suburbs for the insurance money, and bailing out for the open road in a cloud of smoke and rubber dust? And if that is the fantasy, why pick some aged, two-wheeled V-twin throwback that, compared to the best in the world, is too heavy, too slow, too fat, too lumpy, too noisy, and too cumbersome to keep up?

Why indeed? If the Harley is so out to lunch, why have the same Japanese trendsetters been forced to build their own faux Harleys? These feeble counterfeits of the great American icon are better at everything except *being* a Harley-Davidson—the one elemental factor in a core mystique so powerful that only a few brands, such as Rolex, Ferrari, Cartier, Louis Vuitton, and Hermes, rival it worldwide.

While American movie stars, Disney, and Coca-Cola are headliner Yankee products, surveys indicate that when foreigners think of America, they identify products like Stetson hats, Jack Daniel's whiskey, Gibson guitars, and Harley-Davidson motorcycles as the real thing, the heart and soul representatives of the good old USA.

When the brothers Davidson teamed with boyhood pal Bill Harley to create a motorcycle a century ago, producing a worldwide legend was hardly in their business plan. Making a utilitarian machine that would rival the new automobile as a form of cheap, reliable transportation for the average working man was their mission. No hot-rod superbikes, no side-ways-by-the-silo stunt riding, no exhaust blast that unto itself would reach immortality. None of this. Just a simple, pillar-to-post, no frills motorcycle that started every morning and ran until the cows came home.

The crazy, zig-zag growth of Harley-Davidson over the last 100 years makes no sense. From its modest origins in a Milwaukee backyard to its brutal wars with archrivals Indian and Excelsior in the 1920s and 1930s, to its Mad Max reputation in the 1950s and 1960s, to its descent toward oblivion in the 1970s, and its amazing rebirth a decade later, this is the stuff of legend.

How this humpty old motorcycle became the baddest, most fearsome, most ominous machine on the face of the earth is basically an accident. One sunny day in the summer of 1947 in a dust bowl burg in northern California changed it all. There, in little Hollister on the Fourth of July, a small riot involving maybe 200 hard-riding World War II veterans triggered the legend. The Hollister fracas (particularly a single posed photograph from the incident that appeared in *Life* magazine) inspired a short story in *Harpers* magazine and the movie *The Wild One*.

Concurrent with Hollister came the biker gangs from the smokestack towns of California and the Beat movement that would transmogrify into the Hippie screwiness of the 1960's. Drive-in biker movies and Hunter S. Thompson's brilliant, timeless book, *Hells Angels: A Strange and Terrible Saga* set the Harley myth in stone. Other motorcycles, domestic and imported, were at the time embraced by the biker clubs, but the Harley, with its customized chopper setups that caused overt hatred within the Motor Company, became the centerpiece of the movement. The image of the chopped Harley fried into the brains of the American public when Peter Fonda and Dennis Hopper rode choppers in the drug-fogged 1969 epic, *Easy Rider*.

Now over 30 years later, Harley-Davidson is big-time. Its common stock is prized, its management celebrated, and its products compared with the best on earth. The grease-stained, tattooed loyalists who, like it or not, created the entire gritty hell-raiser image, have been displaced. They can't afford $20,000 Harleys. The new breed of owners can hire specialty firms to transport their shiny new V-Rods in 18-wheelers to annual blowouts at Sturgis or Daytona Beach. There they suit up in leather, paste on tattoos, and fake it as real-guy, working class biker grunts for the weekend.

The Harley-Davidson motorcycle has long since ceased to be a simple two-wheeled transportation device and devolved into a social statement. It is hardly coincidental that the Harley is the motorcycle *dujour* of all outlaw biker clubs around the world. Nor is it coincidental that the new

breed of yuppie riders employ Harleys as a kind of dramatic device to demonstrate their manliness (or in the case of woman riders, their classic femaleness). Sociologists have observed that riding a Harley is a form of street theater wherein the rider role-plays as a modern-day outlaw, substituting his flame-belching two-wheeler for a bucking bronco. There is no question that part of the joy of Harley ownership is the inclusion in a loose fraternity of self-styled rebels.

Prescient Harley-Davidson executives identified this mindset as a marketing advantage in the 1970s and answered the call by providing protest models like the Super-Glide, the Low Rider, and the Wide Glide. Family design genius "Willy G." Davidson was a leader in pegging the outlaw riders and the outcasts as the bedrock of Harley-Davidson enthusiasm, and he led his family company into embracing the bad-boy image. Black and orange, first used by the factory racing team, became the theme colors, along with unabashed jingoism. A mood of rebellion and mild anarchism runs deep in the American psyche, and Harley-Davidson, through brilliant marketing and product development, tapped that vein like no other commercial enterprise.

Basic American values of courage, loyalty, and patriotism, linked to the primitive thunder of a V-twin engine, led Harley-Davidson to the Promised Land. Within two decades the motorcycle bridged the gap from being the iron horse of outlaw tough guys to the darling of the upwardly mobile.

The company's 1996 annual financial report headlined the following 10 words, which neatly summarized its unique mantra:

> *Heritage*
> *Quality*
> *Passion*
> *Look*
> *Sound*
> *Feel*
> *Relationships*
> *Freedom*
> *Individuality*
> *Lifestyle*

In a broad sense this composes much of what American culture is all about.

At the end of my book, *Outlaw Machine*, which probed the Harley-Davidson mystique, I puzzled briefly about what, in the middle 1990s, seemed to be a trend toward an androgynous cyberworld. (With perfunctory apologies about quoting myself), I closed the book with the following paean to Harley-Davidson and its subtle impact on our society and perhaps the whole of Western civilization:

> *So what is left? The vacant satisfaction of inner space and the subordination of self to the computer and virtual reality? The docile capitulation to the safety net of the nanny state and the prison ship of political correctness? The mindless goose-step into group-think and New Age frontal-lobe massaging? Perhaps that is our fate.*

Captain America: the quintessential outlaw machine.

But at the end of the bus line, before the last stop on the road to oblivion, lies that crazy, tasteless, violent, bizarre mongrel horde called Americans, with their God-awful music, their horrendous sloppiness and rudeness and their reservoir of aggravatingly cheerful optimism. At the heart of this is the archaic, throwback Harley-Davidson motorcycle, a dreadful, irresponsible machine with no redeeming social qualities—mechanical pornography to decent folk—that simply won't go away despite the sheer, outrageous blat of its fuming exhaust in the face of seamless technology and the orderly, opulent, and essentially soulless brave new world. But if that rumble, that ungodly roar, that death threat to collectivism and convention dies away, it will be time to turn out the lights.

Those lines were written in 1998, when only the peccadilloes of the Clinton administration and the boom in dot-com stocks distracted the nation. Now, in the wake of September 11 and the war on worldwide terrorism, the role of Harley-Davidson as an affirmation of the American spirit has been amplified. Now, more than ever, it is a national symbol and a national treasure unlike any other.

—Brock Yates
Wyoming, New York

Chapter 1

THE EARLY YEARS

By Herbert Wagner

"Speed is, one might say, his god."
—The Boy of Today, 1922

Now and then I'll run into someone who asks if the ghost of Harley or Davidson wanders the old red brick factory on Juneau Avenue. The place is old enough for ghosts. The first 1910 portion went up next to the long-vanished 1906–1909 wood and brick plant, right up the block from the old woodshed behind the Davidson family residence. If a ghost exists, it certainly feels at home.

And doesn't the old Harley-Davidson nickname "Silent Gray Fellow" invoke a phantom that haunts the midnight highway?

Ghosts aside, the spirit of Harley-Davidson's founders still inhabits the old factory in an inspirational sense. Stroll around its red brick walls sometime and you'll know what I mean.

The early years of Harley-Davidson involve ghosts and dreams. Of people and bikes long vanished, people who created and raised the Harley-Davidson motorcycle above all others, leaving in their wake memories, mysteries, and legends.

THE ORIGIN

Relaying a true and factual accounting of Harley Davidson's origins presents a challenge. After 1908, the Motor Company began veering from the facts for marketing purposes. Specifically, the build dates of the first two motorcycles constructed by Harley and Davidson—two totally different designs—were confused, and their respective identities sometimes merged into a single machine.

The founders were too busy building and selling motorcycles to accurately record their early experiences. In 1942, Arthur Davidson recalled the origin of the Harley-Davidson: "It just growed . . . like Topsy . . . with luck." But it wasn't just luck.

In America, the notion of a gasoline-powered bicycle had been kicked around like a carnival freak since the early 1890s, when the shady capitalist-inventor

Edward Joel Pennington promoted his latest device, "the Motor Cycle." In 1895, Pennington demonstrated his gasoline-powered two-wheeler on Milwaukee's Wisconsin Avenue. Onlookers mobbed the scene, including, one might speculate, two 14-year-old chums living in that neighborhood named William S. (Bill) Harley and Arthur (Art) Davidson. Pennington's impractical but mesmerizing invention may have inspired the notion of the motorcycle in the minds of these two boys.

The motorcycle remained a wishing-well fantasy until the lightweight, reliable de Dion-Bouton-type engine arrived from France in the late 1890s. In 1901

the first motorcycles appeared in Milwaukee. That July, 20-year-old Bill Harley drew plans for a "bicycle motor," plans that in part survive in the Harley family today. Harley's 1901 bicycle motor was about the size of a large chain saw engine (7.07 ci/106 cc). According to legend, a "German draughtsman" gave Harley some engine construction tips, then vanished into history without a trace.

Working on the project with Arthur Davidson and another buddy named Henry Melk, who owned a lathe, Bill Harley tinkered through 1902 and into 1903, when Art's brother Walter come home expecting a ride.

Arthur Davidson (right) delivers a Harley to George Dykesten (standing) in 1906. Cambridge, WI, July 5, 1906.

Harley's first stab at building a V-twin in 1909 failed, but the company came roaring back with a winning twin in 1911.

The motor-bicycle wasn't finished, so Walter joined in. Less of a dreamer perhaps, Walter pushed aside old man Davidson's stuff in the backyard shed, and in the summer of 1903 they rolled out their proud creation. The motor-bicycle ran, but its motor wasn't powerful enough for Milwaukee's modest hills.

Here's where myth and confusion blurs the picture. A Motor Company document from 1907 clearly states that the machine finished in the "summer of 1903" was NOT the large, loop-frame bike we recognize today as the original Harley-Davidson, but a more primitive vehicle with a smaller engine attached to a pedal bicycle frame. No photograph of this first machine has ever surfaced. Confusing it with the second, and more advanced, loop-frame model was a natural trap for the unwary and careless, or those who later wanted to score points for advertising purposes. That's what happened.

But don't consider the 1901–1903 motor-bicycle a failure or an object of derision. Our heroes learned fast. First, they needed a bigger motor. They may have found it in the machine shop of Arthur's pal and another Milwaukee legend, famed outboard motor builder Ole Evinrude.

Evidence suggests that Bill Harley adapted Ole's single-cylinder engine for motorcycle service. Striking similarities exist between the Evinrude and Harley engines. This second engine had a 24.74 cubic inches

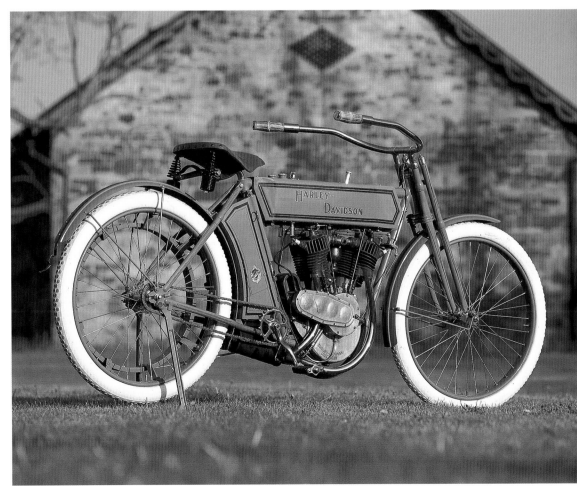

(405-cc) displacement, considerably larger than the previous bicycle motor.

Things were moving fast in the local motorcycle industry. Both the Merkel Co. (Milwaukee) and Mitchell Co. (Racine) started building bicycle-like motorcycles in early 1901. In late 1902 (for the 1903 model year) both firms introduced totally new designs based upon loop (Merkel) or cradle (Mitchell) frames. By abandoning the diamond-style bicycle layout, both the Merkel and Mitchell companies demonstrated a modern understanding of motorcycle engineering.

Thus, in the latter half of 1903, Bill Harley and the Davidson brothers had two innovative motorcycles built

in the neighborhood to guide them. In fact, Harley's second design took strong cues from the Merkel, using a nearly identical extension fork and a very similar frame with a front down-tube flowing around the engine in a continuous loop. As a result, the original Harley-Davidson came into existence using correct engineering principles with strong potential for future development.

One photo of this first "real" Harley-Davidson is known. It resembles, but is not identical to, the oldest bike in the H-D museum collection today.

The first prototype of this second H-D model, according to the previously quoted 1907 Motor Company source, was finished the "next season." Although it was begun

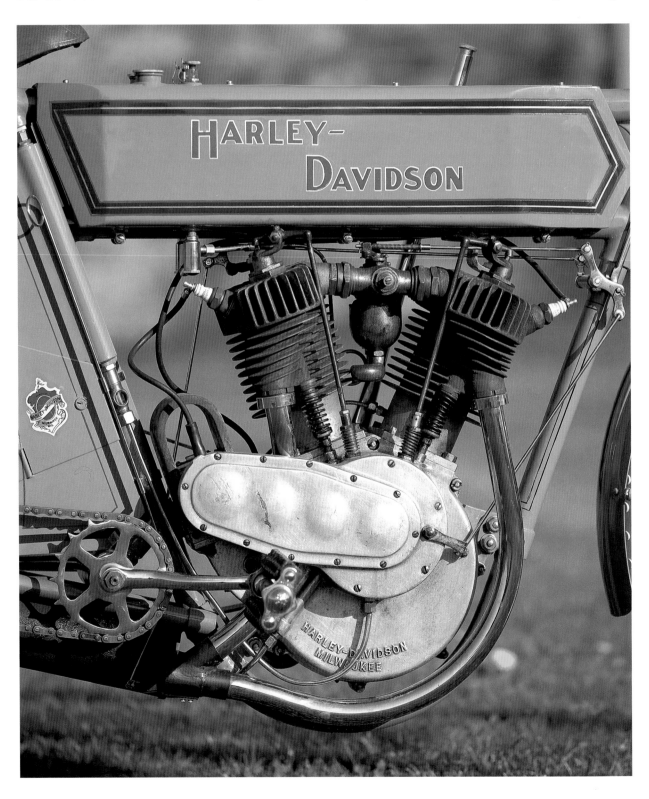

Opposite page
The 1911 singles still had suction-type intake valves. The 500-cc single was good for four horsepower.

Walter Davidson (left) and
William S. Harley in 1914.

For 1912, Harley offered a 988-cc
twin that pumped out a whopping
8 horsepower. The bigger twin
came with chain drive and a clutch
in the rear hub.

Singles still had leather belt drive in 1912.

in 1903, this would technically make it a 1904 model. At the time, however, no one was thinking about labels or model years. The 1904 finish date is almost certainly the reason Harley-Davidson made the 1954 bikes the 50th Anniversary models, rather than the 1953 bikes, as one might have expected. In 1978, when AMF/Harley-Davidson began celebrating anniversaries again, the distinction between the 1903 power-bicycle and the 1904 loop-frame prototype—apparently still recognized in 1954—had been lost.

Early histories and advertising literature handed out by the factory in the 1908–1916 period further cloud the picture, by providing a confusing hash of contradictory origin dates, incorrect model identification, and false claims. To be fair, accurate history was not Harley-Davidson's goal; selling motorcycles in a highly competitive market was.

After completing the second model sometime in 1904, our heroes' hobby took an entrepreneurial turn when a pal named Henry Meyer offered to buy that first machine.

Around that same time, a Chicago motorcycle buff named Carl H. Lang saw the Harley-Davidson. Lang liked the "Harley" so much (or "Davidson" as it was sometimes known) that he offered to sell the motorcycle in Chicago. In 1905 Harley and the Davidsons produced at least five motorcycles, three of which Lang took. In 1906 Lang took 24 out of 50. In 1907 he sold 84 out of 250.

In late 1906 Harley and the Davidsons built a small factory on Juneau Avenue (then Chestnut Street). In 1907, older brother Bill Davidson left the railroad to run the machine shop, instilling some locomotive durability into the two-wheeler. That September the founders formally incorporated as a business under the name Harley-Davidson Motor Co. Its mission statement? "Manufacture and sell motorcycles, motors, marine engines, and fixtures, and appliances."

A New Monarch of the Miles

More power, more speed and greater flexibility are built into the "Master 17"—the new Harley-Davidson motorcycle. From its beautiful military olive drab finish to the very heart of the motor it's a mechanical masterpiece. You will marvel at the smashing power of the new

Harley-Davidson

You will wonder at the smoothness of action; you will be grateful for the mechanical ingenuity which gives you that rare combination of flexibility and power at low speeds and you will fairly gasp with delight when you realize how this wonderful machine throws down the barriers of distance and makes of the whole country one vast recreation ground—for you.

Make it a point to see the new "Master 17" Harley-Davidson motorcycle at your dealers. Write and let us send you the new catalog. Read page two on "Performance"—then you will understand.

HARLEY-DAVIDSON MOTOR COMPANY

Producers of High-Grade Motorcycles for More Than Fifteen Years
Also Manufacturers of Harley-Davidson Bicycles
480 B Street, MILWAUKEE, WIS., U. S. A.

BUILT ON HONOR

Up to that time, Harley-Davidson was largely a Milwaukee-Chicago phenomenon with a few machines sold in Philadelphia, Detroit, Minnesota, and even California. Perry Mack, Ralph Sporleder, and Walter Davidson had entered some Midwestern races and won a few trophies, but they were small fish in a pond increasingly dominated by Indian—the winner of just about every important race in sight.

In mid-1908 H-D's fame took off when Walter won the National Endurance Contest through New York State's Catskill Mountains. Sixty-five riders on 17 different makes of motorcycle, including foreign bikes and the increasingly famous Indian, were entered. Just to show how regional Harley-Davidson was at this early date, the *New York Times* dubbed it the "Howard-Davidson."

Walter finished the contest with a perfect score of 1,000, but so did some others. What was outstanding about Walter's performance was his total time deviation of just eight minutes during the two day, 356-mile course.

While many other machines had broken rims, cracked frames, or seized engines, Walter's bike came through without mishap. The top Indian riders had "Big Chief" Hendee and "Medicine Man" Hedstrom following in a Stevens-Duryea automobile filled with repair parts, but Walter had no back-up vehicle nor any spare parts.

Three days later, Walter went on to win the F.A.M. Economy Contest, going 50 miles on one quart and one ounce of gasoline—even beating bikes of smaller displacement. The judges were impressed. They awarded Walter five additional points for consistency and overall excellence. This *1,000-plus-5* win was one of the highest honors granted in early motorcycle competition.

Back in Milwaukee, Walter brought home a new spirit for Harley-Davidson. The Motor Company soon heralded his Diamond Medal win in full-page

advertisements. This was the beginning of Harley-Davidson's national fame and fanatically loyal following.

H-D sales literature for 1909 touted a "Built on Honor" superior construction theme. The nickname "Gray Fellow" first came into use at this time (the term "Silent" was added later). With a trusty Harley-Davidson, the advertisements announced, a person could ramble at will, exploring the countryside, and safely return home. From moonlit hilltops, one could marvel at America's romantic vastness, knowing it was attainable under the spinning wheels of the Harley-Davidson motorcycle.

Harley's advanced design, robust construction, and good-sized motor pushed Milwaukee ahead at a critical stage when a large percentage of motorcycle riders wanted rugged, economical transportation.

V-twin Mania

The motorcycle was growing up fast. Riders' needs and desires were changing. Some were hitching up sidecars. Others wanted more hill-climbing oomph. Everyone wanted more mile-eating speed. These things were most easily obtained by adding a second cylinder.

The Harley look got its first big update for 1916 with rounded gas tanks.

Glenn Curtiss had done it in 1903 with America's first production V-twin. And although Harley-Davidson had a V-twin prototype finished by late 1906, and advertised V-twins in 1907, 1908, 1909, and 1910, only a handful were produced during that period. Harley was tardy to adopt the V-twin design because demand for the single was so strong that a twin seemed unnecessary. Besides, technical difficulties with the suction intake valves used on all pre-1911 H-D twins tarnished Harley's sterling reputation for reliability.

Once Harley perfected mechanical intake valves in 1911, the twin quickly overtook the single, and by 1913 the majority of Harley-Davidsons sold were V-twins. The bigger and heavier V-twin brought forth new challenges. Riders started their bikes by peddling or pushing and then jumping on, but the heavier V-twin made this run-and-jump-on business difficult. As one angry rider said, "To run along and then throw oneself on is good enough for young boys to do, but for a person over 45 or 50 it is a dangerous practice."

In 1907, Harley-Davidson became the first American motorcycle to offer a clutch as an option. In 1908, Harley offered an optional Lang two-speed transmission. Neither caught on. The vast majority of Harleys rolled out as single-speeds, using a simple belt-tensioning device. By 1912, as the bikes got bigger and heavier, Harley came back with a better clutch. With a clutch, riders could start from a standstill, without any foot or pedal assistance. At a stop, one could disconnect the engine from the drive.

Steep hills, city traffic, and sidecars stimulated the multispeed transmission. In 1914, H-D offered a rear-hub two-speed, and in 1915 it introduced a modern enclosed three-speed running in oil. That same year electric lighting appeared, and in 1916 the kick-starter was first used. With these features, the modern Harley-Davidson platform was established. Except for electric-start and foot-shift, the basic design has not changed significantly to this day.

Bringing Town and Country Together

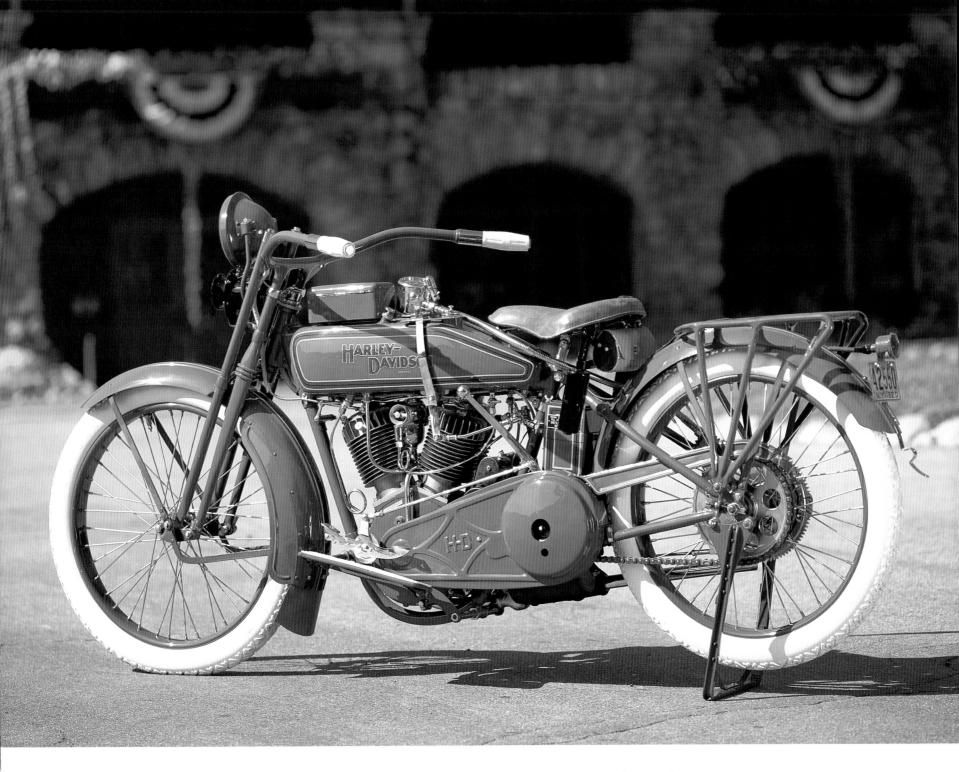

The early teens were a golden era for Harley-Davidson. America was prosperous, the motorcycle market was expanding, and Milwaukee was exporting Silent Gray Fellows around the world. Milwaukee riders were having fun putting on Goodfellowship Tours. These set the pattern for the gypsy tours and rallies of later decades. With a sidecar, the motorcycle could still compete with the automobile's family-carrying capacity. All this helped Harley-Davidson grow from 1,149 bikes built in 1909 to 16,924 in 1916.

That latter year, the original 1904 Harley-Davidson prototype is noted for the last time. In 1912–1913, it had been promoted in advertisements as having accumulated "100,000 miles" under a series of owners, beginning with Henry Meyer and ending with Stephen Sparough. In 1916, it was on display in C.H. Lang's Chicago dealership. Then it disappears from the historical record. For you get-rich-quick types, the original Harley is still out there, somewhere, waiting to be rediscovered.

THE GRAY FELLOW TURNS GREEN

In 1917 America entered World War I. For the first time, Harley-Davidson was drawn away from the consumer marketplace to dabble with motorcycles for war purposes. Bill Harley mounted machine guns on special sidecar rigs that first chased Pancho Villa along the Mexican border and later saw service when America entered World War I.

Harley-Davidson did not actively pursue big military contracts, but catered to U.S. riders. Dealers could get new bikes and replacement parts until the last six months of the war in 1918, when the U.S. Army took about 8,000 H-D motorcycles.

After gaining military fame chasing Pancho Villa in Mexico and the Kaiser's troops in Europe, even civilian Harleys were painted military green.

During the war Harley-Davidson's reliability was again demonstrated. As the late William H. Davidson once told me, "Harley got its deepest breath over in the mud in France."

In 1917 Harley-Davidson switched color from the traditional gray to military olive drab. Since I've never seen a reason given for this critical change, I'll offer one. Because Milwaukee was heavily ethnic German, that city had been slow to jump on the patriotic bandwagon. So slow, in fact, that as American isolationist sentiment changed to support of England and France,

some had branded Milwaukee subversive. In the Harley family, there's a legend of government agents watching the house because Bill Harley had married Anna Jachthuber, whose parents were from Germany.

After 1908, the Harley-Davidson had worn gray paint (before that it was usually black), and the Silent Gray Fellow nickname was world famous. But as patriotic sentiment grew heated against things German (*sauerkraut* became *liberty cabbage* and Milwaukee's *Germania* statue was sold for scrap) one might speculate that "Gray Fellow" was too close for comfort to the fellows wearing field-gray uniforms in Kaiser Bill's army.

And doesn't the word "silent" imply stealth, secrecy, and eavesdropping? These were not desirable attributes in a country suddenly obsessed with enemy agents and espionage, where attacks against citizens suspected of mixed loyalty were common. Goodbye silent gray, hello Army green.

BEST IN THE WORLD

By 1920, Harley-Davidson seemed on top of the world. Milwaukee built what was widely acknowledged as the best heavyweight motorcycle available anywhere. Milwaukee's dealership network was the envy of the industry. Motor Company advertising was lavish, often artistically beautiful. The company had been solvent and profitable in every year of existence. The factory had grown from a 10-by-15-foot woodshed in 1903 to a massive six-story red brick complex stretching along Chestnut Street and around the corner on 37th (now 38th) Street, encompassing a total of 600,000 square feet of floor space.

Because of the demand for more powerful and faster motorcycles, Harley-Davidson came out with a 74 cubic-inch Big Twin in 1921. Some, however, were calling for even bigger motors displacing 80 or 100 cubic inches.

But there was reason to worry. American motorcycle registrations had peaked in 1920, after which a decline of 10,000–15,000 per year set in. In 1921, an economic recession caused Harley-Davidson to show a loss for the first time. Another sales drop in 1924 caused the Motor Company to post another loss. During these years people were switching from motorcycles to four-wheeled transportation. The trend was so serious that Harley-Davidson's founders gloomily predicted, "The pleasure sport riding motorcycle is largely a thing of the past in this country and not to be depended upon for future business."

While some expected the faithful to come back, few would. The founders believed that the future lay in police sales and commercial delivery motorcycles, plus strong foreign demand. Such a policy would have doomed Harley-Davidson in time. The Motor Company needed an entirely new strategy for the American rider. But this would take time and agony to figure out.

In the early 1920s, overseas markets that buoyed up stagnant domestic growth were critical for H-D.

Arthur Davidson (on motorcycle) with northern pike and (possibly?) Oakly Fisher (sidecar) with nice bass, about 1916.

Early woman rider and de facto H-D office manager, Crystal Haydel, 1917.

Following pages
Each year, Harley added features and updates to the F-head twins that made them faster and more civilized. Shown is a 1923.

The distributor on the 1923 twin made starting easier than it was on magneto-ignition bikes.

Having shown its worth in World War I, the Harley-Davidson had largely pushed aside inferior British twins in overseas markets.

The Brits, however, came back strong with a new approach. In the early 1920s, they began building innovative models with more speed in a smaller package; bikes using advanced overhead-valve, single-cylinder technology. In 1924, readers of *MotorCycling* were stunned by a report of the 350-cc *overhead-camshaft* Chater-Lea-Blackburne breaking the 100-mile per hour speed barrier at 6,000 rpm. This was amazing news in a nation where big, low-revving V-twins were the standard. It intrigued the founders, who were trying to fathom a changing marketplace. In 1926, Walter Davidson said, "Way back in 1905–6–7–8...the single-cylinder motorcycle was used partly as a sporting proposition and also very largely as economical transportation. The automobile was high-priced, the cheapest car being in the neighborhood of $1,000, whereas your motorcycle sold in the neighborhood of $200." But times had changed. Milwaukee's Big Twin was now more expensive than Ford's cheapest car!

If you wanted a speedometer on your JD, it was a special-order item. Speedometers weren't standard equipment until 1936.

Harley-Davidson
FACTORIES

By Jerry Hatfield

Harley-Davidson grew explosively during its first decade, roughly doubling its production each year. Managers placed supplies, equipment, and people as close together as possible. They grew the factory vertically, so they could use elevators to move stocks between floors, and handcarts to roll the items on each floor. The heaviest stuff, such as metal bars and sheets, was stored either at ground level or in a basement. There, too, were the heaviest machines, like the big presses that hammered sheets into fuel tank sections.

At first, one man assembled one motorcycle, entirely on his own, starting with the bare frame and proceeding

Newly completed Harley factory about 1915. Faded lettering can still be seen on the side of the building today.

by bolting on parts. In the early 1920s came an assembly line. Sort of. This was an entirely nonautomated setup.

In 1920, Harley-Davidson completed the last of a series of factory additions, making it the largest motorcycle plant in the world. Harley-Davidson had reached the end of achieving efficiency through volume in the vertical factory layout.

THE HORIZONTAL FACTORY

During World War II, a number of new defense industry factories built with a horizontal layout achieved high efficiency by using forklift trucks and roller conveyors. When the war ended, Harley-Davidson bought a Milwaukee plant previously used by Borg-Warner for producing military items. This plant was dedicated to building Harley's lightweight two-stroke single-cylinder model.

In 1969, American Machine & Foundry (AMF) bought Harley-Davidson. Final motorcycle assembly was moved to AMF's York, Pennsylvania, factory, formerly used for making military and bowling equipment. Engine production remained in the Milwaukee factory, while the old multi-storied buildings were transitioned into engineering and administrative use.

With the added total factory space, Harley-Davidson was able to increase production dramatically, from 27,000 in 1969 to 60,000 in 1972. However, quality problems accompanied production growth. Sometimes parts couldn't be found in the overhead system, or parts needed rework, or parts had been made obsolete by engineering changes.

THE TUNED FACTORY

The tuned factory—my term, not Harley's—came in the early 1980s, with the awareness that the people in the factory were more important than the shape of the factory.

THE SPACE-AGE FACTORY

The new Harley-Davidson V-Rod exemplifies space age engineering and factory know-how applied to motorcycles—motorcycles that are in tune with the critical styling department that keeps all things "Harley." To maintain the Harley look and feel in a bike that houses the large and powerful engine sired by the VR1000 road racer meant that frame dimensions were critical.

THE FUTURE

Harley-Davidson now operates three major manufacturing sites, and produces well over 200,000 motorcycles each year. As well as the Milwaukee engine plant and the York assembly plant, the Motor Company now builds all Sportsters and V-Rods at its Kansas City facility. A host of other facilities house styling and engineering people. There may be more plants in the future, but people will remain key.

Harley-Davidson Engineering Department, circa 1923–1924; William S. Harley (right).

Since the single-cylinder motorcycle had largely gone out of existence, the motorcycle was now a Big Twin proposition. The days when youngsters learned to ride on a small bike and then moved up to a larger one were gone. With older riders switching to automobiles, domestic motorcycle sales were eroding at both ends.

THE SINGLE STAGES A COMEBACK

That situation inspired H-D to build a new single-cylinder model in the mid-1920s. It wasn't a decision arrived at easily, as earlier attempts to market bicycles (1918–1924) and the 35-cubic-inch (584-cc) flat-twin Sport Model (1919–1923) had not been successful. This time the nudge came from Harley-Davidson's foreign dealers, who begged for a smaller motorcycle to compete with the increasingly successful European singles.

After evaluating foreign markets, the founders decided to fill the gap with a totally new 21-cubic-inch (350-cc) machine built along the lines of the Big Twin. Study showed a motor of that size with a three-speed gearbox was the best combination. Harley-Davidson introduced the new Single for 1926 in both economical side-valve form that got 70–80 miles per gallon and

50–55 miles per hour, and in sporting overhead-valve form that could top 65.

Harley-Davidson bet big on this new small machine, taking out ads in general circulation magazines. But Harley's strategy to reintroduce the single-cylinder motorcycle to America was not successful. The American public didn't want a motorcycle for basic transportation. It had fallen in love with the automobile, and it wasn't coming back. Overseas, where it might have succeeded, murderous new tariffs in the "Sterling Bloc" soon knocked Milwaukee out of the running.

Disappointment with the Single sent Harley-Davidson reeling back to the other extreme of the market—bigger engines and more cylinders. But while the Single was unsuccessful in the sales department, it would play an unexpected and unique role in H-D's eventual breakthrough success.

A HIDDEN ROOM AT HARLEY-DAVIDSON

Harley test rider and factory racer Albert "Squibb" Henrich tells a story from the 1920s that involves a mystery in the 1911 portion of the Juneau Avenue factory. To date, the mystery has not been solved.

Early class of military mechanics, 1917.

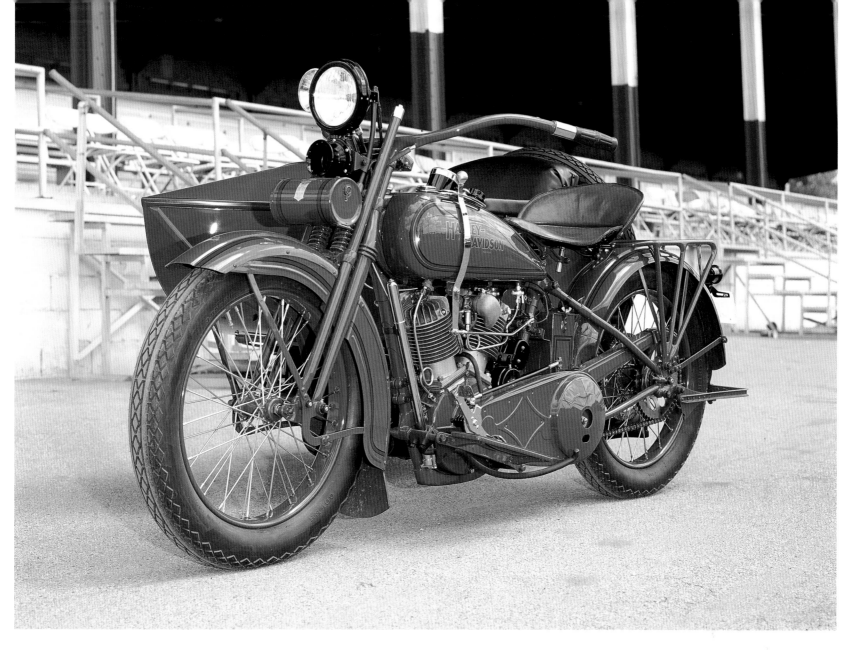

The extra grunt of the JD's 74-inch motor made it a natural for sidecar duty.

During lunch one day, Squibb and Edwin "Sherbie" Becker were talking about old bikes in the Testers' Room in the western end of the factory basement. Then Sherbie asked him to come around the corner near the elevator. Pointing to a spot on the massive concrete walls, Sherbie told Squibb that old belt-drive motorcycles were walled-up back in there.

Squibb was an honest guy. I believe he described the story as best he could remember. So what gives? Is the story myth or true?

Perhaps it's a bit of both.

Squibb believed the "big boys"—the founders— knew about this cache of early bikes walled up in the basement. But in considering it over the years, I don't think that could be right. If the founders had known, you'd expect their descendants would know too—the children and grandchildren of the original Harleys and Davidsons. But I've asked some of them, and none knew of this hidden room story.

After considering the possibilities, I believe that in 1911, when that portion of the factory was under

Harley's first production overhead- valve bikes were the Models AA and BA singles, introduced for 1926. They quickly gained the nickname "Peashooter."

The Peashooter's 350-cc engine was good for about 12 horsepower.

Following page
Harley fans were a little tired of green by 1927, so for 1928, Harley stopped painting engine cases and covers green, offering other colors as options.

The 1928 engines featured several important updates, including an air cleaner and a throttle-controlled oil pump.

The hot-rod of the Peashooter line was the export-only Model BAF with twin exhaust ports. Shown is a 1929 model.

construction, an order came down from the "big boys" to clean up the "old junk" in the existing shop next door. This was a time of major model changes at Harley-Davidson. Two years earlier, it had issued its first replacement parts catalog, covering the 1909 model, but nothing earlier. This suggests that in 1911, H-D considered everything on hand from 1908 back obsolete and not worth saving. Just possibly, that accounts for the old motorcycles or parts that Sherbie was talking about.

I've heard other firsthand accounts of vintage H-D stuff buried in Milwaukee area landfills or dumped into Lake Michigan, so it seems possible that instead of calling the junk man in 1911 to cart that early stuff away, some of the guys—including Sherbie—simply dumped it all into an open excavation of the new factory, where it was soon covered over or walled up. The hidden room may simply have been easy way to dispose of old junk.

REGAINING GROUND

In early 1927, Arthur Davidson took four tanks enameled in maroon, light green, police blue, and light blue to the New York motorcycle show. H-D finally realized that riders wanted livelier colors than military drab.

While Harley was updating styling, it was also instilling new life into the dealer network and club scene. Both had stagnated after World War I. As Walter Davidson told dealers in 1926, "The day of selling motorcycles sitting in your store, waiting for the customer to come to you has gone by." Harley-Davidson tried to eliminate its more complacent and ossified agents. Milwaukee dealer Bill Knuth, who had worked

FLORIDA
HORSELESS
CARRIAGE 400A

Previous pages
A multitude of updates made the 1928 JD an even better bike, whether you wanted to haul a sidecar or tear around solo.

at the Harley factory as early as 1911, founded the Cream City Motorcycle Club for Milwaukee riders. He put on activities like the Badger Derby, Midnight Mystery Tour, and Knuth's Kollege, which combined history, mechanical tips, riding lore, and good food— and brought many new riders into the sport.

FOUR-CYLINDER SHAFT-DRIVE EXPERIMENTAL

Harley's earlier prediction that the sporting motorcycle market was dying turned out to be wrong. More aggressive sales techniques and a revitalized club scene showed there was still great interest in motorcycling. Sales picked up and Harley-Davidson built nearly 24,000 motorcycles in 1929. Further factory expansion was considered. As Walter Davidson reported, "In the pleasure field there seems to be a very great market, and this can be greatly stimulated by bringing out new and better models."

The new and better models that Walter had in mind would retire the old F-head V-twin still built to 1911 designs. The next generation of engines, introduced in 1929, would be side-valves—a configuration Indian had done well with over the years.

But Harley had bigger plans. Much bigger. Late in 1928 the Engineering Department laid out an ambitious strategy in a surviving Motor Company document titled *Report of Meeting to Decide on Models for 1930.* The proposed model lineup was more imaginative than anything H-D

Motorcycle parking at a rally in
Wisconsin, 1930s.

had attempted yet. Six separate models were based upon the following engine types: 21 and 30.50 singles; 45 and 74 twins; and 80 and 90-cubic-inch fours.

The 1928 *Report* gives brief descriptions of the proposed four-cylinder models:

80 Cubic Inch Chain-Drive Model
90 Cubic Inch Shaft-Drive Model

No further construction details are noted beyond a brief mention that both models were to incorporate a new low frame and new tanks.

The four-cylinder motors went beyond anything Harley-Davidson had ever built. It is believed they resembled two compact 45s placed side-by-side in a single crankcase and perhaps with cylinders cast in pairs—almost like something you'd find in an air-cooled automobile engine. The frame for these V-4 models was probably not the single down-tube VL type, but a new double down-tube cradle frame similar to that used with the later 61 overhead-valve Knucklehead. The 90-inch shaft-drive model is the more fascinating of these V-4s. In 1925, the Motor Company had taken out a patent on a shaft-drive system. The 1928 *Report* is proof it considered putting it on a production bike. In 1929, William S. Harley recommended that a four-cylinder shaft-drive model be assembled and tested before deciding whether or not to produce it.

Years ago, Squibb Henrich told another story about his factory test riding days, of taking out an experimental shaft-drive V-engine Harley. At that time he guessed it was a 45-inch V-twin, but now I'd bet anything the shaftie Heinrich rode was the 90-inch V-4.

According to Henrich (who was remembering the event 60 years later), Harley built three prototype machines that were kept at a secret base in Reedsburg, with testing done up near Wildcat Mountain.

When asked what he thought of the shaftie, Heinrich replied, "Oh, I liked it. There wasn't nothing it couldn't do. It was a powerful machine, quiet, smooth,

as smooth as a Henderson Four on takeoff. You didn't have to worry about sand or mud. You could ride axle deep and never wear it out like a chain. The shaft-drive worked beautifully with those rubber cushions to take up the torque."

To date, no factory photos of these V-4 Harleys have surfaced. And as we all know, neither the 80-inch chain or 90-inch shaft-drive V-4 were put into production. Yet if the machine was as good as old Squibby remembered, why wasn't it built? What happened?

The onset of the Great Depression may have been a contributing factor. But might other reasons have convinced H-D to cancel these stunning new models?

Perhaps. In 1929, the long-running lawsuit against Harley-Davidson by the Eclipse Company for infringement of a clutch patent came to a frightful conclusion. Harley-Davidson had been confident should it lose the

This period sidecar leans with the motorcycle.

case, at most $300,000 would be paid out. The judge, however, awarded a heart-stopping $1.1 million to Eclipse. In the final agreement, the founders had two weeks to fork over the money or lose the factory. Old-timers say that Walter Davidson never got over the shock—the worst in the company's history—although harder times were yet to come.

While H-D had enough cash socked away in government securities to pay Eclipse off, it made the necessary high tooling costs of bringing out a completely new motorcycle platform an extravagance in light of the economic downturn, and the founders probably killed the V-4 project as a result.

Perhaps it was just as well. Harley-Davidson entered the 1930s with the uninspiring but cheap-to-build VL as the big bike in the model lineup, and even these would be a tough sell. A luxury V-4 would have had little chance of success in the dismal market environment of the Great Depression.

Thus ended the early years of Harley-Davidson. Starting as backyard dreamers, the founders established the fundamentals of a world-famous motorcycle company based on sound engineering, manufacturing, and marketing principles. During this period, Harley-Davidson gathered a fanatically loyal following that is still going strong 100 years later.

Nineteen twenty-nine was the last year for Harley's F-head Big Twins.

Chapter 2

THE FLATHEAD ERA

By Jerry Hatfield

The side-valve engine, an archaic design now confined to lawn mowers and weed whackers, once powered many of the world's high-performance motorcycles. The "side-valve" name comes from the location of the valves in a pocket off to the side of the cylinder bore. The valves are upside-down and the stems parallel to the bore. The underside of the cylinder head consists of a flat surface into which a slight cavity is formed to allow the valves to open and the combustion process to start. Were it not for the cooling fins, the top of the heads would also be flat, earning this type of engine the nickname "flathead."

For a given capacity, flatheads burn more fuel than overhead valve engines. For a given performance level, a flathead engine needed to be larger, and thus heavier, than a comparable overhead. On paper the flathead design is inferior to an overhead-valve configuration, but until the mid-1920s, inferior fuels narrowed the gap between flathead and overhead performance. Because of the poor quality of gasoline, overhead–valve engines were forced to use low-compression pistons, so flatheads weren't that much weaker than overheads until the arrival of tetraethyl lead at service stations in 1924. The availability of more efficient (and more expensive) fuel along with motorcyclists' rising expectations for performance doomed the flathead design to the scrap heap of history. For a time during the first half of the twentieth century, however, the flathead reigned supreme.

FIRST OF THE HARLEY-DAVIDSON FLATHEADS

As 1920 drew near, Harley-Davidson had the largest motorcycle factory in the world, but H-D sales had leveled off. The heady years of explosive growth, in which the Harley-Davidson factory had annually doubled its output, were behind the company. To keep

The war hog, Harley's Model WLA, gained renown as "the bike that won the war." From 1941 through 1945, Harley-Davidson built tens of thousands of WLAs for the Allied war effort.

growing, Harley-Davidson needed to bring new people into motorcycling.

Harley-Davidson F-head (or inlet-over-exhaust, the combustion chamber design used on most early motorcycles) V-twins were all the things that sporting motorcyclists liked: big, noisy, rough, oily, and fast, which of course meant that the car crowd loathed them. To convert car people into motorcycle people, Harley's new model would be the opposite: shorter, lower, lighter, cleaner, smoother, and quieter. The new Harley would have enough muscle for all normal riding

conditions, yet run quietly to avoid the suggestions of speed and danger.

Harley-Davidson introduced the missionary motor-cycle designed to bring in new riders in 1919. Called the "Sport," the new model featured a 584-cc (35.6-cubic inches), engine, twice the size of the Indian light twin then on the market. The Harley sales catalog proclaimed "Not a lightweight!" This was the first flathead mid-dleweight motorcycle built by one of the three major American companies, Harley-Davidson, Indian, and Excelsior. The Sport, the first American middleweight

Harley's first flathead was the very unusual Model W Sport Twin of 1919. As the name implies, it's a twin, but not in the usual Harley sense. The cylinders are laid down and pointed fore and aft. The 600-cc flathead twin was technically advanced, but the model never caught on among Harley enthusiasts, and it was canceled in 1923.

Howard "Hap" E. Jameson with office class and Sport Model, 1923.

with an opposed cylinder configuration, featured other innovations for the American market, including unit construction of the engine and three-speed transmission, helical gear primary drive, and a wet clutch.

The Sport engine spun as smoothly as a turbine. The sweetly running middleweight seemed to have it all, and first-year Sport sales were brisk. But a year later, Indian brought out the 1920 600-cc Scout V-twin, with the traditional "potato-potato-potato" V-twin sound. The peppier Scout out-sported the Sport, so survival of the Harley middleweight hinged on its missionary effectiveness.

Unfortunately, the Sport cost too much. Equipped with lights, the motorcycle sold for $445, roughly $9,000 in today's money. Used Model T Fords could be bought for less, so the Sport couldn't compete as basic transportation. At $485, the 1,000-cc (61-cubic inches) Harley-Davidson V-twin cost only nine percent more than the 584-cc Sport, so the middleweight couldn't compete with the bigger Harleys for the sporting business. Thus, the Sport was on the market

A 1929 Model D flathead (right) and an overhead-valve twin-port Model BAF (left).

The "three-cylinder Harley," the 45-cubic-inch Model D of 1929, was actually Harley's first flathead V-twin. Why "three-cylinder"? See that black thing sticking up in front of the engine? It's the generator, and some thought it looked like an extra jug.

only through 1923. Sport sales totaled 9,130 over five seasons. As 1923 drew to a close, the Sport missionary movement had failed, and Harley-Davidson again was an all F-head marque.

LET'S TRY AGAIN

Somewhere in the Harley-Davidson dealer network, a rider bought the last Sport in late 1923. Six months later, the company decided to build another bike for commuters and penny-pinchers. Why? For two reasons. First, management viewed the Sport's demise as the result of having produced an over-engineered and overpriced motorcycle. The second reason for a new model was the strength of the foreign markets, particularly British Commonwealth nations, where the

rugged Milwaukee brand was well suited to colonial rough roads. Harleys sold well south of the equator, in Africa, Australia, and New Zealand. These Southern Hemisphere markets had riding seasons the opposite of the United States, and supplying them enhanced Harley-Davidson production efficiency by leveling off peaks and valleys.

Worldwide, the most popular motorcycles were chain-driven 250-cc or 350-cc flathead single-cylinders with three-speed hand-shifted transmissions, the kind of motorcycles that Harley-Davidson could build at rock-bottom prices. The one-lungers came out in late 1925 as 1926 models. Because cost containment was critical, a variation of the single was offered with magneto ignition but no lights. The stateside price of

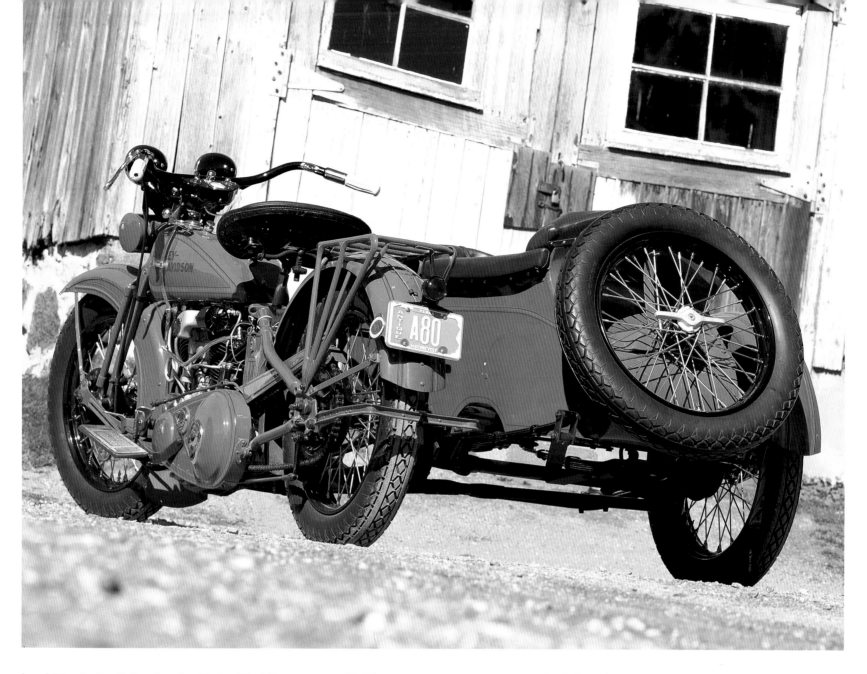

In addition to the flathead motor, Harley fitted the Model V with a new frame, fork, and clutch.

this minimal motorcycle was just $210, about half that of the no-frills Sport once offered.

For 1930, the factory brought out a 500-cc (30.5-cubic inches) flathead single. The 350-cc singles were offered for the seasons of 1926 through 1930 in both flathead and overhead versions, and as flatheads only from 1931 through 1934.

Harley-Davidson singles lasted nearly twice as long as the Sport, and singles sales were about triple that of the Sport, but by 1933, at the bottom of the Great Depression, production and sales of all Harley-Davidsons were down to about 10 percent of plant capacity. Sales of the singles were hardest hit, falling to just over 300. This seems odd on first thought, since a low-bucks bike would seem to have been just the ticket for depression-era buyers, but two factors contributed to low sales of the single. First, newly raised Commonwealth tariffs killed Southern Hemisphere sales overnight. Second, Harley's lightweights competed with their larger models. Customers who could barely

Sidecar in flooded street, 1930s.

Nineteen thirty-one was the last year for the Model D and its "third cylinder." In 1932, Harley introduced an improved Forty-five, the Model R, with a horizontally mounted generator.

afford new singles were just as likely to buy used Forty-fives or Seventy-fours for about the same price. Besides, if you rode a single amid the twin-cylinder crowd, you were considered what today we would call a "nerd." The factory justified continued singles offerings by assembling bikes from stocks of leftover parts.

Over 27,000 singles were sold during the nine seasons of 1926 through 1934, the great bulk of them flatheads. Though singles sales finally dived, one of every four Harley-Davidsons sold during the era was a single. The one-lungers had earned their keep, but it was time to move on with an all twin-cylinder lineup.

THE BIG MOVE

The Harley-Davidson F-heads had put the Milwaukee brand on top in both the show rooms and on the racetrack. But the F-head V-twins were near the end of their development trail. Harley-Davidson began to consider replacing the F-head V-twins with either flathead or overhead-valve V-twins. Several F-head shortcomings motivated a change. The inlet rockers were exposed to benefit from cooling air, which meant that oil mist settled over the engine and collected dust

to produce grime. The exposed rockers promoted rapid wear, because dust mixed with oil seepage to produce a lapping compound. Consequently, F-heads required frequent rocker arm maintenance to keep in top tune. The exposed inlet push rods and rocker arms also produced a clattering that didn't inspire confidence.

Harley-Davidson understood that overhead-valve engines were ultimately going to dominate the car and motorcycle markets. The question was when. Metallurgy in 1925 wasn't what it is today. Exhaust valves were particularly troublesome on air-cooled engines, which is why the Harley F-heads had two exposed rockers and valve stems and why overhead valve motorcycles had four of these sets. For Harley, the appeal of high-performance overhead- valve engines was offset by the prospect of doubling the F-head grime, wear, and noise. Harley-Davidson was impressed by its great rival, Indian. The Indian flatheads had all the moving parts enclosed, side-stepping the F-head problems of wear, noise, and filth. In the street-racing wars, the Indian flatheads held their own. In the end, Harley opted for a near-term sure thing. Its next generation of V-twin motorcycles would be powered by flatheads.

Brakes were a weak point on Harleys until the 2000 models came out. In 1934, they were really weak. That tiny hub is all the front brake it had.

To catch hooligans on hot-rod Harleys and Indians, smart cops got VLDs of their own. That "flying saucer" atop the front fender is a mechanical siren.

A FALSE START

Harley-Davidson decided to launch the new flat-head V-twin concept by entering the middleweight field, which the company had abandoned with the defunct Sport. Its reasoning was simple. At the time, prospective Harley buyers surveyed the dealers' floors and chose between a 270-pound 350-cc single for $235 or a 500-pound 1,000-cc V-twin for $335. Harley designed a 600-cc (37-cubic inches) flathead V-twin to plug the gap between these two machines and to compete head on with the same-sized flathead Indian Scout. Each 300-cc cylinder of the proposed V-twin would generate less stress than the 350-cc cylinder of

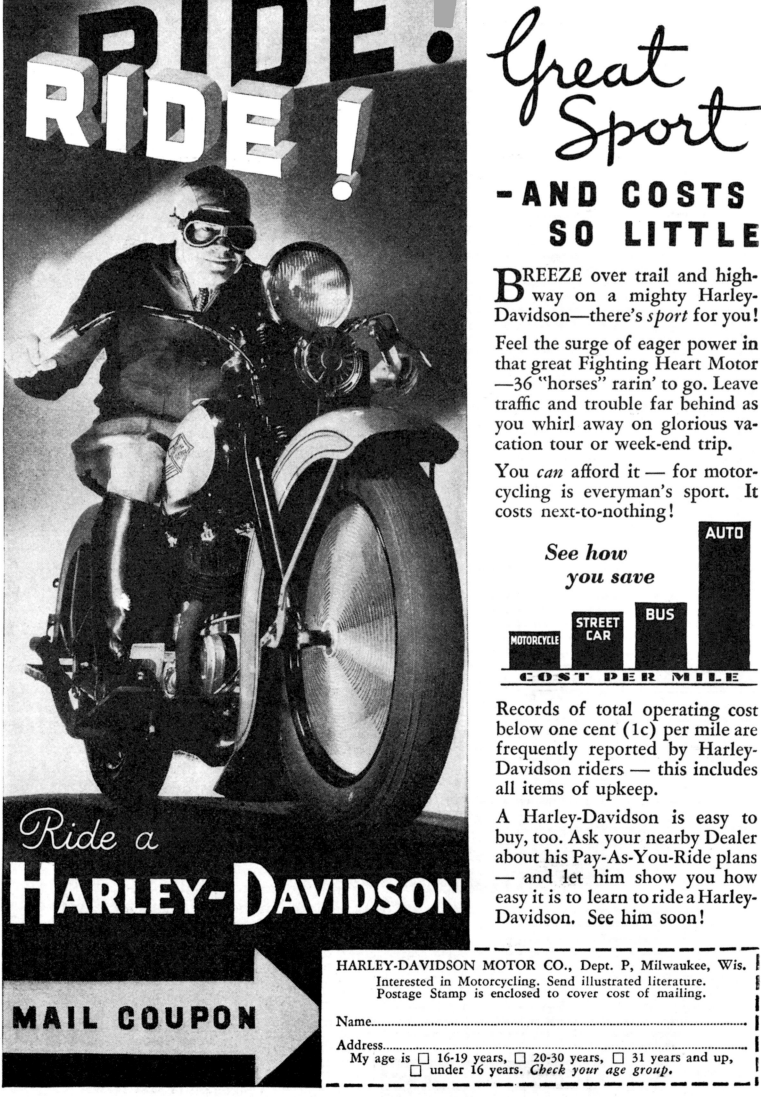

RIDE! RIDE! RIDE!

Ride a HARLEY-DAVIDSON

MAIL COUPON ➜

Great Sport
—AND COSTS SO LITTLE

BREEZE over trail and highway on a mighty Harley-Davidson—there's *sport* for you!

Feel the surge of eager power in that great Fighting Heart Motor —36 "horses" rarin' to go. Leave traffic and trouble far behind as you whirl away on glorious vacation tour or week-end trip.

You *can* afford it — for motorcycling is everyman's sport. It costs next-to-nothing!

See how you save

COST PER MILE

Records of total operating cost below one cent (1c) per mile are frequently reported by Harley-Davidson riders — this includes all items of upkeep.

A Harley-Davidson is easy to buy, too. Ask your nearby Dealer about his Pay-As-You-Ride plans — and let him show you how easy it is to learn to ride a Harley-Davidson. See him soon!

HARLEY-DAVIDSON MOTOR CO., Dept. P, Milwaukee, Wis.
Interested in Motorcycling. Send illustrated literature. Postage Stamp is enclosed to cover cost of mailing.

Name...

Address...
My age is ☐ 16-19 years, ☐ 20-30 years, ☐ 31 years and up, ☐ under 16 years. *Check your age group.*

When writing to advertisers please mention Popular Mechanics

Even the smaller RL 45 got updated streamlined looks for 1934. It also got aluminum pistons, a new oil pump, and a new clutch.

the lightweight single, so many of the lightweight single parts could be used on the middleweight twin, resulting in substantial cost savings. But as Harley proceeded with planning on the 600-cc V-twin, Excelsior introduced the F-head 750-cc Super X V-twin, and then Indian launched its flathead 750-cc Scout 45 V-twin. The appearance of these 750-cc rivals forced Harley-Davidson to increase the size of the proposed middleweight to 750-cc, and this delayed the debut of the model by a year or more.

THE FORTY-FIVE

The new Harley-Davidson Forty-five 750-cc flat-head V-twin, introduced in 1929, was a handsome motorcycle. Part of the credit for the good looks went to the frame, which featured a straight front down-tube. The straight front down-tube left no room to mount a generator in front of the engine, so to accommodate the generator, the factory mounted the unit to the side of the engine. The factory aligned the generator with the front down-tube to keep the lines smooth and flowing.

The abundance of parts from the single-cylinder range emphasized the lightness of the Forty-five and suggested good acceleration and responsive handling. With so much of the weight carried low to the ground, the Forty-five seemed hardly heavier than the flathead single. However, as the fleet of new Forty-fives gathered mileage, the use of so many singles parts proved unwise. The clutch wasn't strong enough, and the engine was so low in the frame that the crankcase bottomed out during turns. Harley halted Forty-five production in the spring of 1929 to correct these problems. Production of the revamped Forty-fives continued through the 1931 season.

THE FLATHEAD BIG TWINS

For the 1930 season, Harley-Davidson replaced the last of the F-head engines with a 1,200-cc (74-cubic inches) flathead design. The new Model V, or "Seventy-four," as it came to be known, was pulled from the market shortly after its introduction in late 1929 because of technical problems, as had been the Forty-Five flathead before it. The flywheels proved too light for American-style riding, and the lighter clutch springs proved too weak for American use. In early 1930, the factory shipped a modification kit to dealers, who rebuilt the Seventy-fours. Dealers had to remove everything from the old frame, disassemble the engine, reassemble all engine parts to the new crankcase, remove and replace the clutch, then install

The rooster-tail muffler and two-tone paint, both new for 1935, made for a fine-looking flathead.

Fifteen years of progress: a 1920 F-head Model J (right) and a 1935 flathead Model V (left).

everything into the new frame. And they did all this on their own dime, because the factory didn't compensate the dealers for the labor involved.

The new flathead Seventy-fours produced about the same power as the last of the F-head V-twins, but since the V series weighed about 100 pounds more, acceleration was disappointing to sporting riders. The saving grace was considerably improved reliability. Dealers promoted long, fast club runs, during which the F-head big twins overheated and shed parts, while the new flathead big twins kept running and stayed together.

The reliable flathead V-twins arrived just as Americans fell in love with long-distance touring. Highways were being paved. Service stations blossomed, and they gave away detailed maps of the newly numbered national and state road systems. Aided by both the new road signs and maps, riders seldom got lost as in the F-head era. The new motel and fast food industries were growing rapidly. Service stations emphasized clean restrooms, so riders and their dates didn't have to "pick flowers," the euphemism for relieving oneself behind the bushes. Along with better roads

The Eighty was back for 1936, but it was cataloged as the VH (low compression) and VLH (high compression).

For 1937, all the flatheads were restyled and given recirculating oiling systems. Shown is a 1938 model.

came faster speeds. Ever-smoother roads throughout the 1930s allowed faster speeds over longer stretches. The flathead V-twins met these new challenges far better than the old F-heads.

The V series continued through 1936 with detail refinements. During this era, California dealer Tom Sifton was a styling pioneer. He fitted virtually all his new Harleys with custom-designed, high-rise, chrome-plated handlebars. The handlebars became part of the "California" look, which became increasingly popular on the West Coast. Harley-Davidson brought out the overhead-valve 1,000-cc (61-cubic inches) Knucklehead in 1936, but the company shrewdly continued to offer both flatheads and the Knuckleheads. For the 1937 season, Harley-Davidson outfitted the Seventy-four and Forty-five with recirculating (dry sump) oiling. These models were designated the U (Seventy-four) and W (Forty-five) series. An 80-cubic inches flathead was offered as the Model VLH for 1935–1936, and as the Model UL for 1937–1940. By the 1941 season, Knuckleheads were outselling flathead big twins, so the Eighty was dropped to avoid competing with the new 1,200-cc (74-cubic inches) overhead-valve machines. After World War II, Knuckleheads dominated sales, and flathead big twins withered. The flathead Seventy-four continued through the 1948 season, and the Forty-five through the 1951 season.

FLATHEADS HELP WIN WORLD WAR II

The United States military used Harley-Davidsons for all its World War II needs. (Indians were limited to test programs and to use by Allied forces.)

**"Keeping a cool head" was
always a challenge on the Harley
side-valve engines prior to the
introduction of aluminum
cylinder heads. These were first
offered on the 1939 WLDD, and
later on the other flatheads.**

The war hog, Harley's Model WLA, gained renown as "the bike that won the war." From 1941 through 1945, Harley-Davidson built tens of thousands of WLAs for the Allied war effort.

During the war, Harley-Davidson built over 80,000 motorcycles for American and Allied forces. The great bulk of these were flathead Forty-fives. Despite the photos and text in many magazine articles of the era, and Harley's proud advertisements, American and Allied forces didn't use motorcycles as combat vehicles. Instead, the army used them for military police activities, such as posting traffic directors along convoy routes. Harley-Davidson's continuous high wartime production rate kept the company running efficiently. Harley's war experience positioned the company for efficient motorcycle manufacturing when peace production returned in late 1945.

THE MODEL K: AN ANSWER TO THE BRITISH INVASION

In the late 1940s, many British bikes arrived on the American scene. Typically, these middleweight motorcycles featured telescopic forks, 500-cc (30.50-cubic inches) overhead-valve engines, hand-operated clutches, and four-speed foot-shifted transmissions. Many Brit-bike riders gave their motorcycles the "California" treatment, which included high-rise handlebars and

An XA model during World War II.

Only minor updates were made to the Forty-fives each year after the war.

cut-down or "bobbed" fenders. These imports weighed less than the Harley Forty-fives, and coupled with more efficient engines and transmissions, performed better. Some imports even included rear suspensions. With the devaluation of British currency in 1949, the imports sold for about two-thirds the cost of Harley's Forty-five. Harley's more costly Forty-five, with its springer fork, rigid rear end, and three-speed, hand-shifted transmission could not last against this competition.

To meet the challenge, Harley-Davidson brought out a new, technologically advanced middleweight, the Model K. The K featured a telescopic fork but upped the comfort ante by tossing in a long-travel swinging-arm rear suspension. The K layout was a trendsetter, and within a few years all rival brands used a swinging-arm rear suspension. High-rise handlebars, the highest ever put on a stock Harley up to that time, conformed to the California style. Harley-Davidson didn't build cut-down bikes in those days, so the K featured full fenders with the classic Milwaukee flair. Yet, the overall lines of the K mimicked the cut-down "bobber" look. Behind the long front fork and high-rise bars was a high-rise fuel tank. But the tank swept dramatically down as it swept back, making the solo saddle seem lower than it was. You didn't sit *on* a K at the local hamburger drive-in; you sat *in* the K. The motorcycle had a look that was right for the times.

The Model K featured a unit-construction engine and transmission that was stronger than the old separate engine and gearbox setup. The four-speed foot-shift transmission met the British opposition head on.

In contrast to these sophisticated features, the K continued with the side-valve engine configuration. The size of the 750-cc K powerplant was supposed to compensate for its antiquated valve-train design. Two facts diminished the comparative performance of the K. First, the Model K weighed 450 pounds, but typical British 500-cc motorcycles weighed about 350 pounds. Second, the K was targeted at the wrong competitors. The British 650-cc (40-cubic inches) overhead-valve entries from Triumph and BSA, which appeared as 1950 models, beat the Harley K to the market. With 30 percent more power than the K, and being hardly any heavier, the new 650-cc imports outpaced the Harley K.

THE KH CLOSES THE GAP

For the 1954 season, Harley-Davidson increased the flathead engine capacity to almost 900-cc, in an attempt to close the performance gap between its flathead middleweight and the overhead valve competition from across the pond. Neither the K nor the KH sold well. One problem was an old one: high price. At around $1,000, the middleweight Harleys were priced only 10 percent under the company's popular big

At the end of the 1951 season, the WL was retired in favor of a next-generation flathead, the Model K.

Following page
The K may not have been a powerhouse, but it sure was lean, a look accentuated by the high, buckhorn bars.

In 1954, Harley bumped displacement from 750 cc to 883 cc and created the Model KH. In 1955 came the KHK, the hot-rod of the line, shown here.

Right
Here's a 1956 KH, the last of the Harley's flathead street bikes (excluding Servi-Cars and racers).

overhead-valve Panheads. As the Sport model had proven in the 1920s, it was dangerous to price a middleweight so close to a heavyweight. But the K and KH pricing problems were especially damaging in the 1950s, because Harley now had serious competition from imported motorcycles.

A Seamless Cloth

After 1945, Harley-Davidson flatheads were few in comparison to the popular Harley overhead valve big twins. But the Milwaukee flatheads were far more important to the Motor Company than mere numbers can convey. Harley-Davidson side-valve bikes kept the company going during the depths of the Great Depression. During World War II, some 80,000 Harley flatheads served the American and Allied forces, and kept the company's motorcycle building expertise at high level. In the meek K and the better KH were the seeds that sprouted the Sportster. For Harley-Davidson, the flatheads were patterns on a seamless cloth called "evolution."

Class C Regulations and
THE MODEL K

By Ed Youngblood

Although the K engine proved dominant on the track, helping riders like Everett Brashear win races all across America, it proved less successful on show room floors. Here Brashear receives a trophy from Jim Davis in 1955.

Geopolitical policies intended to rebuild European industry and stimulate the post-war economy following World War II had the unintended consequence of bringing a flood of British motorcycles into the U.S. market. These bikes were lighter, better handling, and quicker than the traditional American designs offered by Indian and Harley-Davidson, and they were technically more sophisticated, featuring rear suspensions and telescopic front forks. The penetration of these motorcycles into the American market only accelerated when, in September 1949, Britain devalued the pound sterling, effectively reducing the retail prices of goods exported to America—including motorcycles—by 25 percent.

At the time, Indian was still giving Harley-Davidson fits on America's racetracks, but Indian was a company in trouble. After World War II, Indian maintained a tight grip on the prestigious American Motorcyclist Association Number One plate and national championship title, but the Wigwam would not continue to thwart Harley-Davidson on the nation's racetracks for long. In 1953, Ernie Beckman won Indian's last national championship, and production ceased at Springfield the same year.

While Harley-Davidson battled Indian on America's dirt tracks, a flood of motorcycles from overseas presented an entirely new threat on the street. The Motor Company badly needed a new motorcycle to keep up with a rapidly changing and increasingly competitive motorcycling scene. Its answer was the Model K, a revolutionary product introduced in 1952 that borrowed much from its British competitors. Although it retained a traditional V-twin engine, the K had swing-arm rear suspension, unit-construction engine and gearbox, a hand clutch, and foot shift. At 45 cubic inches (750 cc), it was smaller than most of the bikes in Harley-Davidson's model line, although not as light or agile as some of the British bikes with which it hoped to compete. While many features of the K were technologically advanced, the new Harley used one technology that was positively antiquated. Although Harley-Davidson had introduced overhead valves into its Big Twin engines 16 years before, the K relied on ancient side-valve technology.

The K was a beautiful machine, compact and featuring nicely integrated styling. The sleek new motorcycle declared that Harley-Davidson had finally designed a new motorcycle from the ground up. It looked right for a new and more youthful post-war customer, but given a side-valve engine, the K's performance was not outstanding and its sales were disappointing. After several attempts at improving performance, the K was finally replaced in 1957 with the spectacularly successful 55-cubic-inch overhead-valve Sportster, which looked very much like a K with a different top end.

Why had Harley-Davidson not gone with an overhead-valve engine in the first place? In spite of its outdated engine design and lackluster sales performance, the K proved a superb platform for replacing the aging WR racer. AMA rules allowed side-valve engines to displace 750 cc but limited overhead-valve engines to 500 cc, so an OHV 750 would have been ineligible for championship competition. What the K never accomplished on the street, the KR achieved in spades on the racetrack. Hopped up and stripped of every ounce of unnecessary weight, the KR was an outstanding racer right out of the crate. When breathed upon by skilled Harley tuners, it became even better. Paul Goldsmith won Daytona for Harley-Davidson in 1953, and in 1955 Brad Andres launched a seven-year winning streak for the Milwaukee brand. Until the AMA's engine classification rules changed in 1970, KRs won Daytona 11 of 14 times, and with the exception of Dick Mann's championship in 1963, every AMA Grand National Champion earned his title aboard a KR between 1954 and 1966.

Cynics will tell you that Harley-Davidson ran the AMA and that the KR succeeded only because Milwaukee was given a 50 percent displacement

advantage over the British by the AMA rule book, in compensation for its ancient side-valve design. In reality, the AMA's "mixed formula" rules, which were intended to level the playing field between overhead-valve and side-valve technology, were not written for the KR. The formula began in 1926 in an effort to keep Excelsior in the racing game. At that time, Harley and Indian were racing the 500-cc overhead-valve singles. The mixed formula rules did force Harley-Davidson to use the throwback side-valve engine design in the 1952 model K street bike, dooming the K to failure in an increasingly competitive marketplace. The K, however, was not a complete failure. Although not an outstanding motorcycle in its own right, the short-lived K made possible the celebrated KR racer and laid the foundation for the spectacular XL Sportster.

In 1952, Harley had to make its new middleweight sportbike a flathead to comply with AMA racing regulations.

Chapter 3

THE KNUCKLEHEAD ERA

By Greg Field

Ahush fell though the ballroom as the stage curtains slowly drew back. Despite all the hardships brought by the Great Depression, Harley-Davidson dealers from as far away as Japan filled the Green Room of Milwaukee's Schroeder Hotel for the first dealers' convention in five years.

Why go through all that bother when the cash-strapped Motor Company would likely unveil just another year's ration of minor updates and new paint colors to the stale and unpopular flatheads?

Rumors. Hints. Sightings. A buzz.

Through the dealer network, word had spread around the world that an all-new Harley-Davidson was ready to make its debut, a motorcycle so new, so bold, and so exciting that it would power the company and dealers into a full-throttle climb out of the Depression.

Chief Engineer William S. Harley and Harley promotions man "Hap" Jameson stood proudly on that stage, like two stone lions flanking a magnificent wrought-iron gate. I doubt anyone noticed them, however, because between them was what everyone had come to see.

The hush deepened as the crowd absorbed every detail of the new machine. Even from the farthest corner of the room, dealers could see that the new motorcycle was a masterpiece of style—a bold fusion of Art Deco and streamlining that looked like a motorcycle, not another refinement of Harley's first motorized bicycles.

As the silence held for a long, enraptured moment, Bill Harley and the other company founders had to be wondering, "What are they all thinking?"

Seconds later, there was no doubt. From one corner came a whoop of triumph, followed by more, merging with wave after wave of applause. No one recorded whether Old Bill blushed, but certainly we could forgive him a little pride in his new baby's first standing ovation.

Bare-knuckled and brawny, the Overhead engine in this 1940 model isn't all that different from the Evolution engine that powered Harley back into profitability in the 1980s.

That bike was the Harley-Davidson Model E of 1936. The company liked to call its new machine the "Sixty-one" (in honor of its 61-cubic inch displacement) or "Overhead" (in honor of its overhead valves, a first on a Harley production twin).

You and I know it today as the "Knucklehead." That day was November 25, 1935, a defining moment in Harley-Davidson history that marked the real beginning of the Harley mystique. It was the day the Harley-Davidson big twin became more than just another motorcycle.

It was the day the legend began....

A CLOSER LOOK

After their first glimpse of the Sixty-one, the dealers impatiently sat through the rote presentation of the slightly revised flatheads that filled out the 1936 Harley line. The second it was over, they bum-rushed the stage to get a closer look at the Sixty-one.

The sleek styling that was so evident from afar was even more striking at arm's length. The Sixty-one was a looker from any angle. Symmetry defined the new machine. Twin gas tanks straddled the frame's backbone tube, each with its own chrome-plated filler cap and petcock. A new instrument panel with a large, inte-

Harley liked to call the 1936 Model E the "Sixty-one," in honor of its 61 cubic-inch engine, or "Overhead," in honor of its overhead valves. You and I know it as the Knucklehead.

Since the 1930s, Harleys have been famed for the quality of their paint-work and their bold color combinations. The company offered a striking array of color choices starting in 1933, in an attempt to compete with rival Indian Motocycle Company. Indian's motorcycles could be ordered in any color offered by DuPont, because DuPont owned Indian.

gral, 100-mile-per-hour speedometer (placed front and center, right where it would be easiest to read), an ammeter, an oil-pressure indicator, and the ignition switch bridged the gap between the tanks. Twin down-tubes swept back from the steering head to the rear axle clips. The sweeping V of the cylinders, highlighted on the right side by the gleaming pushrod covers, framed the dramatic slash-cut chrome-plated air intake horn. Polished aluminum rocker housings, each with two round, chrome-plated covers over the ends of the rock-er shafts topped those cylinders.

The whole bike had a smooth, streamlined, almost organic look to it, each part so perfectly placed that it seemed the product of divine inspiration. Like the exter-nal changes that distinguish Neanderthal from modern

Here we see the most popular choice—Vermilion Blue and Croydon Cream—shown with perhaps the best-looking choice—Sherwood Green with silver.

Boldest was this combo of Maroon tanks and fenders with Nile Green fender skirts and striping. Those aluminum rocker supports on the top of the heads gave rise to the Knucklehead name, because fans thought they resembled a clenched fist.

man, the differences between VL and Knuckle were subtle but reflected important changes deep inside.

Surprisingly—at least from today's perspective—these great looks were the natural result of great engineering, rather than the result of after-the-fact "styling" by some industrial designer. In the 1930s, Harley didn't even have a formal styling department, let alone the services of someone like Willie G.

That's right, Harley fans. This was a time when Harley's engineers designed the best motorcycles they knew how to build and worried about what they looked like second. The looks evolved with the engineering. Under the leadership of cofounder and chief engineer William S. Harley, function determined form. Period. Contrast this approach with that used to design the Twin Cam six decades later.

Even the new bike's silhouette was right, shaped as it was by the dictates of function. At the time, nature's own teardrop was hailed as the aerodynamically per-

fect form. No accident, then that the Knuckle's profile was defined by teardrop tanks superimposed over the teardrop loop of the frame, with wheels and a sprung seat tacked on. Look at a Softail today and you'll see the same perfect form.

The paint on the new machine accentuated its good looks. Gas tanks and fender crowns were blue; fender skirts, tank pinstripes, and wheel rims were white.

Peeking under the stylish gas tanks, dealers saw overhead valves and springs, promising that the new Sixty-one was more than just a pretty face. From what they could tell, about all the new engine had in common with the old flathead engine was the 45-degree V-angle. They weren't far off in that assumption. The engine looked great, too—all gloss black iron, shiny aluminum, and gleaming chrome.

As they nodded approvingly, rumors circulated that the heads were the latest hemispherical type and that prototypes had already buried the needle on the

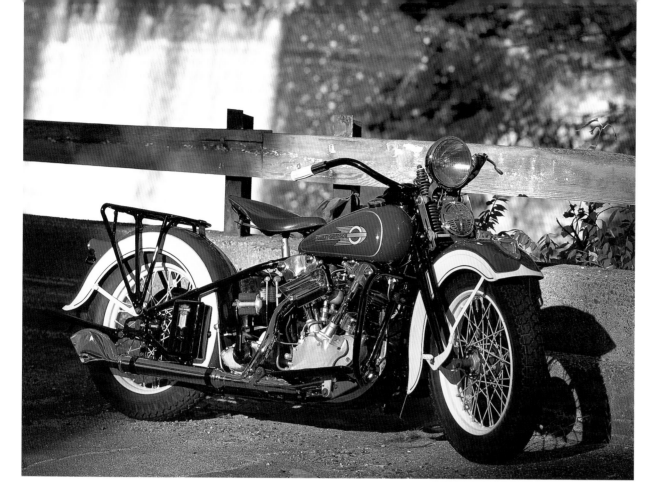

The 1936 Knuckle wasn't just a styling exercise. An all-new engine with overhead valves and hemi heads made it the American hot-rod of the era.

Is it a UPS Knucklehead? No, but many riders and dealers of the time thought the brown and blue paint for 1937 made the bike look as if it were in uniform, or worse, like liver. The scheme was not popular.

New tank and fender stripes modernized the Knuckle look for 1938. What really made fans of the Knuckle happy, though, was that Harley changed the valve covers to keep more of the oil inside the engine and off the rider's legs.

100-mile-per-hour speedo. Both rumors were true. (You didn't think the muscle cars of the 1950s and 1960s were the first "hemis," did you?)

Mounted to the left tank, the shifter gate had five positions—1, N, 2, 3, and 4, front to rear. A four-speed! That was new, too. And Harley pointed out that it was an advanced, constant-mesh design that was quieter, stronger, and more durable than the sliding-gear transmissions found on the competing Indian and foreign motorcycles.

Previous Harley frames had all been single-down-tube types that were really just descendants of turn-of-the-century bicycle frames. On the Sixty-one, twin down-tubes cradled the engine in a cage of rigid chrome-moly tubing. That frame and the beefy new springer front end promised handling to match the power.

Its swoopy new horseshoe-shaped oil tank filled the space under the seat. Its curved front contributed to the rounded, streamlined look of the new machine and hid the blocky battery from view. Savvy dealers noticed it had both feed and return tubes and knew what that meant: the Sixty-one's oiling system circulated oil through the engine and back to the oil tank to be used again. On previous Harleys the oil made a one-way trip through the engine and then dripped—"total loss" it was called.

In the Knucklehead, the dealers saw a knockout combination of cutting-edge looks and performance. It was, like the Model 94 Winchester or the Colt 1911 automatic pistol, an instant classic. It looked so right that it just had to work right. And like the Model 94 and the Colt pistol, the Knuckle's design indeed proved timeless, spawning whole industries of imitators.

One by one, the dealers filtered out of the ballroom with visions of the Sixty-one dancing in their heads.

DISAPPEARING ACT

After the curtains were closed on the stage that day, a curious thing happened: The most exciting new American motorcycle in over a decade disappeared as completely as if it had never been there at all.

For the rest of 1935 and early 1936, Harley insisted publicly that there was no Sixty-one. Harley's 1936 models were announced to the public in the January 1936 issue of *The Enthusiast*, and the Sixty-one was neither shown nor mentioned. Even the magazine's coverage of the dealers' convention ignored the Sixty-one.

Dealers knew better, but they were told to keep the secret because production would be "extremely limited" and that "under no circumstances should this model be ordered as a demonstrator!"

Why the secrecy when the dealers were so pumped and the market was so obviously ready?

Problems. Not big ones but messy ones nonetheless. The early Sixty-ones didn't just leak oil, they gushed the slippery stuff.

For reasons unknown, Bill Harley had left out of his recirculating oil system a return circuit for the oil pumped to the valves and rockers. That oil ended up all over the engines and riders. Also, valve springs broke.

Thus, while dealers clamored for immediate delivery of the Sixty-one, Harley-Davidson denied the new bike's existence while simultaneously working on fixes for its problems and getting the factory geared up for full production. Harley's failure on the 1930 VL had been embarrassingly public. If it failed again on the Sixty-one, Harley wanted it to be a private failure this time.

Fortunately, about the same time the factory was ready, so were fixes for the engine. Harley solved the oiling problem by fitting individual enclosures and

This tyke was meant to grow up to be a motorcycle rider.

Custom paint's not a new thing. You could order your new Knuckle painted just about any way you wanted, or have it painted later.

Cops loved the Knucklehead, too. No flathead Indian would ever get the best of them, once they had Harley's Overhead, especially after Harley added the big-port cylinder heads for 1940.

Along with the extra power came a restyle for the new decade, with new chrome tank badges and half-moon-shaped footboards.

oil return lines for each valve. A switch to a new supplier solved the valve spring problem.

The first Sixty-one demonstrator models shipped in January 1936, still under the cloak of silence.

PUBLIC DEBUT

A month later, the Sixty-one began to blow its own cover by winning formal and informal races and the hearts of Harley fans everywhere. On February 2, Butch Quirk rode a sidecar-equipped Sixty-one to victory in a 350-mile endurance run sponsored by the Rose City Motorcycle Club of Portland, Oregon. Later in the month, the Graves & Chubbuck dealership in Pasadena, California, reported: "There never has been a motorcycle put out that has set the boys to talking so much as the Sixty-one. The news of its arrival was broadcast by the boys from the treetops, and five hours after its setup there was 120 miles on the speedometer."

All the rave reviews quickly eased the company's fears, so on February 21, Harley officially broke the silence and actually encouraged dealers to take orders for the Sixty-one. It also ran an ad for its new Big Twin in *The Motorcyclist*.

Harley offered the Sixty-one in two basic forms: the high-compression Model EL and medium-compression Model E. The base price was $380, but for that you didn't even get a jiffy stand! To get that, you had to pay another $14 for the Standard Solo Group. As an odd aside, Harley even offered the Knucklehead engine to midget-car racers as the 36EM.

Production models featured the same great looks as the prototype shown at the dealers' convention. In addition to the blue and white shown on the prototype, the order blanks listed four other color combinations. Some of these were downright gaudy, especially the Maroon with neon Nile Green panels and rims.

By March, orders for the Sixty-one rolled in faster than Harley-Davidson could build them, despite the ongoing Depression.

PROBLEMS, SOLUTIONS, AND A HAPPY ENDING

Unfortunately, the first Knuckleheads proved anything but trouble free. Certainly, the problems were nowhere near as serious as those of the first VLs, but they were serious enough that Bill Harley spent the next six months modifying part after part to refine the design. Some dealers expressed bitterness that once again the Motor Company used its customers as unpaid testers.

Those dealers were more right than they knew. A powerful combination of Harley-Davidson's need to quickly recoup the bike's high development costs, the financial squeeze of the Depression, and labor laws that prevented H-D engineers from working overtime forced company management into releasing the design before it was fully mature. In fact, it was so immature, you could call the 1936 Sixty-ones "mass-produced prototypes" or "beta" versions in the parlance of the Internet age.

Fortunately, the problems that resulted weren't as severe as those that plagued the early VLs.

Nineteen forty was the first year you could get the fat 5.00x16 tires that soon became such a big part of the Harley look.

The Knuckle motor got an even-brawnier brother in 1941 with the introduction of the FL. Bored and stroked, the FL boasted 74 cubic inches of displacement and more horsepower and torque than the old Sixty-one could hope to produce.

The features that made the Sixty-one engine so exciting also proved the most troublesome. Its oil pump was more than adequate to pump oil all the way to the new OHV (overhead valve mechanism), but adjustment of the oil supply to each rocker arm was critical—and the standardized factory adjustment left some bikes with problems from over-oiled or under-oiled valves.

The consequences of over-oiling were unpleasant but not catastrophic: blue clouds of oil smoke and oil all over the bike and the rider's legs. Some even used more oil than the previous Harleys with total-loss oil systems.

If the adjustment erred on the side of under-oiling, the consequences were much more serious, ranging from

what Harley described as "squeaking" valves to rapid and excessive wear of the valves, rockers, and shafts.

For each of these problems and dozens more, the company quickly came up with fixes. During the year, Bill Harley modified nearly every part at least once, and some he modified three or more times before getting them right. All that is testament to his determination to make the Sixty-one's performance as good as its looks.

Dealers and riders may have griped, but they bought Sixty-ones anyway. They overlooked all of its problems because its over OHV engine gave it unprecedented performance for an American production twin. Even in its mild stock state of tune, the OHV engine could propel the

Sixty-one to an honest 95 miles per hour. With a little work, it easily outran its 100-mile-per-hour speedometer.

And unlike the flatheads from both Harley and Indian, the new OHV could sustain those high speeds indefinitely. Not only was it the best-looking bike on the planet, it was among the fastest. Of its United States-built contemporaries, only the Crocker held a clear advantage.

Harley's original plan was to build and sell 1,600 overheads that first year. By the time the plant switched over to 1937 production in the fall of 1936, it had actually sold between 1,700 and 1,900 of the expensive new model, depending on whose records you believe.

Yes, Harley's flathead big twins did outsell the Sixty-one that year, but everyone knew the Overhead would soon take over.

It was a fitting start to the legend.

1937: THE KNUCKLEHEAD TAKES OVER

If the original Sixty-one was the "beta" big twin, the 1937 version was the ready-for-prime-time Knuckle Version 1.0. It came with a beefier frame, larger rear brake, 120-mile-per-hour speedometer, and more improvements than you care to know about. What matters is that it really was improved, and that it sold even better than before.

Kenosha, WI, Harley dealer Frank Ulicki (center) at a blindfold contest.

The Myth of THE HARLEY & INDIAN "WARS"

By Greg Field

You've read all the Harley books, so you know how Harley and Indian were archrivals, trading blows through the 1910s, 1920s, 1930s, and 1940s until Indian finally folded in the 1950s.

If you read this one, you'll learn that the "war" fable is just another bit of Harley mythology that should finally go to the grave at the end of Harley's first century.

Far from being bitter rivals, Harley-Davidson and Indian were on the best of terms. Did each try to outdo the other, saying, "Gotcha," with every new model? Not at all. Before each sales season, representatives of

the two companies would meet for an opulent meal and discuss each company's new models.

Then, together, they would decide what each company's motorcycles should sell for. That's called "price fixing." I'm not sure it was illegal then, but it sure as hell would be now. And it sure as hell ain't competition, much less "war." Can you imagine Harley and Honda doing the same thing today?

Need more evidence? How about this: Indian founder George Hendee and Harley founder Art Davidson were close friends who visited each other at their homes and bonded over common interests in motorcycles and Guernsey cows.

Need more? When Indian got in financial trouble before DuPont bought the company, the Harley founders discussed ways to help the ailing Company, according to Jean Davidson, in her book *Growing Up Harley-Davidson*. And when Indian finally died, there was mourning in Milwaukee.

All the competition was at the dealership level, where loyalty to each brand ran high. That spilled over onto the racetrack, where all the battles were really fought, with grit and valor and glorious victories on both sides.

Japan bombed Pearl Harbor just as the 1942 Harleys went on sale. Almost overnight, the Milwaukee factory switched production over to the military WLA.

Even if you could get a Knuckle during the war, it was as gray and dreary as the Seattle sky. Black paint replaced all the chrome, and gray was often the only paint available.

And the Sixty-one left its mark on the whole Harley line that year. All the other flathead models were dressed up in Sixty-one style and were fitted with recirculating oil systems. In addition, the big-twin flatties got the four-speed transmission and dual-cradle frame.

It was time to break some records with Harley's hot-rod. On March 13, Joe Petrali, who had helped Bill Harley design the Sixty-one, piloted a specially prepared Knuckle to a straightaway record of 136.183 miles per hour on the sand of Daytona Beach.

On April 8 and 9, a true iron man named Fred Ham took a couple days off from his job as a Pasadena motorcycle cop to assault the record for the most miles ridden in 24 hours. To complicate matters, he planned to do all the riding himself on a stock Sixty-one he'd purchased in October 1936. First, he laid out a 5-mile course on Muroc Dry Lake (the sight of Edwards Air Force Base today). Then, with the help of a crew of 20, oil flares to light the course at night, and quarts of cold milk to keep him energized, Ham proceeded to go 'round and 'round for 24 straight hours, stopping only for gas and to change the chain. In all, he rode 1,825 miles, averaging 76.6 miles per hour, a new record.

In other news, Harley-Davidson production workers voted to unionize in March 1937, which broke the heart of founder and company production chief Bill Davidson. Some believe the struggle against unionization contributed to his quick decline and death on April 21.

1938: "SMOOTHER, QUIETER, CLEANER"

After all the changes of 1936 and 1937, the Knucklehead was a mature design. Harley's theme for

Left
Even police officers had difficulty getting new Harleys during the early years of the war. By 1945, when this beauty was built, they were available to any department that wanted them.

Adolph Roemer, Milwaukee Motorcycle Dispatch Corps, 1941–1942.

The overhead-valve Knuckle engine was a revelation for the California Highway Patrol, because it wouldn't overheat and seize during long high-speed pursuits, as did the old flatheads.

the 1938 Knuckleheads was "smoother, quieter, cleaner." It was time to make the Knuckle more civilized.

The biggest change was a set of new valve covers that completely enclosed the rockers and valves, keeping the oil in and the dirt out. Black pants were no longer mandatory.

For 1939, the changes were mostly cosmetic, including the change to what is perhaps the prettiest two-tone paint scheme ever used on a Harley. Even so, Knuckle sales were way up for the year, while sales of the flatheads were stagnant or declining.

Milwaukee motorcycle police officer Ray Schok, 1940s.

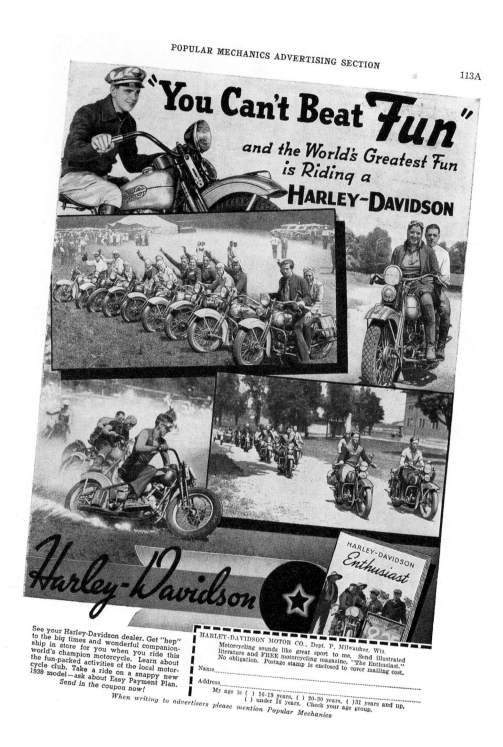

THE BIG-PORT KNUCKLEHEAD, FL, AND WORLD WAR II

Even with war breaking out in Europe, Harley restyled the Sixty-one for 1940, with new sheet metal and tank badges, half-moon footboards, and the option of fat 16-inch tires. Park a 1940 Knuckle next to a Heritage Springer, and I guarantee you'll see the resemblance. The engine got more powerful and more reliable, too, courtesy of larger intake ports, manifold, and carburetor, along with a beefier bottom end and clutch.

By 1941, American industry was gearing up for war. Harley was, too, but the company's engineers still found time to bore and stroke their OHV engine to 74 cubic inches, creating the Model FL engine, known as the "Seventy-four Overhead" to distinguish it from the

After the war ended, Harley wanted to go whole-hog into building civilian models, but the U.S. government gave the steel, aluminum, and chrome needed for production to the European countries under the Marshall Plan.

Following pages
Fifty-plus years of honest wear next to a near-perfect restoration. Who wouldn't want one of each?

Steel and aluminum supplies improved by 1947, but Harley still couldn't get the material to build enough bikes to keep customers happy. Think waiting lists for Harleys began in the 1990s? Think again.

regular Seventy-four, which was a flathead. They threw in an all-new clutch, too, to handle the extra torque of the big FL.

By the time the 1942 models began rolling off the line in the early fall of 1941, America was perilously close to entering the war. American factories were churning out planes, tanks, guns, and other military equipment, to the exclusion of almost everything else. And so was Harley-Davidson. With fat contracts to build bikes for U.S. and Allied forces and shortages of steel, copper, iron, and aluminum, Harley-Davidson only promised each dealer one new bike for the 1942 model year.

The post-war Knuckle engines were basically unchanged form pre-war versions, but they looked spiffy; by 1947 Harley could get enough chrome to dress them up again.

Then came December 7 and the attack on Pearl Harbor. On January 1, 1942, all production of civilian cars, trucks, and motorcycles was halted for the duration of the war. For most of the war years, you had to be a policeman, fireman, essential war worker, or senator's son to get a new Harley.

Those dealers who joined up or were drafted had to worry about keeping their hides whole, while those left behind worried about staying in business. It was a struggle.

While the rest of the country mourned casualties of war, Harley suffered its own. On February 7, 1942, Harley-Davidson President Walter Davidson Sr. died. William H. Davidson, son of the late founder William A., soon took his uncle's place at the head of the company. He would lead the company for the next 41 years.

In May 1942, gasoline and sugar rationing began in the United States. Worse yet, aluminum became

"unobtainium." To get pistons to repair a customer's bike, Harley dealers had to send in the wrecked ones so they could be melted down to build replacements.

To help its dealers stay in business, Harley steered them toward the only sales the government allowed: cop bikes. Dealer bulletins even made suggestions about the perfect Christmas gift to buy the local police chief. Of course, that gift had the Harley logo!

For 1943, Harley built 27,000 military motorcycles, but only about 200 Knuckles. These were civilian or police bikes, but there were a few attempts to dress the Overhead in olive drab. Harley even experimented with joining two Knucklehead motors together to power a light tank for the Canadian army. A true War Hog, eh?

On September 18, 1943, Harley-Davidson cofounder and chief engineer Bill Harley died.

By 1944, restrictions on civilian sales were loosened to allow the sale of more than 500 Knuckles. The

Harley restyled the Knuckle for 1947. Among the new pieces were the instrument panel and speedometer, shown here.

Following page
Rocket-fin mufflers replaced the rooster-tail versions for 1941, but many fans still preferred the older style. The tombstone taillight was new for 1947.

government also surplused many thousands of military motorcycles, and Harley dealers snapped them up and quickly sold them to their eager customers.

By the start of 1945, the battles raged on, but the Allies were confident victory was at hand. The Germans surrendered on May 8, and Japan followed on September 2.

PICKING UP THE PIECES

At the start of the 1946 model year, opportunities abounded for Harley-Davidson and its dealers. The war was won, the boys were coming home by the thousands, and demand was high because most pre-war motorcycles were worn out or scrapped for lack of spares during the wartime years. Time for Harley and the dealers to cash in.

Hard to believe, but Harley didn't offer chrome header pipes until well into the Shovelhead era. Instead, Harley would sell you the stylish chrome flex-pipe covers shown here.

Bill Harley designed an early version of this fork when he was still in college. It was used on all classic Harleys through 1948 and was even licensed for use on other bikes during the 1920s and 1930s.

In 1947, the Knuckle was Harley's largest and most powerful motorcycle, yet it was trim and light by modern Big Twin standards, weighing less than a modern Sportster.

Even better, the flagship of Harley's motorcycle fleet—the Knucklehead—was still the best and most technologically advanced American production motorcycle. Ten years after the Knuckle's introduction, Indian was still peddling flatheads and was rapidly losing market share to the more advanced Harley Overheads.

As a result, Harley-Davidson was able to sell all the motorcycles it could find raw materials to build. Harley built 6,746 Knuckleheads for 1946, more than for any preceding year. The same was true for 1947. After 12 years of production, the Knucklehead was still the American champion.

THEY'RE ALL KNUCKLEHEADS

By November 1947, the champion got a facelift. Harley released its 1948 lineup, including what it called the "biggest motorcycle story of the year," a new version of the Overhead engine to carry the company into the future. The most obvious change was new valve covers that looked like chrome-plated cake pans.

The real story was under the pans, however. Aluminum heads and hydraulic lifters made Harley's OHV motor smoother, quieter, more oil tight, cooler running, and more maintenance free, if not more powerful. In time, it was given the nickname "Panhead."

For 1966, Harley's Overhead was given yet another facelift. It, too, was a top-end job that made the Overhead smoother, quieter, more oil tight, cooler running, and more maintenance free than its predecessor, but not much lighter or more powerful. Enthusiasts soon christened it "Shovelhead."

In 1984 came yet another revision to Harley's OHV, called the V2 Evolution engine. With aluminum cylinders and many other updates, the Evo was a thoroughly modern fulfillment of Bill Harley's original design. When combined with a restyled and updated chassis in new models such as the Softail and FLHT, the Evolution engine once again gave Harley-Davidson's Big Twin true mass-market appeal. As a result, by the early 1990s, the once-ailing Milwaukee

firm would again achieve the same dominance in the American marketplace that it had enjoyed at the end of the Knuckle's reign.

For 1999, the all-new Twin Cam 88 eclipsed the Evo, and the evolutionary line that began with the 1936 Knuckle came to an end. But after 60-plus years of change, during which Harley engineers made thousands of refinements, the basics that made the 1936 Sixty-one engine so appealing remained unchanged.

Knuckle to Pan to Shovel to Evo—all those changes and nicknames make a fascinating story, as you'll read in the following chapters, but we may all be trying to pick fly shit out of the pepper by perpetuating such nicknames.

Truth is, the switch from Knucklehead to Panhead was barely noticed by most riders—and it wasn't accompanied by a nickname change. That came years later. To Harley-Davidson and to Harley riders, the new engines were still just Sixty-one and Seventy-four Overheads. After the Shovel came along, such names were finally useful, and when the Evo came along, even Harley got in on the name game.

Nevertheless, when enthusiasts born during Harley's second century look back on all this, fine distinctions that seem so important to the story of Harley's first century—Panhead, Shovelhead, Evolution, and even Twin Cam—will likely be forgotten.

From the viewpoint of centuries, all those colors bleed into one. They're all just incremental updates of the original Sixty-one engine.

In other words, they're all Knuckleheads.

In front of Bill Knuth's H-D shop in Milwaukee, WI, 1949.

What's in A NAME?

By Greg Field

You probably know how the various Harley engines got all those evocative nicknames like Knucklehead, Panhead, and Shovelhead. Although the Motor Company has trademarked them all, Harley didn't coin any of them. Enthusiasts did.

What you may not know is that with the exception of the Shovel, the names came long after the engines were introduced.

That's right. No one called the 1936 Model EL a "Knucklehead" in 1936. They called it an "Overhead" or "OHV" because of its overhead-valve engine, or they called it a "Sixty-one" because of its displacement. The EL didn't even rate the name "Big Twin" then, that name being reserved for the larger 74- and 80-inch flatheads.

Prior to 1957, the only official name Harley used for its Big Twin was "Overhead Valve."
Note the "OHV" as on the fender.

Harley first gave its Big Twin an official name for the 1958 model year. The "Duo-Glide" refers to the fact that this new model had suspension front and rear.

What, then, did they call the 74-cubic-inch overhead-valve engine when it came along in 1941? Was it a Big Twin? Was it a Seventy-four? Nope. It was a Seventy-four Overhead, because the 74-cubic-inch flathead was still in production. And it didn't inherit the "Big Twin" mantle until the flathead Big Twins were discontinued.

Soon after the demise of the Big Twin flatheads, Harley switched to the engine design later dubbed "Panhead" and then to new "Hydra-Glide" telescopic forks. Harley named the new machines after the forks, so enthusiast didn't need to make up a name. If you bought a new Harley overhead-valve twin in 1949, you bought a "Hydra-Glide," not a "Panhead." And so it went through the "Duo-Glide" years and through the first year of the "Electra Glide." Harley supplied the name, so Harley riders didn't need to.

Then came 1966, with the new engine in the Electra Glide chassis. 'What do we call the old Electra Glide,' they asked?' And now that we're chopping all the old iron, how do we tell each other exactly what we're working on?' That's when the names became necessary and caught on throughout the Harley universe.

From the day of its introduction, the fourth generation of Harley's overhead-valve Big Twin engine had an official name: V2 Evolution. A few months later, in one of the first tests of the engine, a moto-wag jokingly suggested the nickname "Blockhead," just to see if it would stick. That name was in vogue for a while—especially among Harley's detractors. For a while, "Sandwichhead," a name descriptive of the three-piece rocker covers, was even popular. In recent years, the latter two seem to have died out in favor of the simple, evocative "Evo."

When the next engine came along for 1999, Harley named it, too: "Twin Cam 88." Cynical moto-journalists tried to stick it with the nickname "Fathead," but it doesn't seem to have stuck. Instead, enthusiasts currently favor "Twinkie."

For 2002 Harley brought out a water-cooled next-generation machine and named it the V-Rod, perhaps to create some association with Harley's VR1000 road racing bike. Before Harley even showed the new machine, it already had several nicknames—among them "Wethead" and "Sprinklerhead"—courtesy of Internet enthusiast groups.

The jury's still out on what Harley riders will be calling these latest engines when Harley turns 200.

By the time Harley gave its Big Twin electric start, official names were expected, which explains the "Electra Glide" on the front fender of this Shovelhead.

Chapter 4

THE PANHEAD ERA

By Greg Field

Despite the thousands of U.S soldiers killed in World War II, America's jubilation knew no bounds in the fall of 1945. The Allies had soundly trounced Hitler and Tojo, the country's heroes were on their way home, and America glowed with pride that it had proven itself the world's new superpower.

From Harley-Davidson's boardroom, the sunrise of the post war era looked glorious. Spurred on by military sales, the company had revitalized and retooled itself to build nearly 100,000 copies of "The Motorcycle That Won the War." Harley-Davidson was ready to best all previous production records.

And the market for Harley's Big Twins looked as limitless as the Lake Michigan horizon stretching east from Milwaukee. Millions of servicemen—including thousands of former Harley mounted dispatch riders— were suddenly discharged, their wallets fat with money they couldn't spend at the front and their sense of adventure honed keen by war. On the home front, after years of sacrifice, gas rationing, reduced speed limits, and tire shortages, gearheads couldn't wait to cash in their war bonds and drive, drive, drive, in rapid pursuit of the good life.

Unfortunately, that post-war sunrise quickly darkened for the Motor Company. New clouds of war rolled in from the east, as the Soviet Union tightened its stranglehold on Eastern Europe and Mao's Communist forces marched toward victory in China. The terms "Iron Curtain" and "Cold War" gained everyday usage, and Harley-Davidson was once again called on to sacrifice.

The U.S. government's first volley in the Cold War was the Marshall Plan. Implemented to contain the Soviets by rebuilding the war-ravaged economies of Europe and England, the Marshall Plan sent hundreds of millions of dollars in scarce raw materials such as steel and chromium overseas to America's economic competitors.

Harley's designers were and
still are sculptors of chrome.
The headlight and upper fork
shrouds of the Hydra-Glide
were a masterpiece.

In the fall of 1947, when Harley
introduced its 1948 model line,
the big news was a major update
to its Overhead engine.

Following page
See the chrome top hat covering
each head? That was the signature
change to the engine, and the
source of a new nickname:
Panhead. Those pan covers did a
better job of keeping the oil inside
the engine than the old Knuckle
covers ever did.

At the same time, drastically lowered import duties enabled those competitors to ship back goods and undercut U.S. manufacturers, including Harley-Davidson. While the Marshall Plan may have contained Communism abroad, it was a one-two punch that hindered capitalism at home—especially in Milwaukee.

As a result of getting only a fraction of the steel, chrome, aluminum, and rubber it needed, Harley-Davidson couldn't build enough Knuckleheads in 1946 and 1947 to meet the demand. Think waiting lists for new Harleys began in the 1990s? Think again! Guys who wanted a new Harley in the late 1940s often had to wait. Those who didn't want to wait looked to the other makers.

Only one group of makers had a seemingly limitless supply of new bikes to offer.

THE BRITISH INVASION

While the U.S. government was reining in Harley-Davidson, the British government put the spurs to its motorcycle industry by forcing it to export 75 percent of its output or face reduced quotas of the same scarce materials denied Harley.

In style, the 1948 Pan was almost identical to the 1947 Knuckle. One of the rare differences is shown here: a restyled speedo.

Only the United States had the cash to buy all those Brit bikes, and because of the reduced tariffs that were part of the Marshall Plan, those machines were artificially cheap. They were also light, fast, and fun, and there weren't enough Harleys to go around. Instead of the trickle of Triumphs and Nortons that had been imported before the war, 1946 brought a flood of British machinery. England exported nearly 10,000 motorcycles to the United States in 1946 and more than 15,000 in 1947. Many, if not most of those motorcycles were sold to potential Harley customers.

Imagine the frustration in Milwaukee. After barely surviving the Great Depression and helping win the war, they were stabbed in the back by governmental policy. Did the company pout or cry foul, or scream, "That's not fair?" Nope. Those tactics would come later.

Harley chose to compete. That doesn't mean the company's engineers immediately countered the British threat with like machines. That, too, came later, with the launch of the K-models and Sportsters. In that late 1940s, Harley ceded the performance market to the British and steered its Big Twin line down a new road, one that led not to lighter weight or greater performance, but nonetheless to refinement and success.

That more-refined Big Twin made its debut in the fall of 1947, for the 1948 model year. At first glance, the 1948 Sixty-one and Seventy-four Overheads didn't look very new. In fact, nothing was really new,

except the whole top end of the engine. But what a difference a new top end can make.

Most noticeable were the curious new valve covers that looked like chrome-plated cake pans atop each cylinder head. Though Harley didn't even have a name for the new model, Harley enthusiasts soon began referring to it as the "Panhead."

THE PANHEAD MOTOR

With a bulletproof bottom end and decent power, the last of the Knucklehead engines were the equal of all but the most exotic of their contemporaries. Still, they leaked too much oil and were prone to overheating when pushed hard, so Harley engineers applied to the Harley Big Twin some of the lessons learned in the wartime pressure-cooker about making air-cooled motors more reliable.

The Pan took on a whole new look when a modern-looking hydraulically damped telescopic fork replaced the antique-looking springer fork. Harley called the new fork—and the bike—the "Hydra-Glide."

One of those lessons was that aluminum alloy was a better choice of material for the cylinder heads than iron. Aluminum gets rid of engine heat much better than iron, and it is lighter, too. Harley had known all this long before the war (and had even used aluminum heads on some of its flathead motors) but had stuck with iron because aluminum was comparatively expensive. That is, it was more expensive until thousands and thousands of surplus planes were flown home after the war and melted down into light, shiny aluminum ingots. When it began to look as if aluminum would be cheap and plentiful in post-war America, H-D took advantage of the opportunity and used the material for the Panhead.

The new aluminum cylinder heads for the Panhead were completely redesigned to make the whole engine tidier and more reliable. Harley engineers eliminated external oil lines by adding internal passages to oil the cylinders and heads. The valvetrain was redesigned for greater longevity and reduced maintenance, and the aforementioned chrome-plated pans enclosed the resulting assembly. The new covers

The beefy Hydra-Glide fork updated the Harley look so successfully that it still inspires stylists more than a half century later.

Display put on by Milwaukee Motorcycle Club and dealer Bill Knuth, 1949. Note early model.

lent a simple, more modern look to the new heads—and they kept the oil in and dirt out far better than the Knucklehead's separate covers.

Another surprise lurked under those pans, however: hydraulic lifters!

Before the Panhead was introduced, OHV motorcycle engines had purely mechanical links between the cam lobes in the bottom end and the valves in the heads. This simple and effective system required frequent and diligent adjustment to hold the clackity-clacking of loose valves at bay and prevent the heartbreak of burned valves. Nevertheless, valve adjustments were a maintenance hassle that nobody really needed.

Hydraulic lifters solved all those problems by automatically adjusting themselves for proper clearances. Harley engineers put one of them atop each Panhead pushrod. After initial adjustment at the factory, the lifters required adjustment only after major engine repair. Hydraulic lifters meant less time wrenching so the owner of the new Panhead could spend more time riding. It didn't hurt that the new lifters made the engine quieter, so the rider could better enjoy the music of the exhaust note.

The Panhead wasn't the first engine with hydraulic lifters, but what mattered to the Motor Company was that the Panhead was the first *motorcycle* engine with hydraulic lifters, and that they worked, which they did... except when they didn't. We'll get to that later.

The majority of 1952 Pans came from the factory with a hand shift and foot clutch. Many modern riders can't imagine dealing with a hand shift, but they can be fun to ride.

Harley took its Big Twin in a new direction with the Panhead. Instead of spending scarce development money to make more powerful motorcycles to compete with hot-rod British twins, Harley-Davidson concentrated on making its big Overheads quieter, more oil tight, and easier to maintain, so they would appeal to a broader cross-section of Americans. With the 1948 Panhead, Harley's OHV Big Twin began a long rumble down a new byway. The new Panhead was one small step for motorcycling but one giant step for the Motor Company. It was also the start of the most innovative era in Harley history.

HYDRA-GLIDING INTO THE FIFTIES

Nineteen forty-nine was the on-ramp to the paranoid-but-prosperous 1950s. Lines drawn around the world that year culminated in several bloody Cold War skirmishes. Pizza fever began its spread to the heartland. Television began its rise toward becoming the new national pastime. Bikini bathing suits shocked and titillated swimmers across America. The 33 1/3-rpm, long-play record was introduced, and Polaroid's new Land camera began spoiling Americans with photographs

that self-developed in 60 seconds. Roller Derby put pro wrestling on wheels, the first Volkswagen "bugs" hit America's shores, and America's first prefabricated suburb rose out of a Long Island field. And George Orwell's prophetic novel, *1984*, was published to critical acclaim.

It's no surprise that the bike that came to define American motorcycling for the 1950s also made its entrance in 1949: a vastly updated and restyled Panhead called the "Hydra-Glide."

This time, the differences between old and new were anything but subtle. The whole bike was restyled in a bold, modern (for 1949) fashion that was as different from the old springer-forked bikes as the first Knucklehead was from the old flathead it replaced. And the more modern look of the Hydra-Glide was as timeless as that of the Knucklehead that preceded it. Compare one to today's Heritage Softail, and you'll find a lot more similarities than differences. In many ways, the Hydra-Glides were the classic Pans.

Most noticeable was the all-new front end, dominated by massive-looking telescopic forks. Harley-Davidson named its innovative new hydraulic forks "Hydra-Glide." Before long, the Panheads themselves became known by

This rare original 1955 Hydra-Glide featured the Hollywood Green paint option. The toolbox, oil tank, and primary cover were painted to match the tank and fenders.

the Hydra-Glide moniker, and Harley-Davidson encouraged the trend by offering optional front-fender badges featuring the name.

Why telescopic forks when the old spring fork had worked so well for so long? Because, truthfully, springers hadn't worked all that well at all—they had a mere 2 inches of travel and needed constant maintenance—and because most of the competition had already switched to the telescopic forks. BMW built the world's first production motorcycle with a hydraulically damped telescopic fork in 1935, and by 1949, the design had become the industry standard for front suspension design. Harley knew that another tidal wave of Brit bikes with telescopic forks was about to wash over America's shores, so the Panhead needed an immediate suspension and image upgrade to keep from being swept aside.

The Panhead got telescopic forks, but it got a set that could only have come from Milwaukee. Unlike the spindly-looking forks on the foreign bikes, the

Hydra-Glide forks looked stout and muscular. The fork legs were spaced wide to clear the fat front tire and the new front fender. The upper tubes and whole top of the fork assembly were shrouded in black-painted, stamped-steel cover panels that gave the front end the massive good looks that are still so much a part of Harley style. Polished stainless steel covers were optional, but the bright covers looked so good that few bikes were ordered with the plain-Jane black ones.

Ads for the 1949 Panhead emphasized that the new forks were not just about looks, however. "Hydra-Glide sets a new standard in smooth-as-flying, road-hugging comfort," said one, and the ad copy was right. Hydra-Glide forks gave more than twice the travel of the springer forks and their velocity-sensitive valving tamed bumpy roads much better than the old springers. Along with the new fork came a much larger and more powerful front brake.

Continued on page 116

Hummers, Scats, and Toppers

THE MILWAUKEE TWO-STROKES

By Greg Field

To the winner go the spoils. Among the spoils of World War II was a 125-cc two-stroke engine from German maker DKW.

Harley-Davidson, as a member of the winning side, claimed that engine as part of Germany's wartime reparation. Harley put the little two-stroke engine into production for mid-year 1948 as the Model S, a fun little bike with a girder-type front suspension, rigid rear, and a little "peanut" tank that later charmed the world on the XLCH Sportster. It was Harley's best seller that year, with over 10,000 units trailing blue smoke out dealership doors.

In 1951, Harley updated the Model S with a telescopic fork. That fork was of the male-slider type, like all the "upside-down" forks on the latest Buells. In 1953, Harley punched the engine out to a 165 cc and called it the ST. In 1954 Harley added a second model, the STU, which was fitted with a carburetor restrictor to reduce power to under five horsepower, so the kiddies could ride them on the street without a license. In 1955 came a third model, a stripper with the old 125 engine and a "squeeze-bulb" bicycle horn as stock equipment. Harley called its new kiddy bike the Hummer. It didn't need a restrictor, because its little engine was only good for three horsepower.

With the invasion of light, powerful Brit bikes in the early 1950s, sales of the Harley two-strokes steadily declined. Then, came another invasion—an invasion of scooters from Italy—that cut further into sales for Harley's lightweights.

Harley fought back first on the scooter front. The battlewagon of Milwaukee's 1960 counterattack was the all-new Model A Topper scooter.

The Hummer was one of Harley's third attempts to market a motorcycle to the booming youth market following World War II.

Where the Italian scooters were sleek, light, and zippy, the Topper was slab-sided, heavy, and underpowered, with only about five horsepower. For 1961, Harley hot-rodded the Topper to keep up with the Lambrettas and Vespas. The brawny Topper H came with almost twice the horsepower, but by then the scooter craze was played out, and everyone had moved on to small motorcycles from Japan. Sales declined, and the Topper was discontinued in 1965.

For 1962, Harley punched out its two-stroke engine to 175 cc for use on the Pacer streetbike and Scat dual sport, or "scrambler," as such bikes were called at the time. Harley did this in an attempt to give its two-stroke bikes enough power to keep up with the more modern lightweights from Japan and from Harley's Aermacchi affiliate. For 1963, Harley finally gave the Pacers and Scats rear suspension. And what a suspension! As on the later Softail models and Buells, Harley hid the suspension components under the transmission. For 1966, the new Bobcat replaced the Pacer and Scat. The Bobcat was clothed in fiberglass, with its gas tank and boat-tail rear section made from the material.

At the end of 1966, Harley discontinued the little Bobcat and used the full capacity of its Milwaukee plants to build the more profitable Electra Glides and Sportsters.

The Hummers, Scats, Toppers and the rest were good little bikes, but were never really accepted by Harley's hardcore riders and dealers.

continued from page 111

With its shiny Panhead motor and hydraulic forks, the Hydra-Glide was definitely not Grandpa's old Silent Gray Fellow, or flathead, or Knuckle for that matter. It set a new standard for touring bikes of its era, and it was faster, smoother, better handling, and more mannered than any Harley that had come before.

FOOT SHIFT

Though the Hydra-Glide set a new standard for touring bikes of its era, its foot clutch and hand shift made it seem a pre-war relic. All the latest machines from Britain had foot shifters, and the feature was seen as an essential component of a post-war pedigree. Even Indian outshifted Harley on this one, fitting a few Chiefs with foot shifters in late 1949 and early 1950. After swimming against the flow for too long, Harley introduced foot-shift as a Panhead option in late 1951.

Still, Harley's management knew that many of its customers were die-hard traditionalists, so they offered the customer a choice of foot-shift or hand-shift. Most of them wanted foot-shift, and by 1954, foot-shifted bikes outsold hand-shifted machines by a margin of nearly two to one. That margin continued to

Handsome new tank stripes provided aesthetic updates in 1956, but little else was changed.

Near Holy Hill outside of Milwaukee, WI, 1950.

Previous pages
A new color for 1955 was Anniversary Yellow (even though there wasn't an anniversary), shown here. This bike boasts an FLH engine, the new hot-rodded Big Twin for 1955.

The new Sportster grabbed most of the attention for 1957, but the Big Twins got new (plastic) tank badges and new tank panels.

widen every year until only a few hand-shift models were produced each year in the late 1960s.

The Panhead motor itself got a small-but-important update in 1953. In a successful attempt to make the hydraulic lifters more reliable, Harley engineers moved them from the top of the pushrods to the bottom, closer to the oil pump. With this small change, the Panhead's lifters were truly reliable at last. And the basics of this lifter scheme remained in use through the end of the Evolution engines.

Although today the factory celebrates 1903 as its first year, Harley designated 1954 its 50th Anniversary. To mark the occasion, all 1954 Harleys featured special 50th Anniversary badges on their front fenders.

In December 1953, as the 1954 models were rolling off the production line in earnest, H-D's image took a real drubbing in the sensationalist biker flick *The Wild One*. The movie begins with the warning: "This is a shocking story. It could never take place in most American towns—but it did in this one. It is a public challenge not to let it happen again."

The classic hardtail lines disappeared after 1957, and wouldn't return until the advent of the Softail in 1984.

Though the "bikers" in the movie seem almost wholesome now—and their antics in taking over the town probably wouldn't rate a disorderly conduct charge today—the movie really shocked audiences in 1953 and 1954. No longer did the American public think of a motorcycle club as a group of uniformed Shriners riding full-dress Harleys in the Fourth of July parade. A club was now seen as a bunch of unshaven, drunken rowdies, as typified by Marlon Brando's *Wild One* gang, the "Black Rebels MC." Worse yet, the film's villains—Chino (played by Lee Marvin) and his club—rode Harleys and Indians, while Brando's anti-hero Johnny and his group rode Triumphs. After *The Wild One*—and a whole slew of Hollywood imitation—America had a new idea of what kind of people they'd meet on a Harley.

For 1955, Harley-Davidson released its own "Wild One"—the FLH Super Sport. The "H" stood for "high compression." That higher compression combined with ported and polished intakes, boosted FLH horsepower by 10 percent. This extra power helped haul the weight of all the chrome gadgets and touring gear that riders were starting to bolt onto their Hydra-Glides. Bottom ends on all the 1955 Pan engines were beefed up with stout Timken tapered bearings in place of the old roller bearings.

For 1956, the FLH was given even more guts, courtesy of the hot new "Victory" camshaft and even

The sun set on the Hydra-Glide at the end of the 1957 model year.

And the sun rose on a new Harley-Davidson legend in 1958: the Duo-Glide. Its defining feature was the swingarm-and-shocks rear suspension that inspired its name.

Hollywood HOGS

By Mike Seate

Harley-Davidson motorcycles and movies seemed destined to coexist in a symbiotic partnership. Both motorcycles and cinema were among the most dynamic of America's developing technologies during the early years of the twentieth century, making it inevitable that filmmakers would see the potential for two-wheelers on the big screen. It took less than a decade after the first Harley-Davidson motorcycle rolled out of Arthur and Walter Davidson and Bill Harley's tiny Milwaukee garage for one of the spindly single-cylinder machines to make its debut in a silent film.

During the era of thinly plotted action comedies and Keystone Kops farces, quick, agile motorcycles became as common in the silent filmmaker's repertoire of sight gags as tumbling ladders and runaway locomotives. Harley-Davidson, always a media-savvy company, was keen enough to capitalize on the newly established celebrity potential of its machines. In 1918, Seattle Harley-Davidson dealer Harry Trainor saw a chance to showcase the brand's legendary torque and durability when 250-pound vaudeville starlet Trixie Friganza arrived in town for a series of performances. Trainor, eager to show off his new machines, alerted the local press that he'd be chauffeuring the portly Miss Friganza around Seattle's hilly boulevards on a sidecar-equipped Harley-Davidson V-twin.

While the 61-cubic-inch machine called upon all of its available 7.2 horsepower to perform the task, the clever publicity stunt proved worthy of P.T. Barnum himself. Since then, Harley-Davidson's link with movies and show business celebrities has continued unabated, with movie stars from Clark Gable to Larry Hagman flying down Hollywood Boulevard astride customized Milwaukee iron.

Harley-Davidson reaped immeasurable exposure from the association of its products with the film world's biggest names, and directors and producers continued to install America's favorite motorcycle into their works for dramatic effect.

Although in recent years, motorcycles have been cast as universal props for rebellion and antisocial behavior, in the early post-World War II years, Harleys briefly enjoyed a different film role. In the excellent 1953 cop drama *Code Two*, star Ralph Meeker led a squad of Harley riding highway patrol officers over the back roads of Southern California to

Although Harley's had appeared in cinema since the company's earliest years, *Easy Rider*'s Captain America and the Billy Bike were the first Harleys to be featured in costarring roles.

track down a truck hijacking ring. The elegant, police-issue Harley-Davidson Knuckleheads and Panheads in *Code Two* and the serious, crime-does-not-pay message of the film contrasted sharply with the image makeover that motorcycles were about to receive.

With the 1954 release of *The Wild One*, producer Stanley Kramer's epic of post-war angst and black leather insouciance, motorcycles would forever be linked with rebellion in the minds of moviegoers and the general public. Ironically, neither Marlon Brando's pouty gang leader Johnny, nor his drunken jester of an arch nemesis Chino, portrayed by an unshaven Lee Marvin, rode Harleys. Brando's mount was a stock Triumph Thunderbird while Marvin rode a rather oily-looking Indian twin. Nevertheless, *The Wild One*'s tale of a group of bored, restless bikers invading a small out-back hamlet was to become the ghetto from which Harley-Davidson motorcycles would spend the next four decades trying to escape.

Not that Hollywood helped to improve motorcycling's public image. In fact, it only took a couple of years for B-grade studios, principally American International Pictures (A.I.P.), to start cranking out a number of anxious, overwrought motorcycle rebellion flicks. Starting with the laughable *Motorcycle Gang* in 1957, A.I.P. teamed director Roger Corman with former horror-movie maven Samuel Z. Arkoff to create more than a dozen biker exploitation films. Other studios pitched in with other films that all seemed to follow *The Wild One*'s template of invading motorcycle gang versus small town. Drive-in screens lit up throughout the 1960s and early 1970s with movies such as *Devil's Angels*, *Wild Angels*, *Hell's Angels on Wheels*, and *The Savage Seven*. Barely indistinguishable from each other, these so-called chopper operas took full advantage of the headlines generated by real-life biker gangs, who were just then coming to notoriety on the West Coast.

After two decades during which filmmakers suggested that anyone riding a Harley was likely headed for trouble, many motorcyclists had as bad an impression of the movies as Hollywood had of the motorcyclists. Harley-Davidson made great strides to distance itself

from the movie biker image, with many shops refusing to sell or service movie-style choppers or carry the chain wallets and black leathers popularized by drive-in bad-guys.

But given time, even the worst stereotypes have a way of playing themselves out. By the 1980s, the combination of an aging biker population and filmmakers less intent on frightening their audiences at last returned the image of Harley-Davidson motorcycles to something akin to reality. Director Peter Bogdanovich, who got his start on Corman's *Wild Angels* back in 1966, brought to the screen the touching, real-life drama of California teenager Rocky Dennis in 1985's *Mask*. The film centered on the deep sense of family and brotherhood enjoyed by a group of Harley riders and their support of a severely handicapped kid.

With the release of films like *Running Cool* (1993) and *Chrome Soldiers* (1992), bikers were frequently portrayed as heroes of the downtrodden, standing up against crooked cops and, like the cowboys of a generation before, riding romantically off into the sunset. Whether tearing apart a country roadhouse or saving a damsel in distress, movie motorcyclists have almost always been riding Harley-Davidson motorcycles, bringing both fame and infamy to America's favorite motorcycle.

Though Sgt. John Wintergreen, (right) the main character in *Electra Glide in Blue* (played by the infamous Robert Blake), hates his motorcycle (he calls it "that white elephant under my ass"), the bike gave the film its name.

MGM's 1991 release *Harley-Davidson and the Marlboro Man* was so bad it destroyed the career of Mickey Rourke and sent Don Johnson back to the small screen.

higher compression pistons. Also part of the package was a bold "FLH" decal on each side of the oil tank, announcing to all that this was Harley's hot-rod. For 1957, not much changed on the Big Twins, because Harley saved all the glory for its new Sportster.

So ended the Hydra-Glide line. During eight years of production, the King of Bikes—or at least the bike of the King (Elvis bought a tarted-up 1957 Hydra-Glide)—gained weight, power, better lifters, and a stronger bottom end. What it really needed was rear suspension. That would be the headline feature of the Hydra-Glide's successor, the 1958 Duo-Glide.

ENTER THE DUO-GLIDE

While rigid frames and sprung seats provided all the rear suspension anyone had expected when the Knucklehead was introduced in the 1930s, the Panhead's hardtail rear end was an antiquated design by the late 1950s. Even the out-sized saddlebags and crash bars riders fitted to many Hydra-Glides could no longer hide the lack of rear suspension. Worse yet, the new Sportster of 1957 had rear suspension, as had its predecessors, the Models K and KH. How come the lesser twins had rear suspension while the King of the Highway was still a hardtail? Big Twin riders rightfully felt left out. That is

Though the new suspension added nearly 70 pounds, the 650-pound Duo-Glide was still a trim machine by modern standards.

After so many big changes for 1958, little was changed on the 1959 Duo-Glides. Among the few changes were the new "arrow" tank badges shown here (with 1958-style tank panels).

until the fall of 1957, with the introduction of the third iteration of the Panhead, the Duo-Glide.

The "Duo" in Duo-Glide was Harley's acknowledgement of the most important update to its Big Twin since the Hydra-Glide front end of 1949: a swinging-arm rear suspension with a hydraulically damped shock absorber on each side. For the first time, the rear suspension of Harley's Big Twin was as good as the front.

The rear shocks meant a smoother ride on all roads and a real reduction in the pummeling a rider took on the bumpy ones. The addition of a rear suspension turned a good long-haul bike into a great one. The suspenders fore and aft transformed the Panhead into the undisputed King of the American Road.

That suspension also forced a restyle of the whole rear end that made the old Big Twin seem modern again. As a bonus, the Duo-Glide debuted with hydraulic rear brakes for better stopping power.

Little changed for 1959, but the front end was given a facelift for 1960 that updated the Duo-Glide's looks for the new decade. New aluminum fork shrouds enclosed the headlight in a massive, streamlined unit that proved an essential part of the Big Twin look from the 1960s through the last of the real FLHs, in 1984. Later, Willie G. revived that look with the Road King models.

ELECTRA GLIDE: THE PUSH-BUTTON PANHEAD

Even as late as the mid-1960s, Harley-Davidson still considered its FLH the company "hot-rod." Everyone else knew that Harley's Big Twin had long ago lost the

H-D Service School instructor, John Nowak (listening to engine), 1960.

performance war to the smaller Sportster and to British hot rods, such as the Triumph Bonneville and Norton Dominator. Worse yet, Harley's Big Twin began losing yet another skirmish in the early 1960s to a new foe.

That skirmish? The push-button wars. The foe? Honda, and soon a slew of other Japanese companies.

In the early 1960s, Harley-Davidson was selling about 10,000 motorcycles a year to hard-core enthusiasts. Upstart Honda, on the other hand, had been in the U.S. market just a few years, yet it was selling bigger and bigger motorcycles by the hundreds of thousands to mainstream Americans.

Sure, there was a huge price difference between Hondas and Harleys, but that didn't really explain the even huger disparity in sales figures. What really distinguished the Honda from the Harley in the eyes of the general public was much simpler: If you wanted to ride your Honda, all you had to do was turn the key and push the start button, but if you wanted to ride your Harley, you had to go through an arcane starting

By the early 1960s, scofflaws and speeders no longer feared Harley police bikes. Riders on any number of motorcycles could thumb their noses at an officer aboard a Panhead, but they couldn't outrun his radio.

ritual that looked to the uninitiated like equal parts exercise and exorcism. Part of Soichiro Honda's genius was his realization that motorcycles would never appeal to the masses until they were just as easy to start, and as reliable as a car.

Harley-Davidson caught the push-button vibe for 1965. Outwardly, the 1965 Harley Big Twins looked a little pudgier, but not all that different from the 1964 Duo-Glides. That's because the good stuff was hidden from view behind new covers and cases, but chrome script on each side of the front fender named Harley's new era in a dialect all Motor Company fans were sure to understand: *Electra Glide*. That's "Electra" as in electric start—and more than anything Harley-Davidson had ever done, this change had a cultural impact.

Kick-starting had always been an honored rite of passage among Big Twin riders. The standard answer to a son's/little brother's/nephew's/neighborhood pest's longing pleas of "When can I ride it?" were answered (in condescending tones) with, "Maybe some day—if you can kick-start it." At least that was the answer I got. And it looked like a man-sized job to me at the time. Here's the drill: Choke on one or two clicks. Retard the spark. Open the throttle all the way. Leap up and give a priming kick, and then another. Turn on the ignition. Push slowly down on the kick-starter until you feel the compression build. Gather your strength. Then leap up and come down on the lever with all the force you can muster, while still keeping your demeanor as nonchalant as possible.

If all is well, the mighty beast springs to life and you feel like a hero.

If not, you kick some more and swear to the gods of V-twin thunder that you'll give the bike a complete tune-up this Sunday, right after you go to church. And this is not something you want to go through after stalling at an intersection, with a bunch of honking cars behind you.

Die-hard traditionalists were seriously unhappy with the new "Push-Button Pan." Not only had the Motor Company taken away their central initiation rite, but the starter and huge new battery added over 75 pounds to an already portly machine. Say hello to the Hog.

Everyone else was thrilled, despite the extra weight, and sales rose by 26 percent. The new E Glide was the biggest-selling Harley Big Twin since 1951, when the British invasion began in earnest.

The Electra Glide was a Harley Big Twin for the motorcycling masses. It was not just for the young and strong. Anyone who could swing a leg over it could start and ride it. Older riders, smaller riders, and those with weak knees could join the sport and cruise America on the ultimate long-haul touring bike of the day.

Unfortunately, it was the last stretch for the venerable Panhead. For 1966, Harley's Overhead Big Twin motor was given yet another top end, and a new era in Motor Company history began: the Shovelhead era.

The last year for the Panhead— 1965—marked the first year for the Electra Glide.

The Italian Job

AERMACCHI H-D

By Greg Field

For a time in the 1920s, "Aer Macchi" was the "Air Jordan" of seaplane racing, and it built the world's fastest airplanes. Its full name was "Aeronautica Macchi."

Later, Macchi built some very respectable fighters for Mussolini's air force, but those fighters weren't good enough to prevent American flyers from bombing the factory into rubble during World War II. After the war, Aermacchi dusted itself off and began building the small motorcycles that were then the backbone of the Italian transportation system.

When Harley-Davidson wanted to diversify into production of more midsized motorcycles in 1960, Aermacchi seemed a perfect fit, so Harley-Davidson

In 1961, Harley began importing rebadged Aermacchi singles to compete with the small-displacement motorcycles coming from Japan.

The little 250 cc powerplant in this 1967 Sprint H provided spirited performance, but not up to the level of the 250 cc competition.

bought 49 percent of the company for a paltry $260,000. (Aermacchi kept 49 percent, and Lockheed owned the "tie-breaking" 2 percent.) For 1961, Harley began importing rebadged Aermacchi singles and pushing them on reluctant Harley dealers.

By 1966, Harley was importing more than 20,000 Aermacchi two- and four-strokes a year. Most were two-stroke M50s, and they were sold at fire-sale prices. After that, the four-stroke Sprint caught on and had decent sales and racing success through 1974, when it was canceled.

By then, American Motorcycle Federation owned all of Aermacchi, and AMF directed it to build a series of two-stroke street-scramblers and motocrossers, which stacked up in dealerships. Despite that, AMF kept Aermacchi going fullbore. Why?

Vaughn Beals explained: "Italy had this crazy law where you could cut production, but you couldn't lay off employees. AMF thought, 'We have to pay them, so we might as well have them build bikes.' One day we discovered all these bikes warehoused in Italy, the U.S., Brazil, and all over that we hadn't sold. Now we couldn't sell them because they hadn't been prepared for storage, so they were all rusted. I finally convinced AMF to shut it down and sell it."

In June 1978, AMF closed the Aermacchi factory. Remnants of Aermacchi live on today, because AMF ultimately sold the factory to the Castiglioni brothers, who built Cagiva and Ducati motorcycles there.

While ultimately proving disastrous for Harley, the Aermacchi connection resulted in some nice motorcycles.

Chapter 5

THE HELL'S ANGELS

By Hunter S. Thompson

I am not in a mood tonight to introduce a very strong book that I wrote pretty nicely a long time ago. Was it 1966? Yes, I think it was — published in January of 1967, to great acclaim. Yes sir, those were very fast times. But so what, eh? I shit on the chest of acclaim. Probably it's a far, far better thing, I suspect, for you to pick up **Hell's Angels** *and read it. Do it now. Mahalo. Res Ipsa Loquitor.*
-HST, April 10, 2002

(Excerpted from *Hell's Angels: A Strange and Terrible Saga* and re-edited with permission from the author.)

California, Labor Day weekend…early, with ocean fog still in the streets, outlaw motorcyclists wearing chains, shades and greasy Levi's roll out from damp garages, all-night diners and cast-off one-night pads in Frisco, Hollywood, Berdoo and East Oakland, heading for the Monterey peninsula, north of Big Sur…The Menace is loose again, the Hell's Angels, the hundred-carat headline, running fast and loud on the early morning freeway, low in the saddle, nobody smiles, jamming crazy through traffic and ninety miles an hour down the center stripe, missing by inches…like Genghis Khan on an iron horse, a monster steed with a fiery anus, flat out through the eye of a beer can and up your daughter's leg with no quarter asked and none given; show the squares some class, give'em a whiff of those kicks they'll never know…Ah, these righteous dudes, they love to screw it on…Little Jesus, the Gimp, Chocolate George, Buzzard, Zorro, Hambone, Clean Cut, Tiny, Terry the Tramp, Frenchy, Mouldy Marvin, Mother Miles, Dirty Ed, Chuck the Duck, Fat Freddy, Filthy Phil, Charger Charley the Child Molester, Crazy Cross, Puff, Magoo, Animal and at least a hundred more…tense for the action, long hair in the wind, beards and bandanas flapping, earrings, armpits, chain whips, swastikas and stripped-down Harleys flashing chrome as traffic on 101 moves over, nervous, to let the formation pass like a burst of dirty thunder…The run was on, "outlaws" from all over the state rolled in packs toward Monterey: north from San Bernardino and Los Angeles on 101; south from Sacramento on 50…south from Oakland, Hayward and Richmond on 17; and from Frisco on the Coast Highway. The hard-core, the outlaw elite, were the Hell's Angels…wearing the winged death's-head on the back of their sleeveless jackets and packing their "mamas" behind them on big "chopped hogs." They rode with a fine, unwashed arrogance, secure in their reputation as the rottenest motorcycle gang in the whole history of Christendom.

From San Francisco in a separate formation came the Gypsy Jokers, three dozen in all, the number-two outlaw club in California, starved for publicity, and with only one chapter, the Jokers could still look down on such as the Presidents, Road Rats, Nightriders and Question Marks, also from the Bay Area, Gomorrah…with Sodom five hundred miles to the south in the vast mad bowl of Los Angeles, home turf of the Satan's Slaves, number three in the outlaw hierarchy, custom-bike specialists with a taste for the flesh of young dogs, flashy headbands and tender young blondes with lobotomy eyes; the Slaves were the class of Los Angeles, and their women clung tight to the leather backs of these dog-eating, crotch-busting fools as they headed north for their annual party with the Hell's Angels, who even then viewed the "L.A. bunch"

with friendly condescension…which the Slaves didn't mind, for they could dump with impunity on the other southern clubs—the Coffin Cheaters, Iron Horsemen, Galloping Gooses, Comancheros, Stray Satans and a homeless fringe element of human chancres so foul that not even the outlaw clubs—north or south— would claim them except in a fight when an extra chain or beer bottle might make the crucial difference.

Motorcycling's outlaw image goes back to the earliest days of the sport.

Until an Angel earns his death's-head wing, he's just a prospect, and can only wear the club rocker patch.

The customized bobbers of the 1930s and 1940s prefigured the choppers used by the Hell's Angels in the 1950s and 1960s.

The California climate is perfect for bikes, as well as surfboards, convertibles, swimming pools and abulia. Most cyclists are harmless weekend types, no more dangerous than skiers or skin-divers. But ever since the end of World War II the West Coast has been plagued by gangs of young wild men on motorcycles, roaming the highways in groups of ten to thirty and stopping whenever they get thirsty or road-cramped to suck up some beer and make noise. The hell broth of publicity in 1965 made the phenomenon seem brand-new, but even in the ranks of the Hell's Angels there are those who insist that the outlaw scene went over the bump in the mid-fifties, when the original faces began drifting off to marriage and mortgages and time payments.

The whole thing was born, they say, in the late 1940s, when most ex-GIs wanted to get back to an orderly pattern: college, marriage, a job, children—all

the peaceful extras that come with a sense of security. But not everybody felt that way. Like the drifters who rode west after Appomattox, there were thousands of veterans in 1945 who flatly rejected the idea of going back to their pre-war pattern. They didn't want order, but privacy—and time to figure things out. It was a nervous, downhill feeling, a mean kind of *Angst* that always comes out of wars…a compressed sense of time on the outer limits of fatalism. They wanted more action, and one of the ways to look for it was on a big motorcycle. By 1947 the state was alive with bikes, nearly all of them powerful American-made iron from Harley-Davidson and Indian.

The concept of the "motorcycle outlaw" was as uniquely American as jazz. Nothing like them had ever existed. In some ways they appeared to be a kind of half-breed anachronism, a human hangover from the era of the Wild West. Yet in other ways they were as new as television. There was absolutely no precedent, in the years after World War II, for large gangs of hoodlums on motorcycles, reveling in violence, worshiping

"Support your local Hell's Angels," admonishes the sticker on this bike's ignition module.

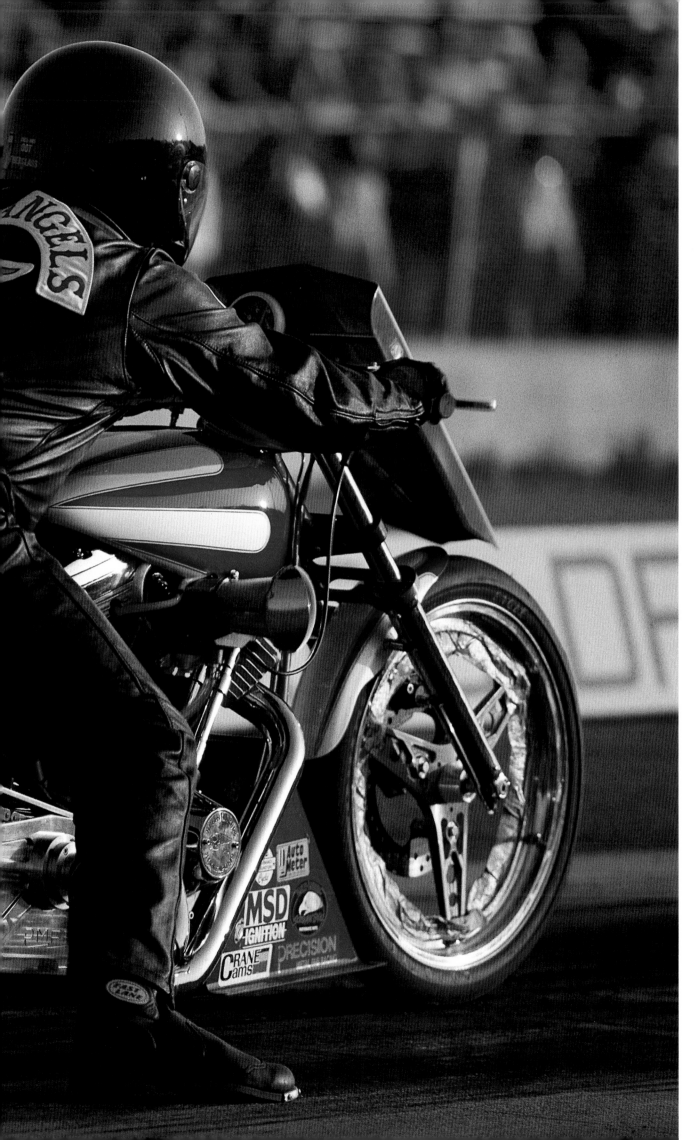

Today the Hell's Angels are fixtures on the Harley-Davidson drag-racing circuit.

mobility and thinking nothing of riding five hundred miles on a weekend…to whoop it up with other gangs of cyclists in some country hamlet entirely unprepared to handle even a dozen peaceful tourists. Many picturesque, outback villages got their first taste of tourism not from families driving Fords or Chevrolets, but from clusters of boozing "city boys" on motorcycles.

The farther the Angels roam from their own turf, the more likely they are to cause panic. A group of them seen on a highway for the first time is offensive to every normal notion of what is supposed to be happening in this country; it is bizarre to the point of seeming like a bad hallucination…and this is the context in which the term "outlaw" makes real sense.

To see a lone Angel screaming through traffic—defying all rules, limits and patterns—is to understand the motorcycle as an instrument of anarchy, a tool of defiance and even a weapon. A Hell's Angel on foot can look pretty foolish. Their sloppy histrionics and inane conversations can be interesting for a few hours, but beyond the initial strangeness, their everyday scene is as tedious and depressing as a costume ball for demented children. There is something pathetic about a bunch of men gathering every night in the same bar, taking themselves very seriously in their ratty uniforms, with nothing to look forward to but the chance of a fight or a round of head jobs from some drunken charwoman.

But there is nothing pathetic about the sight of an Angel on his bike. The whole—man and machine together—is far more than the sum of its parts. His motorcycle is the one thing in life he has absolutely mastered. It is his only valid status symbol, his equalizer, and he pampers it the same way a busty Hollywood starlet pampers her body. Without it, he is no better than a punk on a street corner. And he knows it. The Angels are not articulate about many things, but they bring a lover's inspiration to the subject of bikes. Sonny Barger, a man not given to sentimental rambling, once defined the word "love" as "the feeling you get when you like something as much as your motorcycle. Yeah, I guess you could say that was love."

With rare exceptions, the outlaw bike is a Harley 74, a giant of a motorcycle that comes out of the Milwaukee factory weighing seven hundred pounds, but which the Angels strip down to about five hundred. In the argot of the cycle world the Harley is a "hog," and the outlaw bike is a "chopped hog." Basically it is the same machine all motorcycle cops use, but the police bike is an accessory-loaded elephant compared to the lean, customized dynamos the Hell's Angels ride. The resemblance is about the same as that of a factory-equipped Cadillac to a dragster's stripped-down essence of the same car. The Angels refer to standard 74s as "garbage wagons," and Bylaw Number 11 of the charter is a put-down in the grand manner. "An Angel cannot wear the colors while riding on a garbage wagon with a non-Angel." A chopped hog, or "chopper," is little more than a heavy frame, a tiny seat and a massive, 1,200-cc (or 74-cubic-inch) engine. This is nearly twice the size of the engines in the Triumph Bonneville or the BSA Lightning Rocket, both 650-cc machines capable of 120 to 130 miles an hour. The Honda Super Hawk has a 305-cc engine and a top speed of just under 100. A columnist for the *Los Angeles Times* once described hogs as "the kind of cycle the German couriers used to run down dogs and chickens—and people—in World War II: low brutish machines, with drivers to match."

As this funeral in Amsterdam shows, Hell's Angels have set up chapters around the world. According to Sonny Barger, "the sun never sets on the Angels' patch."

CHOPPERS

By Mike Seate

The 1930s and 1940s offered few options to bikers hoping to make their Harley-Davidson motorcycles faster—there were no showcases filled with the latest carbon fiber and billet aluminum parts. The most expedient path to higher speed was to lighten the bike, since shedding pounds was as simple as pulling out the old hacksaw and going to work.

Among the first items to go were the heavyweight steel fenders. They were either removed entirely or had several inches chopped off—a practice that coined one of motorcycling's most distinctive and, occasionally, notorious movements.

However functional these early choppers—sometimes called bobbers or bob jobs in reference to short-cropped or "bobbed" fenders—were meant to be, func-

tion played little part in later chopper design. The idea of removing, lightening, or downright altering parts on a stock Harley-Davidson motorcycle took on near-baroque dimensions over the next half-century. A movement borne of necessity and simplification gradually evolved into a wild, psychedelic merging of pop art and uniquely American mechanical craftsmanship.

Only 20 years separated the rugged, primer-covered bobbers of the immediate post-World War II period and the candyflake, chromed-out stretch choppers of the *Easy Rider* era, but the two schools were eons apart in looks and function. Early choppers were utilized for everything from cross-state touring to weekend drag racing and even off-road hare-and-hound races. Later versions of the chopper were more of an aesthete's dream: long on looks and eye-pulling potential, but often short on performance.

Whether customized for go or show, these highly personalized machines demanded a skilled, dedicated rider, and their striking image helped make choppers some of the most beloved Harleys on the road.

Some aficionados claim the chopper movement emerged as a close relative of the custom car scene that blossomed in Southern California in the 1950s and 1960s. Visionary car customizers such as brothers Sam and George Barris turned already ornately designed automobiles from the likes of Mercury and Chevrolet into dazzling, sometimes bizarre, exercises in form over function.

Some customizing artists, such as cartoonist Ed "Big Daddy" Roth and beatnik painter Von Dutch, quickly realized the customizing potential of American-made motorcycles, taking up where Southern California's inventive street riders left off. Where riders had replaced Harley-Davidson's unwieldy buddy seats with small, spring-mounted solo saddles, the customizers one-upped them with elaborate hand-stitched vinyl upholstery.

Exhaust pipes, which early chopper riders had crudely sawed off for additional noise and top-end horsepower, became the source of endless experimentation for chopper builders; by the mid-1960s, ornate

This chopped Panhead is typical of the motorcycles preferred by outlaw clubs like the Hell's Angels back in the day.

pipes that wouldn't look out of place behind the organ in a Byzantine cathedral were blasting down America's boulevards. Chrome and deeply layered lacquer covered all available surfaces, while seats grew narrower and taller, and often featured chrome "sissy bars" to keep passengers from falling off the motorcycle. Front forks were lengthened, sometimes by extraordinary spans. This practice may have destabilized low-speed handling, but hey—it looked cool and ran fine in a straight line on the highways.

Harley's old, rigid rear suspension frames, which had been made redundant by the introduction of swinging arm rear-suspensions in the late 1950s, suddenly became hot property for their low seat height and simple lines. Even front brakes were discarded as unnecessary; they cluttered the looks of a classic chopper front end.

Like hot rods a decade before, choppers were helped along by cultural forces outside of motorsports. During an era of political and cultural upheaval, chop-

pers took on other roles besides providing a moving showcase for a gearhead's talents. Extended front forks, laid-back riding positions, and designs that, in most states, existed in open defiance of motor vehicle codes imbued choppers with a reputation as a true rebel's steed.

Stock Harley-Davidsons were derided as "garbage wagons" (or worse) by the chopper crowd, who boasted that they'd rather walk than ride a stock machine. Similarly, many Harley-Davidson dealerships steadfastly refused to service choppers or sell chopper parts, further deepening the rift between the two camps.

Rock stars from Janis Joplin to Jimi Hendrix were photographed on their choppers, and *Life* magazine depicted movie starlet Ann Margaret unwinding on her chopped Harley Sportster in between Las Vegas shows. The anything-goes culture of the 1960s also led to choppers becoming forever associated with outlaw biker gangs, who were among the first to

Choppers experienced a resurgence in popularity in the late 1990s.

The mother of all choppers: Captain America from the film *Easy Rider*.

adopt the sleek, in-your-face longbikes as their own.

But all of this freewheeling, backstreet engineering did not go unnoticed by the prying eyes of state legislatures. Just as choppers were entering the cultural mainstream, spawning lifestyle magazines and a burgeoning parts manufacturing trade, lawmakers began outlawing specific chopper designs such as tall "apehanger"-style handlebars and long forks, which were deemed unsafe for public roads.

The sight of a chopper pulled over for an impromptu roadside inspection became a common sight in the 1970s, prompting the rider of many a chopped Harley to slowly revert their machines back into less elaborate (read: less noticeable) customs. The chopper might have remained a curious relic of 1960s culture, if not for a new generation of custom Harley craftsmen who emerged a quarter-century later to rekindle American's love affair with the chopper. In resurrecting the often-maligned machines, builders like Jesse James, Billy Lane, and Paul Yaffee managed to make roadworthy, popular, and even respectable a style of Harley that often was anything but.

At least half the Hell's Angels are war babies, but that is a very broad term. There are also war babies in the Peace Corps, in corporate training programs, and fighting in Vietnam. World War II had a lot to do with the Hell's Angels' origins, but you have to stretch the war theory pretty thin to cover both Dirty Ed, in his early forties, and Clean Cut from Oakland, who is twenty years younger. Dirty Ed is old enough to be Clean Cut's father—which is not likely, though he's planted more seeds than he cares to remember.

It is easy enough to trace the Hell's Angels' mystique—and even their name and their emblems—back to World War II and Hollywood. But their genes and real history go back a lot further. World War II was not the original California boom, but a rebirth of a thing that began in the thirties and was already tapering off when the war economy made California a new

Valhalla. In 1937, Woody Guthrie wrote a song called "Do-Re-Mi.". The chorus goes like this:

> *California is a garden of Eden*
> *A Paradise for you and for me,*
> *But believe it or not,*
> *You won't think it's so hot,*
> *If you ain't got the Do-Re-Mi.*

The song expressed the frustrated sentiments of more than a million Okies, Arkies and hillbillies who made a long trek to the Golden State and found it was just another hard dollar. By the time these gentlemen arrived, the Westward Movement was already beginning to solidify. The "California way of life" was the same old game of musical chairs—but it took a while *Continued on page 148*

You didn't have to be an outlaw to ride a motorcycle in the early days, but it helped.

The customized motorcycles favored by the outlaw clubs varied widely in style. The one common denominator was chrome.

Unlike the ornately customized bikes seen in today's motorcycle clubs, in the early days the Hell's Angels tended to ride simple customs with clean lines.

Even in death, a biker remains part of his club. Along with the Banditos, the Sons of Silence are one of the largest remaining outlaw motorcycle clubs.

Continued from page 143

for this news to filter back East, and meanwhile the Gold Rush continued. Once here, the newcomers hung on for a few years, breeding prolifically—until the war started. Then they either joined up or had their pick of jobs on a booming labor market. Either way, they were Californians when the war ended. The old way of life was scattered back along Route 66, and their children grew up in a new world. The Linkhorns had finally found a home.

Nelson Algren wrote about them in *A Walk on the Wild Side*, but that story was told before they crossed the Rockies. Dove Linkhorn, son of crazy Fitz, went to hustle for his fortune in New Orleans. Ten years later he would have gone to Los Angeles.

Algren's book opens with one of the best historical descriptions of American white trash ever written. He traces the Linkhorn ancestry back to the first wave of bonded servants to arrive on these shores. These were the dregs of society from all over the British Isles—misfits, criminals, debtors, social bankrupts of every type and description—all of them willing to sign oppressive work contracts with future employers in exchange for ocean passage to the New World. Once here, they endured a form of slavery for a year or two—during which they were fed and sheltered by the boss—and when their time of bondage ended, they were turned loose to make their own way.

In theory and in the context of history the setup was mutually advantageous. Any man desperate enough to sell himself into bondage in the first place had pretty well shot his wad in the old country, so a chance for a foothold on a new continent was not to be taken lightly. After a period of hard labor and wretchedness he would then be free to seize whatever he might in a land of seemingly infinite natural wealth. Thousands of bonded servants came over, but by the time they earned their freedom the coastal strip was already settled. The unclaimed land was west, across the Alleghenies. So they drifted into the new states— Kentucky and Tennessee, their sons drifted on to Missouri, Arkansas and Oklahoma.

Drifting became a habit; with dead roots in the Old World and none in the New, the Linkhorns were not of a mind to dig in and cultivate things. Bondage too became a habit, but it was only the temporary kind. They were not pioneers, but sleazy rearguard camp followers of the original westward movement. By the time the Linkhorns arrived anywhere the land was already taken—so they worked for a while and moved on. Their world was a violent, boozing limbo between the pits of despair and the Big Rock Candy Mountain. They kept drifting west, chasing jobs, rumors, homestead grabs or the luck of some front-running kin. They lived off the surface of the land; like armyworms, stripping it of whatever they could before moving on. It was a day-to-day existence, and there was always more land to the west.

While lawyers, guns and money might be the traditional tools in an outlaw-biker's kit, these days the lawyers and money see a lot more use than the guns.

Some stayed behind and their lineal descendants are still there—in the Carolinas, Kentucky, West Virginia and Tennessee. There were dropouts all along the way: hillbillies, Okies, Arkies—they're all the same people. Texas is a living monument to the breed. So is southern California.

Algren called them "fierce craving boys" with "A feeling of having been cheated." Freebooters, armed and drunk—a legion of gamblers, brawlers and whore-hoppers. Blowing into town in a junk Model-A with bald tires; no muffler and one headlight…looking for quick work, with no questions asked and preferably no tax deductions. Just get the cash, fill up at a cut-rate gas station and hit the road, with a pint on the seat and Eddy Arnold on the radio moaning good back-country tunes about home sweet home, that Bluegrass sweetheart still waitin', and roses on Mama's grave.

Algren left the Linkhorns in Texas, but anyone who drives the Western highways knows they didn't stay there either. They kept moving until one day in the late 1930s they stood on the spine of a scrub-oak California hill and looked down on the Pacific Ocean—the end of the road. Things were tough for a while, but no tougher

than they were in a hundred other places. And then came the war—fat city, big money even for Linkhorns.

When the war ended, California was full of veterans looking for ways to spend their separation bonuses. Many decided to stay on the Coast, and while their new radios played hillbilly music they went out and bought big motorcycles—not knowing exactly why, but in the booming rootless atmosphere of those times, it seemed like the thing to do. They were not all Linkhorns, but the forced democracy of four war years had erased so many old distinctions that even Linkhorns were confused. Their pattern of intermarriage was shattered, their children mixed freely and without violence. By 1950 many Linkhorns were participating in the money economy; they owned decent cars, and even houses.

Others, however, broke down under the strain of respectability and answered the call of the genes. There is a story about a Linkhorn who became a wealthy car dealer in Los Angeles. He married a beautiful Spanish actress and bought a mansion in Beverly Hills. But after a decade of opulence he suffered from soaking sweats and was unable to sleep at night. He began to sneak out of the house through the servants' entrance and run a few blocks to a gas station where he kept a hopped-up '37 Ford with no fenders…and spend the rest of the night hanging around honky-tonk bars and truck stops, dressed in dirty overalls and a crusty green T-shirt with a Bardahl emblem on the back. He enjoyed cadging beers and belting whores around when they spurned his crude propositions. One night, after long haggling, he bought several Mason jars full of home whiskey, which he drank while driving at high speed through the Beverly Hills area. When the old Ford finally threw a rod he abandoned it and called a taxi, which took him to his own automobile agency. He kicked down a side door, hot-wired a convertible waiting for tune-up and drove out to Highway 101, where he got in a drag race with some hoodlums from Pasadena. He lost, and it so enraged him that he followed the other car until it stopped for a traffic light—where he rammed it from the rear at seventy miles an hour.

The publicity ruined him, but influential friends kept him out of jail by paying a psychiatrist to call him insane. He spent a year in a rest home; and now, according to the stories, he has a motorcycle dealership near San Diego. People who know him say he's happy—although his driver's license has been revoked for numerous violations, his business is verging on

Unlike the pristine trailer queens seen at motorcycle shows today, early customized bikes were built to ride.

bankruptcy, and his new wife, a jaded ex-beauty queen from West Virginia, is a half-mad alcoholic.

It would not be fair to say that all motorcycle outlaws carry Linkhorn genes, but nobody who has ever spent time among the inbred Anglo-Saxon tribes of Appalachia would need more than a few hours with the Hell's Angels to work up a very strong sense of *déjà vu*. There is the same sulking hostility toward "outsiders," the same extremes of temper and action, and even the same names, sharp faces and long-boned bodies that never look quite natural unless they are leaning on something.

Most of the Angels are obvious Anglo-Saxons, but the Linkhorn attitude is contagious. The few outlaws with Mexican or Italian names not only act like the others but somehow look like them. Even Chinese Mel from Frisco and Charley, a young Negro from Oakland, have the Linkhorn gait and mannerisms.

The widespread appeal of the Angels is worth pondering. Unlike most other rebels, the Angels have given up hope that the world is going to change for them. They assume, on good evidence,

The Hell's Angels emerged from the rough-and-tumble motorcycle culture of post-war America.

that the people who run the social machinery have little use for outlaw motorcyclists, and they are reconciled to being losers. But instead of losing quietly, one by one, they have banded together with a mindless kind of loyalty and moved outside the framework, for good or ill. They may not have an answer, but at least they are still on their feet. One night about halfway through one of their weekly meetings I thought of Joe Hill on his way to face a Utah firing squad and saying his final words: "Don't mourn. Organize." It is safe to say that no Hell's Angel has ever heard of Joe Hill or would know a Wobbly from a bushmaster, but there is something very similar about the attitudes. The Industrial Workers of the World had a serious blueprint for society, while the Hell's Angels mean only to defy society. There is no talk among the Angels of "building a better world," yet their reactions to the world they live in are rooted in the same kind of anarchic, para-legal sense of conviction that brought the armed wrath of the Establishment down on the Wobblies. There is the same kind of suicidal loyalty, the same kind of in-group rituals and nicknames, and above all the same feeling of constant warfare with an unjust world. The Wobblies were losers, and so are the Angels…and if every loser in this country today rode a motorcycle the whole highway system would have to be modified.

There is an important difference between the words "loser" and "outlaw." One is passive and the other is active, and the main reasons the Angels are such good copy is that they are acting out the day-dreams of millions of losers who don't wear any defiant insignia and who don't know how to be outlaws. The streets of every city are thronged with men who would pay all the money they could get their hands on to be transformed—even for a day—into hairy, hard-fisted brutes who walk over cops, extort free drinks from terrified bartenders and thunder out of town on big motorcycles after raping the banker's daughter. Even people who think the Angels should all be put to sleep find it easy to identify with them. They command a fascination, however reluctant, that borders on psychic masturbation.

The Angels don't like being called losers, but they have learned to live with it. "Yeah, I guess I am," said one. "But you're looking at one loser who is going to make a hell of a scene on the way out."

Hunter Thompson leads a heavily armed yet peaceful existence among the flora and fauna of Colorado, surrounded by strong whiskey, fine motorcycles, bombs, hashish, and beautiful naked women with good credit.

When an outlaw-biker club goes out for a ride, people tend to notice.

The
OUTLAW IMPULSE

By Darwin Holmstrom

Since Hunter S. Thompson wrote his seminal book on outlaw motorcycle culture, *Hell's Angels: A Strange and Terrible Saga*, the entire world has been turned inside out. Today, sex and drugs, and anything else that hints at pleasures of the flesh, are taboo subjects, while war and rigid adherence to the status quo are considered the highest goals toward which a human can aspire. What was once deemed obscene is now noble.

Where does the motorcycling culture fit into all this? Like society at large, the motorcycling world has been flopped on its watery head. When Thompson wrote *Hell's Angels*, Harley-Davidson motorcycles were archaic remnants of an earlier time, well on their way to becoming jokes to the broader motorcycling community. Riding a Harley was not sport; it was a political statement. Harley riders knew their machines were fat, slow, unreliable, overpriced, and what the hell were you going to do about it? Trying to debate functionality with many Harley riders was as likely to find you picking your teeth out of your own lower intestinal tract as it was to instigate meaningful discourse. If you wanted to meet nice people, you associated with Honda riders, not Harley riders.

Then things changed. We got Richard Nixon and Watergate; we got Ronald Reagan, AIDS, and the war on drugs. And we got the Harley-Davidson Evolution engine. It still looked like a Harley engine, sounded like a Harley engine, shook like a Harley engine, and even smelled like a Harley engine. But it was a completely

different animal. No longer did you need to have the ability to overhaul the top end alongside the road in the dead of night with nothing but an adjustable wrench and a Zippo lighter. Suddenly any mechanically inept fool with a good line of credit could park his bad ass aboard the quintessential outlaw machine.

This changed everything. People were becoming more conservative; they were forced to lead more rigidly conforming lifestyles. Yet the basic human instinct to rebel against conformity remained intact, if buried deep within our collective psyche. In the mid-1980s, finding expression for that urge grew increasingly difficult. It was no longer socially acceptable to go out and have promiscuous sex for fear of contracting some horrible disease, or to go out and indulge in the drug of your choice for fear of having annoying friends and family members do an intervention and admit you to some mind-numbing rehab clinic. Here comes Harley-Davidson at just the right moment, with a machine that carried the stench of outlaw, minus the real baggage of life outside societal norms, and minus the need for any prerequisite mechanical aptitude. Outlaw lite.

Fast forward 15 years. We are in the initial spasms of a new millennium. Hedonism is making a cautious comeback attempt, but by and large we are a nation of aging boomers too old for serious debauchery, and Reagan babies who do not even know the meaning of serious debauchery. Your average biker is about as much a rebel as Ward Cleaver. He goes to work on time, pays his taxes, and seldom fornicates outside the sanctity of marriage. He even drives the speed limit, often while hogging the left lane. Though he enjoys his Budweiser and may, on occasion, still burn a fatty when his old high-school buddies come to visit, his only real vice is using the cell phone while driving.

Yet each weekend he dons his leather vest with the "Harley Owner's Group" patch, applies his henna tattoos, starts calling his domestic partner "the ol' lady," drops the g's from his gerunds and roars off on his Harley, parading along at 5 miles per hour under the legal limit from tavern to tavern with his peers.

This man has likely earned, at the very least, a degree from a technical college. He may even be an accomplished professional, though the lawyer and doctor bikers are nearly as mythological as the few remaining one-percenters who populated Thompson's book. More likely he hangs Sheetrock, drives a Metro Transit bus, or manages a restaurant. He may even be a she, since many more women ride today than did in 1967, when *Hell's Angels* was first published. And for all his (or her) attempts to portray an outlaw image while aboard his Harley, at best he portrays a caricature of an outlaw biker. His riding is not sport; it is a pantomime performance of his outlaw biker ideal.

This may seem silly, but it is understandable. For most of us, the option of continuing to live the real outlaw lifestyle was not there. Our bodies gave out, we became impoverished, we landed in prison. Billy and Wyatt died at the end of *Easy Rider* for a reason. Had they lived, they likely would have ended up in some dismal trailer court in Fontana, penniless and bikeless—if they were lucky. In an even more likely scenario, they would have ended up in a hideous southern prison, serving life sentences for passing bad checks under some draconian three-strikes-and-you're-out law. Or else they would have become fat old men, pontificating in various 12-step groups. They would have long since ceased being the beautiful biker poets depicted in the movie. No, it was better they went out in a blaze of glory at the hands of redneck duck hunters in some nameless Louisiana swamp. Sometimes it really is best to "ride hard, die young, and leave a good-looking corpse."

But for most of us, our corpses would not have been good-looking enough to warrant an early death. We soldiered on, accepting the ever-increasing limitations placed on us by a more conservative society. We abandoned the sex, drugs, and rock and roll of our youth and accepted the yoke of responsibility, sacrificing our free-wheeling ways in the name of comfort and security. Still, somewhere deep inside, we feel that old outlaw itch, an itch most of us are unwilling to scratch with reckless abandon. Harley-Davidson provides us with a socially acceptable poultice to help alleviate that itch.

Chapter 6

THE SPORTSTER ERA

By Allan Girdler

What we have in the Sportster is a success story. From 1957 through 2002—45 years—the Harley-Davidson Sportster has won races on the track, in the showroom, and on the street. The Sportster has also won the hearts of hundreds of thousands of owners and riders.

This success has come despite some flaws, despite some missteps in both engineering and marketing, despite having begun life with genes that originated in 1929, and despite having been introduced to a market that shifted as soon as it was targeted.

Let's begin with those genes. In 1929 Harley-Davidson introduced a line of middleweight twins. In classic H-D form, they featured a 45-degree V angle, but they displaced only 45 cubic inches. They were flatheads, with in-head side valves operated by four one-lobed camshafts arranged in an arc at the engine's lower right, a design used by no Harley or Indian before.

Aside from the side-valve design, the rest of the bike, named the D series, was state of the art for 1929. There were modest changes and revisions, but the basic engine design carried on through 1951.

In 1952, Harley engineers reworked the basic engine. Engine and gearbox were now unit construction, the transmission sported four cogs in the place of three, and a hand clutch and foot shift replaced the foot-clutch hand-shift setup of the old flathead 45. By no coincidence, this arrangement mimicked the setup used by Harley's rivals from England. The new model, the K, had a rear swing arm and shocks, and telescopic forks. This was new technology for Harley-Davidson, but standard fare for its rivals.

What the K didn't have was enough power, so in 1954 the engine was given a longer stroke, creating a displacement of 54 cubic inches (or 883 cc, so it could be more easily compared with the 650-cc English sports bikes).

The 1957 Sportsters were styled and marketed as "junior" versions of the Hydra-Glide.

**Harley-Davidson service school
with a model K, 1952.**

The larger engine did perform better, especially when it was tuned, but the K, KH, and KHK were better lookers than performers (or sellers).

ENTER THE SPORTSTER

For the 1957 model year, Harley-Davison introduced the XL Sportster.

The Sportster retained all the modern features—the telescopic forks, swing-arm rear suspension, hand clutch and foot shift. Brakes were drum, front and rear. The frame was similar to the KH frame but not identical.

The XL engine had the same displacement, 883 cc or 54 cubic inches, as the KH, but it wasn't simply a KH with overhead valves. The XL had a larger bore and shorter stroke for better breathing, higher revs, and a higher cruising speed.

The narrow V and the four-cam arc were retained, along with the dry clutch, sealed off (or so they hoped) inside the primary drive cavity, which was filled with lube.

But the XL engine had some odd features. First, the heads and cylinders were cast-iron. Most makers, including Harley with its Panhead, used alloy heads, because they ran cooler and lasted longer. The reason for this has never been explained. Perhaps because the Panheads leaked and gave trouble at first, H-D engineers decided they didn't have the foundry expertise to make aluminum heads and took what they considered a safer path.

The second odd feature was simply odd. With this one exception, all Harley-Davidson engines and families began with one letter, as in J, F, D, W, K, and E. But the Sportster arrived bearing the letters XL.

Historically, the L usually indicated higher compression ratios, as in the EL and the DL. Perhaps the model that appeared in 1957 was a higher-compression version of an earlier X prototype. Or perhaps not.

The rest of the new model was current. Because this was the day of "Bigger is Better" in the car world, the original XL arrived looking like a junior FLH, with a large fuel tank, fully valanced fenders, and a large headlight mounted in a nacelle like the one found on the

bigger twins. The Sportster was aimed at the guy who wanted a Panhead but couldn't afford the payments.

This wasn't exactly wrong, and the new XL sold well. It was attractive and much faster than the KH, even though claimed horsepower rating had only gone from 38 to 40.

Although Harley continued to race its side-valve KR models rather than the XL-based overhead valve machines, the company's engineers developed some overhead-valve racers based on the XL. They combined the KR's ball bearing lower end, magneto ignition and open pipes with the XL's cylinders and an improved version of the XL's heads, with larger valves and higher compression ratio. They added a racing carburetor and hotter camshaft timing.

The model was named XLR, which was logical, and it was introduced for the 1958 model year.

Meanwhile, when the California dealers saw the new XL they were impressed with its potential. They told the national guys that fans riding in the woods and

deserts back home in the West needed and deserved something better than the Hummers and 165s the Motor Company offered.

To provide these dealers with a competitive motorcycle, Harley took the peanut tank, open pipes, and skimpy fenders from the XLR and installed a nearly stock XL engine, minus generator and lights but with the KR magneto.

This model was named XLC. California dealers Armando Magri and Len Andres said C was for their state, but it most likely stood for "Competition."

The XLC didn't appear in the history books for years. Harley only sold a handful during the two years it was in the catalog. The XLR barely got a mention. Perhaps a few hundred were built and sold during the years the model was offered for sale (1958–1969). Still, both models proved influential. The motorcycle world of the later 1950s was kind of like a small town. People knew what other people were up to, and word of the XLC and XLH got out.

Harley added the "sport" in "Sportster" for 1958, on the Models XLC and XLCH.

The XLC and XLCH engines were lightened somewhat by a sheet-metal primary cover in place of the cast one used on the XL and XLH.

By 1959, the XLCH was a street- bike with head and taillights. Even so, it still had the original's bobbed rear fender and the peanut tank borrowed from the Hummer.

ENTER THE SUPERBIKE

Harley engineers had learned that the 9:1 compression ratio of the XLR was safe in street use, with the normal gasoline of the day, so for 1958 they introduced a higher-compression H version of the XL.

For the ultimate XL model, Harley engineers combined or expanded the best features of the XLC, XLR, and XLH, creating a machine with the normal street-livable lower end of the XL, the tuning of the XLH, and the bare bones appeal of the XLC. There was the little tank, open pipes, skimpy fenders, and magneto ignition, but the engine on the new model used a rollers-and-bushings lower end that would run for years.

Its name was XLCH.

No motorcycle ever looked better than this minimal machine, with its classic, muscular profile.

That first year, 1958, the XLCH came stripped, and with the low, separate open pipes of the KR and XLR. All the dealers knew their customers and reported to the factory, so for 1959 the XLCH came as a road bike, with lights, generator, and points-and-coil timer atop the gear case.

The factory fitted the XLCH with a siamese exhaust system. The stock muffler didn't muffle much, so sound and performance were fine. Even so, the first thing the XLCH buyer did was remove the siamese pipe and fit a pair of low shorty duals, as seen on the KR, because that was what looked cool. Today, a stock high exhaust is a Sportster restorer's dream find.

The big nacelle and headlight on the XL were too large for the rest of the XLCH, so someone came up with an eyebrow mount for the smaller headlight. (The eyebrow mount is still with us, on both the XL and FX model lines.) The XLCH ruled. The CH was sparse and tuned to a point where it would outperform anything in the English stable, and even the sporting Japanese machines. It simply destroyed any car on the road. While not the absolutely most powerful or the fastest motorcycle a person could buy, the XLCH was the highest-performance motorcycle anyone could find at a nearby store. And everyone knew it.

The CH could be temperamental. A magneto produces more power with more rpm, which means less power at lower speeds, making kick starting a challenge. Spark timing was manually adjusted, which meant if the rider forgot, he was reminded by a literal kick in the shins. Or the sometimes-weak spring wouldn't engage the ratchet, and he'd kick against no resistance, which also hurt. And the XLCH required a lot of kicks, especially after the adoption in 1966 of a radical new carburetor, which worked fine once the tricks had been deciphered.

Nor was daily operation trouble free. The clutch was supposed to run dry, allowing relatively soft springs for ease of operation. But the seals leaked. The oil pump's drive pin was known to shear; the ignition timing gear could slip on its shaft; the right rear case half was weak. All of these traits established the XLCH rider as a man of skill and determination, a motorcyclist who paid his dues.

Early XLCHs weighed 480 or 490 pounds but in 1967 the XLH, with a larger fuel tank and electric start, weighed 510 pounds. All versions of the XLCH would cover the standing-start quarter-mile in less than 15 seconds, and would top 110 miles per hour with an occasional burst up to 120, and they returned 40 to 60 miles per gallon and about 250 to 500 miles per quart of oil.

Gentler, Kinder…and Bigger

By the late 1960s, the superbike market segment was larger, and faster. Triumph and BSA came out with 750-cc four-stroke triples. Kawasaki's ferocious two-stroke triples were even faster and scarier than the British four-strokes, and in 1970, Honda introduced the 750-cc four.

Harley-Davidson took a different tack. In 1970, the XLCH got coil-and-points ignition, which made it easier to start. That year there was an optional fiberglass seat/fender that was used for the 1971 Superglide, in spite of the fact that nobody ordered one for a Sportster. In 1971, the ignition timer was replaced by points inside a housing on the gearcase cover, and the dry clutch was replaced by a wet clutch—harder on the hand but easier on maintenance. Boring the cylinders to 3.188 inches gave the 1972 XL more displacement, increasing capacity to 61 cubic inches, though the

larger XL engine was called a 1,000, probably because the competition used metric measurements.

By this time Harley-Davidson was a division of AMF (American Machine & Foundry), and because the XL line was outselling the FL line, AMF allowed annual improvements but no major changes. Many of the model year variations were matters of style. The CH's peanut tank was standard for both models, and the standard seat was a skimpy plank, replacing the thicker and softer dual saddle. Comfort went down but sales went up.

The front brake was converted to disc in 1973, and in 1974, thanks to federal mandate, the throttle got a return spring. That same year, the feds dictated that motorcycle shift levers were to be located on the left side rather than the right. Since the XL gearbox had been designed to mimic its English rivals, the shift shaft emerged on the right side of the cases. Harley used a system of linkages to move the shift lever from

right to left. In 1976, Harley revised the cases and gearbox so the shift shaft emerged on the left.

In a clear case of good intentions, the 1976 line included another model, the XLT, a touring bike. It had the lovely 3.5-gallon teardrop fuel tank first seen on the Italian sprints, rather than the 2.25-gallon peanut tank, and the dual seat was thicker. Final drive was geared higher for a relaxed highway gait. It didn't sell, and the XLT was dropped after two model years.

As Samuel Goldwyn said, "If people don't want to go to the movies, you can't stop them."

Late in the 1977 model year came something really different. The XL frame was derived from the KH frame. This wasn't as stiff as it could have been, but the frame was good enough for 1950s-era tire and suspension technology. When tires and suspensions improved, and the addition of the electric starter and larger battery added weight and moved things around,

For 1970, Sportsters could be had with the optional boattail shown on this XLH.

the space between the shocks and the engine were so cramped that on occasion the chain would saw through the corner of the oil tank.

When the racing and engineering departments were working on the XR-750 racer, they drew up a vastly better frame. It was stiffer and more predictable, and there was room behind the engine.

THE XLCR

While the XR-750 project was under way, William G. Davidson, third-generation member of the founding family and Harley's head of styling, believed the

Motor Company needed additional models and more press coverage, and it needed to achieve both on a tight budget.

The XLCR project began with a redesigned XR frame.

Into this frame went a blacked-out XL engine. The bodywork was vaguely based on the XR-750, with solo seat and a tapering tail, low bars, rear set pegs, and a bikini fairing. A bit before this time, the English bike nuts had begun modifying sports models to mimic road racers, with low bars, rear set controls, and souped-up engines. They used the machines on the street, racing from hangout to hangout, and the bikes

For 1977, Willie G. Davidson and company tried to cash in on the "café racer" trend, with the introduction of Willie's take on the theme, the XLCR. With a new frame, new gas tank, Siamese exhaust, and blacked-out good looks, it was the biggest change to the Sportster line since the original XLCH.

were known as "café racers." Willie G. knew of this trend, and because some elements of the modified XL were in that vein, the new model was named XLCR. The XLCR came with a better seat than did the normal XLH. The gearing was lower so the dragstrip times were better. As the XLCR came from the factory, it was a good machine, an improvement in important ways. But after it left the factory, it didn't sell. For its second year, the XLCR got an optional passenger seat, and it still didn't sell. In the long run, the XLCR became a collector's bike and has held its value much better than others in its class, but at the time, the model was a commercial failure.

Model year 1979 marked the last year for the XLCH, which really hadn't been a distinct model since the loss of the magneto and the acquisition of electric start. In its place came the XLS, another attempt to make a new model from existing parts. The name of the new XLS was Roadster, chosen via a nationwide contest. Featuring drag bars on risers and mildly extended forks, the Roadster was marketed as a Sportster version of the popular FX Low Rider.

Willie G. took the frame, exhaust, and other bits off the CR and used them on the whole line of redesigned Sportsters starting mid-year 1978. Unfortunately, these "Disco Sportsters" bombed, because of the new frame and triangular covers that spoiled the traditional Sportster look.

Opposite Page
Unfortunately, the CR was too "café" for the Harley traditionalist and too "Harley" for the real sportbike enthusiasts, and it never found a market.

Living with

THE XLCR

By Peter Egan

When you own a Harley Café Racer, you hear two familiar lines over and over. One is "If you ever decide to sell that thing, let me know," and the other is "If I ever owned a Harley, that would be the one."

While this curbside appreciation is nice, it probably comes a little too late for Willie G. Davidson—who made it his personal project to design the XLCR—and for the Motor Company itself. When these bikes were brand-new in 1977, they were either snapped up immediately by collectors or left to languish on showroom floors. I, myself, almost bought one brand-new after it sat unsold for a year at a local Harley shop, with the price reduced from its original $3,595 list (expensive at the time) to a mere $2,499. And the dealer had *two* of them at that price.

But I didn't buy an XLCR, even at this bargain-basement price. And why, you ask, not?

Well, probably for the same reason many other sport bike/café racer-types didn't buy them. First, while the bike was admittedly beautiful and charismatic, it didn't have the top speed or cornering clearance of contemporary exotics such as the Ducati 900SS, BMW R90S, or Moto Guzzi V7 Sport, and it was not much of a two-up mount, even with the optional dual saddle. The XLCR had a vibratory top speed of 106 miles per hour, at a time when an

The author with his XLCR.

R90S or 900SS would smoothly surge to 130-plus miles per hour and cruise at an easy 100 miles per hour all day.

Just as importantly, this was a time when the famous baby boomers hadn't yet reached that financially secure point in their lives when they could afford more than one motorcycle. And the XLCR was not a very practical "Only Bike." Harleys of the AMF-era had a very spotty reputation for build quality and reliability. All of this together conspired against high sales figures. Kept me from buying one, too.

Until two years ago.

So what changed?

Well, I am one of those boomers who can finally afford more than one bike. And I have always loved the look and sound of the XLCR. So when a nice clean, lightly restored example with 12,000 miles on the odometer showed up in the Sunday want ads a few years ago, I bought it.

I've ridden the bike regularly for more than two years now, and can make at least a provisional consumer report on my own experience with the Café Racer:

First, the dreaded AMF reliability factor.

So far, so good. In two seasons of riding, nothing has gone wrong. Not one thing. I've spent entire Saturdays batting around the hilly back roads of southwestern Wisconsin at fairly high speeds, as well as commuting regularly into the Big City to buy guitar picks and motorcycle magazines (those twin staples of life) without so much as a loose part or burned-out light bulb. Compared with a few other vintage bikes I've owned (from an island nation that shall remain unnamed), the Harley has been a paragon of reliability.

The XLCR has never failed to start, either. You turn on the gas, pull out the choke, hit the button (there's no kick starter) and it fires after one or two revolutions of the crank, throwing out a big glorious cloud of unburned (and burned) hydrocarbons. That quickly clears, and then you push the choke off immediately and it settles down to an easy, loping idle.

Head on down the driveway and you find the footpegs slightly behind you and the bars at a comfortable forward lean, quite mild and civilized by modern sport-bike standards, almost like my BMW R100RS. A gentleman's sporting position. The solo seat is well shaped, but the foam is somewhat soft, so you find yourself moving forward and back on a long ride to occasionally change your position.

As you accelerate onto the highway, you discover that the black Harley may not have an astronomical top speed, but it accelerates like the hammers of Hell and pulls like a truck at real-world velocities. Suddenly you have to remind yourself that superbikes of the mid-1970s were not slow by any standard, and that this was the fastest and quickest stock Harley road bike made up to that point. The XLCR has abundant, user-friendly, concussive torque and moves out smartly at any speed between 45 and 95 miles per hour, the place where most of us ride most of the time.

A fifth speed would have been nice, just to dial down the highway revs a bit, but cruising in fourth gives you a nice sweet spot in the engine vibration (which is only moderate and much overstated—I think—by critics) around 62 miles per hour, or about 3,600 rpm, and another one between 70 and 75 miles per hour. Highway travel at those speeds is quite pleasant.

Road tests from the 1970s are rather hard on the XLCR's handling capabilities, but I think that is probably because the OEM Goodyear tires were nothing to write home about. With modern Metzler sport tires on my own bike, however, handling is effortless and intuitive, with nice balance and stick. If you really wick it up, you'll start to drag pipes and pegs, but cornering clearance is adequate for smooth, swift road riding.

But then the XLCR has good chassis lineage, with its back end and swing arm coming off the XR dirt-trackers and the front end from the regular Sportster, so there's nothing tricky or odd about the frame geometry. The bike simply tracks wherever you point it, and never shakes its head or twitches. It's stable, planted, and easy to ride.

Unless the corner is bumpy. Then the slightly stiff rear springs and under-damped OEM rear shocks let the rear end patter and bounce around a bit, but even then they don't upset the bike's directional stability. Brakes? The dual-front and single-rear discs are slightly underwhelming

by modern standards. Not much feel, but they slow down the bike well on the safe side of panic. They are good enough that you don't have to think about them when you are riding.

Fuel mileage is pretty good, generally between 45 and 52 miles per gallon, depending on how it's ridden, and the surprisingly large 4.0-gallon fuel tank gives it excellent range, with normal pre-reserve fill-ups coming around 160 miles. My own bike—still on its original unmolested factory engine—uses a little oil. After a 200-mile Sunday ride, I usually have to add about a half-pint of the required 60-weight Harley oil.

Oil changes, like most maintenance on the bike, are easy. There's no oil filter, so you merely pull the drain plug on the left-side oil tank and refill it. Valve adjusts, too, are dead simple once you remove the air cleaner and get the knack of removing spring clips from the pushrod tubes. You lift the tube to expose a threaded adjuster and locknut at the bottom of the pushrod, then adjust it until the pushrod just spins in your fingertips when the same valve on the opposite cylinder is full open. No gap gauge needed. Lube the chain, and you're ready to ride.

That ride will most likely be solo, of course, as the optional dual seat is nothing but an alternate pad and cover that snaps over the tailpiece with passenger pegs threaded into the rear axle. My wife—who cheerfully rides on almost any sportbike—has pronounced the rear seat and pegs "impossible." She won't ride on it.

That feature excepted, the XLCR has proved to be a much more inviting and useful daily rider than I expected. When I bought it, I half suspected it might end up as a sort of garage artifact, but that has not been the case. The bike is easy to start and makes no special demands on the rider. It gets used a lot, even with three more modern bikes in the garage.

These practical considerations, of course, don't really get to the root appeal of the XLCR, which is its tactile charm. The bike is narrow and compact, with a solid mechanical feel that almost seems to be the product of a machine shop rather than an assembly line. There's a little locomotive in its blood, yet it never lets you forget for a moment that you are on a motorcycle.

The 1979 (and later) XL frame extended all the way back to above the rear axle. It was stiffer, which helped handling.

New noise regulations dictated the 1979 air cleaner would be bigger and less graceful than the earlier versions.

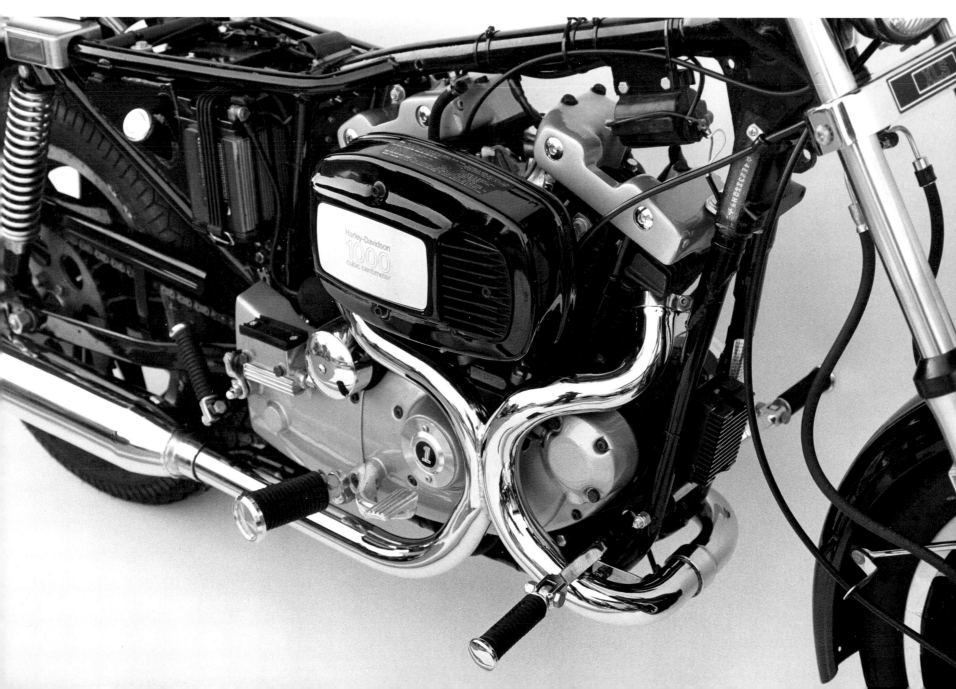

TWO MOVES, OPPOSITE DIRECTIONS

AMF invested a ton of money in H-D's plants, and into planning for improved products, but AMF executives weren't good with people. Some bad feelings remain among Motor Company fans and former employees over the unrest and labor troubles from the AMF years. But, the improved infrastructure and the money for research and development gave Harley a base from which to launch better motorcycles, which it did.

After a group of investors bought Harley-Davidson from AMF, the first thing the new owners did to the sportster family was introduce what's known in the retail world as a loss leader.

For 1983, Harley introduced a stripped Sportster model with a peanut tank, solo seat, and low bars. It came only in black and had hardly any chrome, even on the exhaust pipes. Harley named its new Sportster the XLX-61—none of this metric foolishness—and the suggested retail price was $3,995, marginally less expensive than an optioned XLH and much less expensive than a Harley Big Twin. The price was right in the neighborhood of comparable imports. The model run sold out. Fast.

To create another Sportster-based model, H-D's racing department took two-carb aluminum-alloy XR-750 cylinder heads, made special alloy cylinders,

For 1983, Harley tried to woo the performance crowd with real performance on the new XR-1000, rather than the look of performance, as on the XLCR.

The XR featured aluminum heads and twin carbs on the right like those on the racing XR-750s.

and adapted the top end to a modified version of XL cases. They mounted two carburetors on the right and two exhaust pipes on the left, just like an XR-750.

They put the mix-and-match engine in an XLX frame and tagged the model the XR-1000.

Actually, it was a bit more complicated than that. The XL and XR engines had diverged in major ways since their common ancestry began, and the actual XR heads wouldn't fit on the XL cases, while the XR heads were too tall for the XL frame.

The new model needed new cases and a whole lot more, most of which wasn't readily apparent to the naked eye. Thus, when the XR-1000 appeared as a 1983 model, it was priced at $7,000—nearly twice the asking price for the XLX—while it only had 10 or so more horsepower than the stock XL-1000 engine. And while

the tests showed the XR-1000 to be the quickest Harley ever, it wasn't close to the times turned by the 750-cc fours in the rival showrooms. Worse yet, the engineering department had done the work too quickly. There were serious flaws in the XR-1000's basic design: They broke early and often.

What might have been the true third strike against the XR-1000 was that it didn't look all that different from the XLX or an XHL. It featured no bodywork, no streamlining, no road-going fairing, nor anything besides those two carburetors sticking out on the right side to indicate it was anything more than a pedestrian XLX.

The XR-1000, like the XLCR, didn't sell and was dropped from the lineup after two years.

But the XR-1000 wasn't a total disaster. The XLX may have sold like hotdogs at halftime, but the profit

The XR-1000 also had twin high exhausts on the left. Its high price kept it from the best-seller list.

Right

No more iron—this Sportster engine is all aluminum, and quieter, more oil tight, and more powerful. The Evolution engine brought the Sportster out of the 1950s and into the future.

Following pages

The 883 Sportster was reliable, oil tight, and great fun to ride. It was the hit of the sales year, outselling all the Big Twins.

Though the engine was all new, the rest of the bike was pure XLX Sportster, right down to its $3,995 price tag. It was the bargain of the decade.

margin was terribly thin. The XR-1000 sold like sand in the desert, but because of its big markup, the XR-1000 actually put some money in the bank when the banks were about to call in the loans. And like other models the public didn't want, the XR-1000 is now a collector's item—so valuable that owners show them rather than ride them.

COMES THE EVOLUTION

From the Motor Company's beginning, it's been an H-D policy to make improvements one or two at a time. For the 1986 model year, the Sportster got a new Evolution engine. In something of a break with Harley tradition, just about everything about the Evo engine was new.

The profile and the general outline were the same, but the new engine's cylinders and heads were aluminum alloy, at last, and because they would let the engine run cooler under load, they could be more heavily stressed to produce more power. A few weeks after debuting the XLH-883, the factory introduced the XLH-1100 Sportster. The 1100, created by increasing the cylinder bore, was quicker than the old Ironhead XL-1000 and as quick as rival 1,000-cc twins from across either ocean.

Priced at $3,995 for a stripped model with solo seat and black paint, the Evo-powered XL-883 was a bargain. The 1100 was priced $1,200 higher than the 883, although the 1100 didn't come in a stripped version. Besides, the 1100 still sold for $2,000 less than the least expensive Big Twin.

In 1991, Harley redesigned the Sportster engine to include a five-speed transmission. "Hell Freezes Over" exclaimed the moto mags of the day when it appeared.

THE HUGGER'S SECRET

Women have been riding motorcycles since the motorcycle was invented, but it wasn't until the 1980s that manufacturers began to recognize this fact. Harley-Davidson also recognized some basic physical differences between men and women, most notably that women usually aren't as tall as men. Beginning with the 1980 model year, Harley offered an XLH with shorter rear shock absorbers, the fork tubes slipped up in their clamps, and less padding in the seat. These minor changes resulted in the lowest static seat height on the market. The new model was named Hugger, and it was just like any other XLH except for the suspension and the seat. The Hugger has been a strong seller since it was introduced, and a sizeable portion of that market segment is female.

THE 1200

The 1,100-cc Sportster had performed well and proven reliable, so for 1988, the bore was increased again, raising the displacement to 1,200.

This time, though, there was more involved than a larger bore. The 1200 used larger valves and ports, along with a larger combustion chamber.

FIVE SPEEDS...AND MORE

The 1991 XLH got two major improvements.

First, the engineers figured how to put five pairs of gears where four had been since the first Model K appeared in 1952. When the engineers were packing

The 1100 Sportster was the fastest motorcycle in Harley's 1986 lineup.

All that work was worth it, because the five-speed transmission brought the Sportster into the 1990s.

that fifth set of gears inside the cavity, they revised and improved the shift drum and linkage, so the 1991 and subsequent XLs are much easier to shift, with lighter controls and fewer grinding noises.

The second major modification was a switch to belt drive, long a feature of the Big Twins. The belt drive first arrived on the 1,200-cc Sportster. This proved so popular that for the 1993 model year all the XLs came stock with belt drive, which is much cleaner, needs virtually no maintenance, and lasts two or three times as long as the best chain ever did.

The next few years saw mostly minor changes such as larger fuel tanks, until the introduction of the Custom and Sport versions of the 1,200-cc model in 1996. The Custom came with raised handlebars, stepped seat, and a 21-inch front wheel. It sold well. The Sport had stickier tires, low bars, and tunable suspension, and didn't sell as well.

The big Sportster news for 1999 was the introduction of an 883-cc version of the Custom. For 2002, Harley introduced the XL-883R, a racy-looking Sportster with a stock two-into-one exhaust and big muffler, a streamlined seat and low bars, and perhaps

By 1993, all Sportsters came with belt final drive.

Want more show or more go in your Sportster? Harley had your answer for 1996: the new 1200 Custom and 1200 Sport.

On the go side, the 1200 Sport had an adjustable cartridge fork, adjustable gas piggyback shocks, sticky tires, and triple floating discs.

best of all, the darker orange paint seen on the VR-1000 and XR-750 factory racers.

THE UNBROKEN CIRCLE

The more things change, the more they remain the same.

When the Sportster appeared in 1957, it arrived as an air-cooled, narrow-angle, V-twin with modern suspension, brakes, and controls, and with a profile that somehow combined the traditional and the radical. As

the Sportster appears on the eve of the Motor Company's second century of building motorcycles, it's an air-cooled, narrow-angle, overhead-valve V-twin with modern suspension, brakes, and controls, and with a profile that still combines the traditional and the radical.

But in the intervening years, all the details have changed. The Sportster's lifespan has been a time of major technical improvement. The 2002 Sportster is an incomparably better motorcycle than the 1957 XL was, never mind what Granddad says.

On the show side, the 1200 Custom was given high chromed risers and drag bars, a slotted rear wheel, a skinny 21-inch front tire on a chrome rim, and a chrome bullet headlight.

Harley's
SPORTSTER PARADOX

By Kevin Cameron

The Harley Sportster has been, from 1957 to the 2001 introduction of the V-Rod, the Motor Company's sportiest machine. However, the classic Sportster look has frozen its mufflers in a form that is today incompatible with high horsepower. I'm referring, of course, to the infamous "shorty duals," the little 3-inch diameter, 18-inch-long mufflers that preserve the raunchy,

provocative look of loud, straight-through, hot-rod glass-packs.

The problem is how do you meet modern noise standards with these small-volume mufflers, without completely choking the engine? No compromise is possible—people really like the way shorties look and lately they also like performance. Now what?

The old straight-through muffler was just a slight enlargement in the pipe with a perforated tube running through it, with the space between tube and muffler body filled with a dissipative material like packed fiberglass. Sound pulses—in trying to expand into the fiber—lost some energy, and so there was some muffling effect. Today, the bark of glasspacks can't even come close to meeting required sound levels.

Effective muffling today makes use of what are called "quarter-wave tubes." These divert part of a sound wave and delay it, so that it emerges 180 degrees out-of-step

Harley engineers can use any exhaust system they want on a Sportster, as long as it's shorty duals.

with the original sound pulse. The two now neatly cancel each other. A typical automotive muffler may have four such tubes, each tuned to attenuate a particular range of frequencies. Through choice of tube lengths, the muffler engineer can tailor the resulting sound. It can be essentially silent, or the muffler can pass some desired sound character to suit market demand.

The trouble is, there isn't room to do all this inside shorty duals. Therefore, Harley's mufflers have had to be made quite restrictive to achieve sound level compliance. This seriously limits horsepower. The Motor Company may even have resorted to measures such as slowing the initial rate of exhaust valve lift to make the emerging sound pulse less steep and therefore less rich in the higher frequencies that light up sound meters. A restrictive muffler limits power by forcing the engine to pump its exhaust out against the back pressure of the muffler's flow resistance. This back pressure delays the

intake process, thereby reducing the amount of fresh charge taken in. This, in its effect, is like reducing the engine's displacement.

Almost everyone hates the look of the large-volume mufflers that are necessary to combine power and quiet—such as the infamous "Corvair muffler" hung under some Buell models. When I asked Erik Buell about these big, ugly depth charges, he replied, smiling, "Performance is good."

What to do? A large-volume muffler can be concealed under the bike, with the shorties preserved for looks only. There might be some value in so-called "laminar flow" mufflers, which fit better into small volumes but are prone to plugging. Noise cancellation— generating an equal and opposite sound with an internal loudspeaker—would be too expensive. How about education? Get used to it—high performance and low noise mean big mufflers.

Although other types of mufflers have been used throughout the Sporty's long history, only the shorty duals have been accepted by most fans.

The 1,200-cc Sportster was the first Harley model to offer belt drive.

Which brings us, if not quite to the future, to at least wondering what the Sportster's future will be. The Sportster is limited, if not quite imprisoned, by the success of the model line and the parent Motor Company. When the grandparent D-series 45s arrived in 1929, they were an answer to rival Indian's middleweight Scouts.

When the water-cooled V-Rod arrived in 2001, it was an answer to the rival big-engine sports-cruisers from overseas. In an H-D dealership near you, there's the single-cylinder Buell Blast, and the Buell Twins to compete against the sporting twins from east and west. The Softails and Dyna Glides take the factory chopper further than the XL Customs will ever dare to go.

Not long before the V-Rod was introduced, H-D's chief engineer made a point of stressing the Motor company's commitment to air-cooling. "Never mind the federal mandates for emissions and noise," he said. "We can meet those requirements, and we'll never surrender the simplicity and reliability of using the air stream for cooling."

What this means, at this time and in this context, is that the Sportster doesn't have many directions in which it can go. If the models got much smaller or much larger, they'd compete with other Harleys. If Sportsters had four cylinders or radiators, they wouldn't be Sportsters.

What we can expect is continued improvement, evolution if you will, with perhaps a version of the Buell's isolation engine mounts to tame the vibration that remains the XL's only true drawback.

Beyond that, as long as the Sportster sells, the Sportster will be produced. If the Sportster ain't broke, don't fix it.

No one outside the Motor Company knows what the future holds for the Sportster, but no matter how much Harley improves the mechanical parts, you can bet the bike will look a lot like this.

Chapter 7

THE SHOVELHEAD ERA

By Greg Field

For most of its first century, the motorcycles Harley-Davidson built defined the company, but that was not the case between 1966 and 1984. The drama that played out within the Motor Company during the Shovelhead era overshadowed the motorcycles it built. That's not to say Harley-Davidson didn't build some great motorcycles during the era, because it produced some very important models. But as important as those models were, they paled next to the importance of the battles that raged at the very top of Harley-Davidson's corporate hierarchy.

This was a time when the clannish family owners first sold shares to the public, before the clan splintered and put the whole company on the auction block. It was the era when Harley's board of directors fought off a corporate vampire bent on sucking the company dry, and found a white knight to take over under favorable terms. In time, that white knight started looking more like the wicked witch, as it expanded production beyond all imagining, clashed mightily with its workforce, ripped the company in two, and shredded its good reputation. Most importantly, it was the era when a core group of heroes bought back the Motor Company after everyone had written it off for dead, then took the company to undreamed of heights.

It was the Shovelhead era. Like all eras worth looking at, it began long before the history books say it did, so let's rewind to the real beginning.

IT WAS A CLAN THING

By beginning, we really mean beginning, as in 1903 through 1907. Bill Harley and the Davidson brothers were tight, but the Davidsons ran everything while Harley was off earning an engineering degree.

The Davidson boys were sons of Scottish immigrants, so "clan" was not just a word. They had been raised on the principle that if you need help, you turn

A new era for the Motor Company began when the 1966 Shovelhead engines made their debut.

Harley created the Shovelhead engine by bolting a new top end onto the old bottom end. Its signature feature was a set of new rocker boxes shaped like the Sportster's. Some thought they resembled the end-view of a coal shovel, which inspired the Shovelhead nickname.

Opening image
Like the first of the breed, the last FLHs were trim and unencumbered by bags or fairing.

to your clan, which in this case was the extended Davidson family in and around Milwaukee.

When they needed more space, Dad built a shed for them. When they were hungry, Mom cooked for them. When they needed someone to paint the company name on the building or on the new machines, a sister did it. When they needed someone to keep the books, another sister pitched in. When they needed a loan, they turned to a bachelor uncle. Though they didn't go so far as to paint their first bikes tartan plaid, the Davidsons were Scots to a fault.

When Harley-Davidson incorporated in 1907, its board of directors became the clan chieftains. The clan grew as the families grew, and all management positions were filled from sons of chieftains. In turn, the chieftains managed the company to maximize profits back to the clan. The clan's first loyalty was to the company, and the company's first loyalty was to the clan.

That clan stayed tight and grew rich through the gravy years of the 1910s and 1920s. During the tough years of the 1930s, the growth years of the 1940s, and the British invasion of the 1950s, this clannishness served the company well. "If a problem came up, they could just get the family together in a room and solve it," explained Vaughn Beals, the man who would later lead Harley back to glory.

By the early 1960s, however, the clannishness wasn't working so well. Clan loyalty to the company had been diluted over three generations, the new clan chieftains weren't necessarily the best men for the jobs, and clannish emphasis on paying shareholders before investing in new equipment and designs had left Harley with outdated factories and designs—just as the Japanese moved in.

It could be said that Harley's clannishness had turned a proud, kilted Highland piper into the toothless, inbred banjo picker of the motorcycle industry.

What We Have Here is a Failure to Diversify

Most of the Harley and Davidson clans neither worked for the company nor cared about the motorcycles. The predominant attitude was, "My entire fortune is tied up in some stupid motorcycle company founded by my father (or grandfather or husband's father), and I think I could make more money if that money was invested in Coca Cola or McDonalds."

These later generations had also grown financially savvy. They knew it was risky to have all their financial eggs in one basket. What they and Harley-

Davidson needed was to diversify. Harley's first steps toward diversification came in 1960, when it began building scooters and bought into the Italian firm Aermacchi to get a new line of lightweight motorcycles. In 1962, Harley bought the Tomahawk boat works and began building golf carts and boats.

Further diversification and upgrades to the plants required capital that neither the company nor the stockholders had. And the stockholders couldn't diversify for themselves because no one else in the clan had the money to buy their stock. That put clan chieftains Gordon, Walter, and William H. Davidson and William J. Harley in a real bind. Their own fortunes were tied up, too, and the folks breathing down their necks were kin, not anonymous investors. And if they didn't find some money soon, clan and company would probably wither and die together.

Going Public

The only way out was to break with clan tradition and sell stock to the general public for the first time. Harley's directors split the stock two-for-one and made a first offering of 75,000 shares for the company and about 24,000 from its shareholders, which all

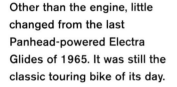

Other than the engine, little changed from the last Panhead-powered Electra Glides of 1965. It was still the classic touring bike of its day.

quickly sold. Harley-Davidson spent its share on plant expansions in Italy, Milwaukee, and at Tomahawk, boosting its workforce by 20 percent.

Despite the infusion of cash, money was still very tight, according to Tom Gelb, then plant superintendent and later one of the saviors of the company. "They let me buy one machine tool a year. Nobody believes this now, but we still used box wrenches on the production line because there was no money for pneumatic tools. I had a feeling the company wasn't going to last, so I left."

THE FIRST SHOVELHEAD

That brings us to the namesake of this era, created when Harley updated the Panhead engine for 1966. Like the Panhead before it, the new engine wasn't all that new. Mostly, it was a new top end on the old Panhead bottom end. Its marque feature was a set of U-shaped rocker boxes that enclosed the valve gear but left more head area exposed for better cooling. Squinted at from the bike's right side, after a few too many beers, the covers shape resembled the back of a coal shovel, earning the nickname "Shovelhead."

With the investment brought in by the stock sale and the sales bump brought on by the new engine, 1966 was the most successful in company history. Sales rose to 36,310, the most the company had ever sold in one year. True, many of these were the lightweights built by Aermacchi, but revenue and profits were the best they'd ever been.

For 1967, Harley once again gave the Electra Glide a few updates. Sales were down a bit compared to 1966, but profits were up because the expensive Electra Glides and Sportsters sold as well as before. Little was changed for 1968, but sales remained steady, leading to record revenue and great profit margins.

An outside observer could easily think all was well in Harleyland. Unfortunately, all was far from well.

BREAKING UP THE CLAN

Despite diversification and good profits, the stockholders wanted more. Problem was, there was no longer a quick way to raise the money to diversify. After the last issuance of "print-and-sell" stock, members of the clan only owned 53 percent of outstanding shares. If they sold stock or the company printed more, the clan would lose its majority control.

This crisis split the clan into two camps. "We could diversify two ways," explained John Davidson, board member and son of then-president William H. Davidson. "We could start building lawn mowers and so on, or we could get sucked up. The merger group held the majority and won, so we began looking for someone to buy the company."

SEARCHING FOR A SUGAR DADDY

Harley quietly sent feelers out in its search for a buyer, and the major companies that responded included Caterpillar, John Deere, OMC, and Chris-Craft.

One by one, these potential buyers backed out, some after seeing the sorry state of the company's plants and processes, others after personality conflicts with the clan. In one case, the suitor decided it didn't want to be associated with the "criminal" element attracted to Harleys. Some say all the deals were sabotaged by President William H. Davidson, who didn't want to sell at all.

ALL HELL BREAKS LOOSE

One impatient Harley stockholder finally forced William H.'s hand. Through a broker, that stockholder approached the rapidly growing conglomerate of Bangor Punta (BP), and soon, all hell broke loose.

On May 24, 1968, BP quietly approached Harley's board with an offer to buy H-D for $27 per share. It was a pretty good offer, because H-D stock typically traded for $14–20 at the time.

Suddenly, it was high-pucker time in the Harley boardroom. BP had been in the news lately because it was just then acquiring another Milwaukee institution, Waukesha Motors. And BP was widely viewed as a corporate Count Dracula that moved in quickly to suck a company dry whenever it smelled blood. Harley would need to find a white knight to beat back the vampire.

Little would be changed through the end of the 1960s, because Harley-Davidson management had its mind fixed on one goal: finding a suitable buyer for the aging Motor Company.

The FLHs built in 1969 were the last Big Twins with the flat-sided timing cover and generator shown here.

CORPORATE VAMPIRE?

The characterization of BP as a corporate vampire may or may not be fair. BP was a highly diversified company, the result of a *ménage à trios* between potatoes, sugar, and railroading. It was formed when the Bangor & Aroostook Railroad merged with the Punta Alegre Sugar Corp.

Vampire or not, BP was an unstoppable acquisition machine that was virtually sheltered from taxation after Castro had seized the company's Cuban sugar factories, giving it a $54 million "paper" loss that the company used to great advantage. By 1968, companies it controlled built products as varied as guns (Smith & Wesson), chemical mace, breathalyzers, motor homes, boats, and industrial machinery. Most of these companies are still around, so it's doubtful that BP's reputation matched reality.

That doesn't matter, though, because William H. Davidson and the board believed that reputation. As the last dyed-in-the-plaid remnants of the clan, they loved both the company and their jobs, so they unanimously rejected BP's offer and intensified their search for other suitors.

Spurned in its friendly takeover attempt, BP bared its fangs on October 1, and took its offer directly to the shareholders. This time the offer was upped to about $32 per share, nearly 50 percent above market.

Harley fought back, calling the offer "inadequate" and emphasizing that the exchange was taxable. Despite that, BP was able to buy or get options on 16.3 percent of the Harley stock, most from boat builder Chris-Craft, which had earlier looked at buying H-D.

WHITE KNIGHT?

Harley-Davidson found its white knight in American Machine & Foundry, better known as AMF, and announced on October 31 that it had already struck a deal for a tax-free exchange of 1.23 shares of AMF (worth about $29) for each share of H-D stock.

Like Harley-Davidson, AMF was a turn-of-the-century company, and like BP, it was hell-bent on diversification. "AMF was the result of an antitrust action in the early part of the century, in which the tobacco makers were forced to divest themselves of manufacturing the machinery that processed tobacco and made cigarettes," explained Vaughn Beals. "They then began acquiring leisure businesses." Those businesses included boats (Hatteras) and bowling pin setters.

What set AMF apart was its chairman, Rodney Gott, who in his pitch emphasized that he was a long-time Harley fan and offered advice on fending off BP's hostile takeover. "Rodney Gott was a great pitchman," remembered John Davidson. "He sold us a real bill of goods, telling us he would keep Harley-Davidson's management in place and that we would be autonomous."

BIDDING WAR

A big formality remained, however. Under Wisconsin law, a proposed merger took effect only if at least two-thirds of a company's shares approved. BP's goal became to get one third of the shares so it could stop the AMF merger. Accordingly, it offered $40 per share.

That started a comical bidding war between BP and AMF that resulted in a doubling of company value. (BP's final offer was $49 per share, tax-free; AMF's was 1.5 shares, worth about $40 per share, again tax-free.) Though BP's offer was by far the best, Harley's board stuck with AMF and drove a stake through the vampire's heart by calling a shareholder's meeting for December 18, 1968, to vote on the AMF merger.

Undeterred, BP rose again to file suit against Harley for $7 million, the amount BP claimed shareholders were losing by accepting AMF's offer.

THE FATEFUL VOTE

When William H. Davidson called the shareholders meeting to order on December 18, BP's president, David W. Wallace, was allowed to speak first. He showed his chutzpah by making one last offer: BP

The 1970 FLHs featured the new "cone" Shovelhead engine, named for the cone-shaped timing cover shown on this 1971 Electra Glide.

In 1971, Harley turned the motorcycling world upside down with the introduction of its factory custom, the Super Glide. The fiberglass rear fender helped earn this model the nickname "Night Train."

would drop the lawsuit if AMF would raise its offer to two full shares for each one of Harley's. That motion was rejected, the polls opened and closed, and the meeting was adjourned, all inside 20 minutes.

When the results were announced later that afternoon, 78 percent had voted to merge, even though AMF's offer was 20 percent less than BP's.

All that stood between Harley-Davidson and the merger was a vote of the AMF stockholders, a formality scheduled for January 7, 1969, in New York. Inside members of the clan advised each other to sell quickly. Could they have known what AMF had planned?

PAPER EXCHANGE

On January 7, AMF's stockholders met at Carnegie Hall and approved the merger. The next day, the Harley-Davidson Motor Company Inc. became AMF Harley-Davidson. Based on the prices that day, AMF paid $38.80 per share, or $27,685,895 total.

But that's on paper.

At the same meeting, AMF's board approved the issue of 20 million new shares of AMF stock. All they needed was just more than 1 million to cover the buy-out of H-D, leaving enough new stock to cover about 18 similar-sized buyouts in the future or to invest in the business.

AMF's actual cost for Harley-Davidson was the expenses to negotiate and consummate the deal and print some stock. AMF's shareholders paid, though, especially the new ones from Harley-Davidson, through dilution of equity. Those members of the H-D clan who sold out right away did OK, but those who didn't saw their fortune decline with AMF's.

THE HONEYMOON

Like most marriages, that between AMF and Harley began well. As soon as the merger papers were signed, AMF began pumping money into Milwaukee, allowing Harley to update facilities, redesign the XR-750 to make it a winner, and to improve the Big Twins and Sportsters.

At first, anyway, AMF even seemed to follow through on the promise to let Harley run itself.

THE "CONE SHOVEL"

The first and most obvious update came for 1970, when the Shovelhead engine was revised to replace its external generator with an alternator inside the primary case, and to replace the external ignition timer with an automatic-advance ignition inside a new cone-shaped cover on the right of the engine. That cone-shaped cover inspired a new nickname: "Cone Shovelhead."

Other than the cone, little changed on the Electra Glide. It was still an old man's bike amid the greatest youth market the world had ever known.

SUPER GLIDE: "THANK GOD FOR THOSE CHOPPER GUYS!"

Nineteen seventy-one was a huge year for Harley. It was the year the glaciers thawed, the guard changed, production exploded, a new star rose, and a new legend began.

Before 1971, Harley's attitudes were seemingly still stuck in the 1930s and 1940s. To Harley, the words "motorcycle club" still meant AMA clubs riding in formation with their squeaky-clean matching uniforms, and the word "motorcycle" meant a decked-out Big Twin.

Harley's managers knew that the growing clubs were the so-called "outlaws," and those who aped the fashion. And they knew those guys loved stripped and chopped Harleys. Harley could have cashed in on the movement from the start, but president William H. Davidson and the others went far out of their way to avoid any association with the chopper boys.

Harley-Davidson accessory catalogs of the day prove how out of touch the company was. Want "bologna-slicer" bumpers, extra lights, or saddlebags? "We've got every color and style in stock." Want a tall sissy bar or a skinny front wheel (let alone a 10-inch-over fork)? "Get the hell out of my dealership, kid!"

Bad as that was for the H-D's bottom line, the real problem the chopper movement presented was that

The FX 1200 Super Glide of 1971 was Willie G. Davidson's announcement to the world that he'd arrived as a designer. Shown is a 1972 model without the boat-tail rear fender.

Despite steady improvements to the Electra Glide through the 1970s, it fell further and further behind each year. Shown here is the big improvement for 1970: the "cone" version of the Shovelhead, with an alternator in place of the generator.

these guys intended to strip off so much of the FLH anyway that they saw no need to buy new, getting by quite nicely with the cast-off Knuckleheads and Panheads of yesteryear.

Fortunately, at least one person at Juneau Avenue was watching—Willie G. Davidson. He'd been watching for a while, too, first when he was in design school in California, and later at events he attended after joining the Motor Company in 1963. Even more fortunate: He held the keys to the styling department.

For 1971, he gave the chopper guys what they wanted: the FX-1200 Super Glide. There Willie G.™ (Yes, Harley even has a trademark on his name; the "G" is for "Godfrey") was, innocently wheeling a Sportster front end down to the styling studio, when he turned a corner and, Bam! He ran smack into another guy wheeling a forkless FLH the other way. Instant karma again. So he took it all back to "Willie World" (not yet trademarked) and started bolting it together.

Front end and chassis looked great together, so he played with the rest. Clunky bits, like the footboards, starter, big battery, and fat rear fender were banished to the scrap bin. Same with the exhaust, replaced by a two-into-one that fit the theme. The tanks seemed a bit fat, so he fitted the smaller 3.5-gallon versions. For the final custom touch, he bolted on the optional boattail seat-fender from the Sportster. Then, he painted it all up in red, white, and blue as a nod to both patriotism and the Captain America chopper from *Easy Rider*.

It was the first factory "custom" and the boldest, most original styling statement from Harley-Davidson since the 1936 Knucklehead. It wasn't quite a masterpiece, mostly because of the boattail, which most people quickly replaced with a regular Sportster rear fender, but it was the start of a whole new line and whole new legend for the Motor Company.

It melted the glacier between the chopper guys and the Motor Company forever. Suddenly, Harley had a new bike the chopper crowd wanted, and Harley dealers had a compelling reason to invite them in. "Thank God for those chopper guys," said John Davidson, then executive vice president in charge of marketing. "They're the most loyal customers in the world, and they kept the company alive for a lot of years."

It was also the debut of a new star for Harley. The Super Glide announced Willie G.'s arrival. Tom Gelb remembered, "In later years, Willie G. was given a lot of credit for things that Louie Netz (Willie's right-hand man in Styling) actually did, but the Super Glide was his baby."

For 1972, the Electra Glide was given hydraulic disc brakes up front. A rear disc was added the next year.

Reportedly, Willie had refined the concept and had it all ready to go by about 1967, but H-D management still despised the chopper crowd too much to ever build a bike for them, and also they thought the new model would only take away from Sportster sales. Thus, it didn't come to market until 1971, when AMF twisted the throttle.

CHANGING OF THE GUARD

And AMF truly was in control by late 1971.

Rodney Gott's pitch about autonomy for Harley-Davidson turned out to be "a load of B.S.," according to John Davidson.

President William H. Davidson was "promoted" to chairman of the board, but it was really just a ceremonial position, because there really was no board. "They told William H., 'Go travel the world. Do whatever you want, but get out of our hair,'" explained John Davidson.

In William H.'s place, AMF installed John O'Brien as president, and he ramped up production and brought in battalions of AMF experts. "Every day an expert on something would show up at our door," said John Davidson. "They thought they could do everything better."

The change in the balance of power was plain for all to see when the 1972 models were released: "AMF" had pride of place preceding "Harley-Davidson" on the new tank badges. Balancing that out was the change to hydraulic disc front brakes, which everyone lauded as a huge improvement over the old drum brakes.

HARLEY OR HONDA?

Before long, AMF and O'Brien revealed their real plan: "They actually thought they could turn us into another Honda," guffawed John Davidson. AMF screwed the factory's throttle full on and tried to catch Honda.

AMF offered up mod, new tank decal graphics each year through the mid-1970s. Shown is the 1974 version.

Willie G.'s next classic came in the form of the 1977 FXS Low Rider. Lowered, raked, and blacked out, the Low Rider was the styling high point of the 1970s.

That caused immense problems in Milwaukee, as experienced foremen and workers got tired of being told what to do and being forced to work overtime. Many retired or moved on, taking hundreds of years of cumulative experience with them. This "brain drain" later came back to bite AMF Harley.

Fix this Fucking Place!

To its chagrin, AMF realized it would take more than adding a second shift to make twice as many motorcycles. "It didn't work because the processes were so screwed up," said Tom Gelb, who had rejoined Harley-Davidson as manufacturing engineering manager after the merger.

The brain drain exacerbated the problem by shifting too much responsibility to new people. That loss of experience was critical, according to Vaughn Beals, who was later president of the company: "The new people tried making everything according to the prints. All the experienced people knew that 'you don't make them to the prints; you do this, and it works.'"

Before long, quality fell victim to the production push, and so did good relations between management and the workers. So, after 10 years of peace at H-D, the workers struck for 25 days. On both sides, the whole experience had a hardening effect on attitudes that would later hound the company.

Despite all those problems, the company cranked out over 34,000 Big Twins and Sportsters for 1972, a 50 percent increase.

Harley was busting at the seams, AMF was pushing for even greater production, and more problems surfaced every day. It got so bad that John O'Brien called Tom Gelb into his office and screamed at him, "Fix this fucking place!"

THE MILWAUKEE HOG BECOMES "YORK PORK"

Fixing the fucking place meant moving assembly out of the decrepit Juneau factory. "Harley had run out of space," remembered Gelb, "so we put together a plan to build a new plant (next to the Capitol Drive plant) to build 75,000 motorcycles a year." Unfortunately, that plan was doomed because, Gelb continued, "AMF didn't like bricks and mortar."

Shortly after proposing the new factory, Gelb was told by president John O'Brien, "This is between you and me. Pack your bags; you're going to York, Pennsylvania. We're going to move assembly to our plant there." Gelb went to York to assess the

In the late 1970s, Harley reached back for more classic styling and paint combinations for the FLH. This is a 1978 model with sidecar.

equipment and to set the factory up for motorcycle production. "Not much was usable," he remembered.

AMF's York plant was largely idle because the two products made there—munitions and automatic bowling-pin setters—were no longer in demand as the Vietnam war wound down and the bowling craze of the 1950s and 1960s died. On the surface the move made sense.

To Gelb and others in Milwaukee, though, the numbers didn't add up. Gelb remembered, "They put together the economics to justify the move, and they were total B.S., saying they'd save 25 percent on labor costs by moving. The basis of that was they'd take away the 25 percent bonuses we had in Milwaukee for meeting productivity goals. They were deluded in thinking they would move and get the same productivity without the bonuses! I fought it and got in deep shit! I had to get with the program or leave."

Gelb "got with the program" after realizing the issue had already been decided by Jack Crim, AMF's group executive in charge of Harley-Davidson. "Jack wanted to be president of AMF," explained Gelb. "To get in good with Rodney Gott (chairman of AMF) he told Rodney, 'We've got this plant in York that's not doing anything. We'll avoid building in Milwaukee and fill up York, and get rid of the dirty, rotten unions in Milwaukee and go to Pennsylvania where we don't have any trouble with the unions.'" Gott, who had a strong dislike for unions, endorsed the plan.

In October 1972, just as the 1973 models began rolling out in earnest, President John O'Brien announced the move publicly, saying that Harley-Davidson would soon transfer some of its assembly from Milwaukee to York. He emphasized that no jobs would be lost in Milwaukee.

The unions remained calm after the first announcement, but that all changed when AMF trucks began hauling away not only the tooling to assemble chassis, but also the punch presses and other equipment to manufacture the chassis components. Within a month, AMF's plan became clear: Only engines would be built in Milwaukee, and everything else would be built in York.

"AMF told the union no one would lose their job," said Tom Gelb "but then they let a bunch of people go. They lied through their teeth."

Gallows humor, then current at the factory, predicted that the Milwaukee "Hog" would soon be pure "York Pork."

A New HAWG

A group soon formed who called themselves "HAWG," an acronym that stood for Harley Action Workers Group, and they started a program of passive resistance (by refusing to work overtime). Other workers took a more militant stance. "It was a bad scene," explained Tom Gelb, "and we had sabotage—ball bearings in cylinders and such. It was minimal, but it was very traumatic."

In April 1974, AMF announced it would invest, $5.5 million in machine tools for the Capitol Drive plant. Certainly the tools were much needed, but AMF also hoped the investment would reassure the union that AMF wasn't abandoning Milwaukee.

It didn't work because at the same time, AMF refused to negotiate with the union on a new contract after Harley's union insisted on having representative of AMF's other unions in on its bargaining team. "AMF's attitude toward the union was, 'Screw 'em!'" remembers Tom Gelb.

THE 100-DAY STRIKE

On May 31, when their old contract expired, Harley's workers walked out. Production stopped, and things got ugly. The company brought in replacement

Hand shift and foot clutch added by the owner enhances the classic appeal of this sidecar rig.

The Myth of
H-D VS. JAPAN

By Greg Field

You already know that the Japanese motorcycle manufacturers were big, bad bullies who conspired to kill off America's last motorcycle company. And you know how Harley fought back and got tariffs against these insidious outsiders, then went on to borrow their manufacturing methods, and ultimately went on to teach them a thing or two about motorcycles.

It's a great story—an American underdog against foreign giants. One of Mom and Pop and apple pie patriotism. And one that every book on Harley tells. But as is often the case in tales about Harley, it's more feel-good mythology than truth.

For example, did you know:

That Harley actually helped start the whole Japanese motorcycle industry? The Motor Company sold plans and tooling and sent over production experts in the 1930s to help Sankyo build its "Rikuo" line of VL clones.

That Harley used the money from Sankyo to help fund development of the Knucklehead?

That Harley also offered to sell the Knucklehead design to Sankyo, but that Sankyo rejected it as too leaky and too fragile? Imagine how history might have been changed if Soichiro Honda started tinkering with Knuckles instead of tiddlers!

That the Japanese Army rode khaki Rikuos to war against Yanks on olive-drab Harley WLAs?

That the Japanese manufacturers actively avoided taking on Harley directly until the market crashed in the early 1980s.

That when Kawasaki took over the market for police motorcycles, it was on the initiative of American racing legend Dan Gurney, and not Kawasaki?

That the glut of Japanese bikes in the early 1980s was a result of war between Yamaha and Honda, not any desire to put Harley out of business?

That the Japanese manufacturers had privately offered loans and technical assistance to Harley even before the tariff battle (including the offer to sell Harley an updated V-twin engine design), but that Harley rejected their help?

That Harley tried to use the tariffs to squeeze loan guarantees from the Japanese?

It's all true.

Harley kickstarted the Japanese motorcycle industry by selling plans and tooling and sending over production experts in the 1930s to help Sankyo build its "Rikuo" line of VL clones. Harley used the money to design and refine the Knucklehead and then offered to let Sankyo build the Knuckle, too. After testing early Knuckles and seeing how much they leaked and broke, the Japanese said, "No thanks, Yanks." Then Sankyo started building VLs, most of which ended up in the Japanese Army.

After the Japanese took over the U.S. market, they feared an anti-Japanese backlash, so they carefully avoided direct confrontation with Harley. Even though they sold police motorcycles all over the world, they didn't offer them in the United States until Dan Gurney's company, American Racers, outfitted Kawasakis and started peddling them to police departments.

When the bottom fell out of the motorcycle market in the early 1980s, the Japanese should have cut back production. Instead, Yamaha's CEO declared it was time to wrest the lead from Honda, and Yamaha ramped up production. When Honda's CEO heard about that, he vowed to bury Yamaha, and did, under huge warehouses filled with unsold bikes. That's why there was a glut. It wasn't because the Japanese wanted to bury Harley. After the tariff, though, the Japanese turned on Harley, first with a new version of the

Yamaha Virago, which was restyled for 1984 to make it look more Harley-like, followed by many others. By then, it was too late, because Harley was on a roll.

Before the tariff was even implemented, Harley offered to drop its bid if the Japanese would give Harley loan guarantees of about $15 million to fund development of the Nova project. After getting the tariffs, Harley offered to ask for an easing of the tariffs in exchange for the loans. Don't believe me? Look it up for yourself in the *Wall Street Journal* (which reported that Harley was asking $40 million) in April 1983. When the story broke, Harley denied it, stating in the *Milwaukee Journal*, "There have been no discussions between Harley and the Japanese." In July, Harley came clean in the *Milwaukee Journal*, admitting that they were negotiating with the Japanese for loan guarantees and that these negotiations had started before the tariff was imposed. (Ultimately, Harley didn't get the loans.)

In my opinion, the tariffs were justified, but to say Harley was at war with the Japanese is as false as to say there ever was a war between Harley and Indian (though at least one whole book has been written on that subject).

The real war all along was between Harley and itself, as the company's leaders discovered when they implemented Japanese management and manufacturing techniques in the 1980s. Harley won that war, and it has the Japanese to thank.

Though Harley-Davidson appeals to our national pride—it is America's motorcycle—in reality, the Motor Company is an international corporation, with ties to many countries, including Japan.

workers. "All's fair in love and war, and this is war," crowed Harley's industrial relations director F.T. Swain. A federal mediator was called in to broker a deal, but the union members overwhelmingly rejected it on July 31.

That rejection shocked both the company and union leaders, and gave both an education on how angry the workers were with AMF.

By early September, AMF Harley-Davidson was over a barrel. It had already introduced the 1975 line-up to dealers and the press, but none had been built because of the strike. With no other choice, Harley agreed to the workers' demands.

A New Attitude

Bad as it had been, the strike was good, because it forced AMF to rethink its handling of Harley. Just before the strike AMF had assigned Ray Tritten, the company's hotshot fix-it guy, to turn things around in Milwaukee. After the strike, Tritten got to work on the core problems and brought in two people who were key to reviving the company.

The first was Jeff Bleustein, a former engineering professor who was the "golden boy" of AMF's corporate engineering unit. Tritten charged him with building a real engineering department at Harley-Davidson. Bleustein began hiring professional engineers and improving the motorcycles.

Then Tritten hired Vaughn Beals as his deputy in late 1975. Instead of dictating from New York, Beals would work within the system in Milwaukee. His first job would be to form a business plan and a long-term product strategy.

The 10-Year Plan

To formulate that strategy, Beals flew the company's top officers to North Carolina for a retreat at the Pinehurst Country Club in April 1976.

In between rounds of golf, they decided Harley-Davidson should, in Beals' words, "ride two horses at once." That meant Harley would update its traditional V-twin and also work on a family of sophisticated water-cooled engines. Both those horses—the Evolution engine and the NOVA—were scheduled to

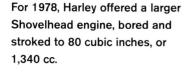

For 1978, Harley offered a larger Shovelhead engine, bored and stroked to 80 cubic inches, or 1,340 cc.

Along with the larger engine came the larger breadbox air cleaner shown on this 1979 FLH-80.

debut in the 1980s. In the short term, they would "Band-Aid" the Shovelhead to get the company through the 1970s.

Beals and company wrote up the plan and presented it to AMF. Shortly thereafter, AMF approved it, and turned on the money tap, starting another honeymoon period. "You told AMF what you wanted, and you got it," remembered Beals. "They invested in major, major upgrades at Harley and let us hire lots of people."

With the new plan, the new investment, and all the new engineers Beals and Bleustein hired, everyone in Milwaukee got the sense that Harley-Davidson was suddenly a company on the mend.

WILLIE G. COMES THROUGH

The boys in engineering got all the money, but Willie G. stole all the glory by doing more with less. With clever juggling of parts, paint, and decals, he quickly expanded Harley's line with distinct new models.

For 1977, he released a new model so gorgeous everyone forgot it was "an AMF" (which at the time was a slur because of all the quality problems). That bike was the FXS Low Rider, created by lowering and raking the Super Glide and fitting a new tank-mounted dash with tandem speedometer and tach.

In 1979, he scored again with the Fat Bob. In 1980 came the one-two punch of the Sturgis and Wide Glide. He also reintroduced classic Harley style to the Electra Glide with sprung seats, fringed leather saddlebags, Art Deco tank emblems, and special editions like the Anniversary, Classic, and Heritage models.

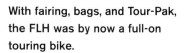

With fairing, bags, and Tour-Pak, the FLH was by now a full-on touring bike.

Willie's new models brought in new customers, and his successful new takes on classic Harley style gave the traditional Harley buyers reason to stick around.

UPDATING THE SHOVELHEAD

While Willie kicked butt on the styling front, Bleustein's boys attacked the Shovel's major problems—all the while working on its replacement.

For 1978, they bored and stroked the Shovel to 80 cubic inches and offered the larger engine alongside the old 74-inch models. They also added electronic ignition and made subtle updates every year after to make the engines quieter, cleaner burning, and more oiltight.

Along the way, they developed smooth, great-handling new models like the FLT, FXRS, and FXRT. These sophisticated motorcycles helped polish Harley's tarnished reputation. Unfortunately, these bikes were "aesthetically challenged," as John

Davidson tactfully describes them, and they didn't sell as well as expected. Later, Harley engineers found a way to mount the classic "batwing" Electra Glide fairing on the FLT. The resulting FLHT Electra Glide proved a winner in both sales and styling.

QUALITY WAS JOB "NONE"

To pay for all the updates, AMF pushed for even greater production. In 1970, AMF's first full year of ownership, Harley's workers built just over 16,000 Big Twins and Sportsters. By 1976, AMF had tripled production to 48,000 Big Twins and Sportsters. The higher production rose, however, the lower quality sank.

"We had to report our shipments at the end of every month," explained Tom Gelb, who ran production in Milwaukee, "and we had to make the numbers. The last 5 to 10 days of the month, people did stuff they shouldn't have done, just to get the bikes out the door."

Tank badges for 1979 were flanked by the "speedball" emblems from the 1930s.

For those who wanted a simpler Electra Glide, Harley offered the FLHS.

"Quality suffered baaaad," remembered John Davidson, who was then president of Harley-Davidson. "I've been angry about that ever since. AMF wanted product out the door, whatever the cost. We shipped bikes without parts, just to get them in the revenue stream. After the bowling business stalled, they needed every penny."

Another factor that harmed the company was the complete lack of coordination between Milwaukee and York. "John Davidson was the president of Harley-Davidson," explained Tom Gelb, "but York didn't work for him. York reported to AMF, so Harley-Davidson didn't even control its final assembly. That caused all kinds of problems with quality and costs, and there was no accountability. The York move was a bad deal, for a lot of reasons."

Harley's reputation suffered horribly. Dealers often had to spend many unpaid hours getting just-delivered bikes to run right. And customers suffered the hassle of

Willie G. really made his mark for 1980, with two new classic customs: the FXB Sturgis and FXWG Wide Glide. This is the limited edition Sturgis.

Besides long, low, and very black looks, the signature features of the Sturgis were the rubber primary and drive belts.

returning their new machines repeatedly to dealers for warranty work and the indignity of breaking down or having parts vibrate off on every short ride. Motorcycle magazines stopped testing new Harleys to save the company the embarrassment or retelling how many times the bike broke down during the test.

The really sad part of the whole thing was how unnecessary it was. AMF revved up Harley for maximum production as the whole market was throttling down. Overall motorcycle sales declined steadily every year after 1975, but AMF forced Harley to keep pushing motorcycles out the door anyway.

GETTING DUMPED ON

The Japanese operated under the same assumption that AMF did—that the downturn in the motorcycle market was a temporary thing, rather than a function of baby boomers selling their bikes, getting married, and raising families.

Unsold bikes began stacking up in dealerships across the country, so Harley filed suit in April 1978 against the Japanese makers, claiming they were dumping excess production in America. Instead of small bikes, the Japanese had shifted their focus to bikes like the 1,000-cc Honda Goldwing and a succession of even larger touring and musclebikes. In other words, the Japanese makers were battering each other for dominance on Harley's turf. From World War II through the early 1970s, Harley's share of the heavyweight motorcycle market had always been 75 percent or more. By 1978, it was in the mid-30s.

In hearings with the International Trade Commission (ITC), Harley proved its dumping allegations, but wasn't able to prove how the dumping injured the company, so the ITC took no action.

ANOTHER CHANGING OF THE GUARD

The whole dynamic of the newly supportive relationship between AMF and Harley-Davidson changed when AMF Chairman Rodney Gott retired and was replaced by Tom York. York was an accountant, not a motorcyclist, and he decided to refocus AMF.

"It got harder and harder to get money out of AMF," explained Vaughn Beals. "About mid-1980, I understood the name of the game. York was a bean counter and had hired a planning firm to develop a strategic plan. They convinced him that AMF should be half industrial and half leisure. (At the time, AMF was about two-thirds leisure.)

"He tried to get to 50/50 by acquisition, leaving no cash. At that time, we were one of 40 companies in AMF, but we brought in one-fifth of the revenue.

Though not a classic of styling, the FLT-80 set a new standard for function.

The all-new frame of the 1982 FLT featured rubber mounts for the engine and an integral fairing. Unfortunately, the FLT's looks weren't popular. Its frame was fitted with a new version of the FLH batwing fairing in 1983 to create the FLHT, which was an instant hit.

Beals got 11 of the other top execs and outside counsel Tim Hoelter together and convinced them that if they could scrape together a million bucks among them, they really could do it. It was tough, but they found the money. Some say that former president William H. Davidson even helped by lending money to Willie G., his son.

That settled, Beals worked on securing the financing and finalizing the deal with AMF's negotiator, Merlin Nelson, whom Beals described as "a stuffed shirt." Nelson wanted "in the range of one to two million from us," he continued. "Naturally, they thought two, and I thought one. We had to scrounge like hell to get a million bucks. There was no way we were gonna get two million without bringing in more people."

Beals and Nelson reached an impasse over the million. Then, Nelson made a critical mistake. "He accused me of duplicity," Beals explained, "and I don't take that well. I bounced off the wall, and told him to shove the company and walked away."

Nelson later approached Beals about resuming talks. "That was my chance," said Beals. "I asked him to cut our equity from $2 million to $1 million, and he agreed. The price we settled on was nominally $71 million, about 25 cents on a dollar of revenue. You could never buy a company for that today."

With a letter of intent signed, Beals and company flew home to Milwaukee to triumphantly announce the buyback, which was consummated June 16, 1981.

THE EAGLE SOARS ALONE

After a huge celebration of Harley-Davidson's independence in York, Beals, Willie G., Bleustein, and the other owners fired up their bikes for a triumphant ride to Milwaukee, stopping at every Harley dealership along the route. "Every one of them had a big cake and celebration," Beals said. "I never wanted to see a cake again."

During the ride back, president Charlie Thompson called Tom Gelb and promoted him to vice president in charge of operations. It was a move that would prove critical to the company's future.

The new owners were excited and apprehensive, because they knew the reality that awaited them in Milwaukee. They were obscenely in debt, the company's reputation was in tatters, the whole country was in recession, the company and its dealers were already overstocked with motorcycles they couldn't sell, and the motorcycle market was in a death spiral. The one positive aspect was that they could convincingly blame all the ills of the recent past on AMF, giving Harley-Davidson the opportunity of a fresh start.

LEARNING FROM THE COMPETITION

The whole team worked to pull Harley-Davidson together. Money was nonexistent, so only really high-priority projects, like fixing the Shovel's oil leaks and

When he shut off the money valve, I knew we were gonna die and take AMF with us."

THE WHITE PAPER

In September 1980, Beals wrote a "white paper" to Tom York, proposing a radical idea: "AMF could get to the 50/50 objective easier by divestiture than by acquisition. AMF should sell Harley-Davidson."

York liked the idea and put AMF man Gary Ward in charge of the sale. After about two months, explained Beals, "Gary came to me and said, 'You and I both know nobody's going to buy Harley. Would you and the other managers consider a leveraged buyout?'"

"I felt like a kid, because I understood conceptually what a leveraged buyout was, but I had no idea of the numbers," Beals continued. Gary Ward had a neighbor who worked for Citicorp, and he set up a meeting. Afterward, "Citicorp was hot to trot," according to Beals.

continuing development of the Evolution engine, got funded. Everybody looked for ways to save money.

Tom Gelb looked at Japanese manufacturing methods and immediately saw the potential of just-in-time inventory, statistical process control, and employee involvement techniques. Within a few months after the buyback, Gelb tried such techniques out in a pilot program and then expanded them gradually throughout the company.

Gelb's changes saved the company. In the long term, it was the key to improving quality. It was too

late to help the 1981 model year, though, and sales fell to the lowest level since 1973. Disaster loomed unless Harley's managers could turn everything around—and quickly.

SILENT SPRING

Then came 1982, the year spring never sprung for the Motor Company.

"A semirecession had hit automotive earlier," remembered Tom Gelb, "and all of a sudden in March 1982, it hit us. At the time, the Japanese manufacturers

The Sturgis remained in the lineup through 1982, though it lost some of its dragster looks.

had about 18 months' worth of finished inventory in the country, and they were selling two- and three-year-old bikes right out of the crate and discounting them, so the bottom fell out of the market.

"I remember we had a policy meeting, and in the next weeks we cut our production rate in half, laid off 40 percent of our workforce, and cut all the salaries of the officers by something like 12 percent and the salaried workforce by 10 percent."

DODGING BULLETS

If all that wasn't bad enough, Harley's production was now below the minimum level specified in the agreements with its lenders. Those banks were free to foreclose at any time.

Fortunately, they chose not to, and here's where Gelb's Japanese-inspired changes became key: They saved Harley $20 million in inventory costs for 1982. Said Vaughn Beals, "In essence, the cash freed up from inventory offset the operating loss for 1982. Absent that, I'm absolutely sure our lenders would not have supported us."

How close was it? Engineer Dave Webster left Harley in 1982 after being told by a friend and fellow Kiwanis Club member who sat on the board of one of the banks, "Harley has about 30 days before they'll have to close the door. Beat the rush!"

With Gelb's help, Harley dodged the first of many bullets. The company survived, but production fell to just over 24,000 units, about half the total for 1981.

CAUGHT IN A CROSSFIRE

Harley's big losses for 1982 were the result of more than a recession and the company's still-poor-but-improving reputation for quality. Harley was caught in the crossfire of a grudge match between industry leader Honda and pushy rival Yamaha.

You're looking at one of the last of the *real* FLHs.

The last few Shovel-powered, four-speed, solid-mount FLHs were built in 1984.

Yamaha had staked its corporate reputation on winning dominance from Honda in 1982. In turn, Honda staked its corporate honor on retaining the lead. Honda and Yamaha crashed together in the U.S. market like two sumo giants, and starved-to-the-bone Harley was crushed between them. Chairman Vaughn Beals fought back with the only tool left. On September 1, 1982, he petitioned the ITC for relief.

RONNIE TO THE RESCUE

As point man for the tariff battle, Vaughn Beals was the focus of scathing criticism from the motorcycling press and from the buyers of Japanese bikes. He never dreamed Harley-Davidson would actually win its case, but he started the action to "get us through to the spring." That is, spring of 1983, when the Evo engine was scheduled to debut.

What made the criticism so galling was that anyone could see Harley's charges had some merit. Unsold Yamahas and Hondas piled up and were blown out at ridiculous prices.

The ITC heard arguments on Harley's petition on November 30, 1982. Beals brought powerful friends to the meeting, including a congressman and a senator. The Japanese made a fatal error before the hearing even started. "They had one attorney represent all four companies, which was tangible evidence of Japan Inc.," Beals said. "I can't conceive of anyone dumb enough to do that, but they were."

The ITC adjourned the hearing and deliberated for months before recommending tariffs of 45 percent on all Japanese motorcycles over 700 cc (after the first 7,000 imported) the first year, with diminishing percentages in the following four years. On April 1, 1983, President Ronald Reagan signed the tariffs into law.

Overall, the tariff was more symbolic than directly helpful. Anticipating the possibility that they might lose, the Japanese had stepped up production and shipment of their large 1983 models to get them on shore before the tariff took effect. A few months later, the Japanese reworked all their 750s into tariff-evading 700s, and Honda and Kawasaki avoided tariffs on their larger models by shifting assembly to their U.S. plants.

As a result, Harley's sales for 1983 were even worse than in 1982. Citicorp held off on foreclosure, but everyone involved knew that if there weren't real improvement in the situation soon, it was all going to fold.

THE END OF SHOVELHEAD ROAD

It was spring of 1983, and the Evo motor was ready for introduction in the 1984 line. Vaughn Beals and the cash-strapped company had to wonder, "What if big problems surfaced with the Evo? Should we bet the whole year's production that it would be trouble-free and accepted?" Because of lessons learned from its history, Harley-Davidson made a sensible compromise: It decided to keep the old engine in production, along with the new one.

Several FX models also carried the Shovelhead engine for 1984, while the all-new Softail and the rubber-mounted models carried the new Evolution engine.

An Ironic End for AMF

By Greg Field

Long into Harley's second century, Motor Company fans will still be arguing over whether AMF saved or wrecked Harley-Davidson. No one really knows to a certainty what would have happened had AMF backed out. Everybody says Bangor Punta would have sucked it dry, but BP also owned Smith & Wesson at the time, and S&W is still making hog-legs.

A better question to ask is, "Who got the better part of the deal: AMF or Harley?" The answer to that is easy: Harley-Davidson, by a mile. Harley got millions of dollars worth of updated facilities, tooling, and designs, along with a corps of professional engineers and managers. Best of all, Harley was able to point its finger at AMF and say, "He did it," on the quality issue.

What did AMF get? A meager profit on the sale after a decade of headaches and horrible PR.

In fact, buying Harley-Davidson was the start of a long, fatal slide for AMF. Some would even say Harley ruined AMF. That may be going too far, but it's truthful to say that purchasing Harley weakened AMF. Once weakened, AMF then fell of its own arrogance.

The story goes that a well-known corporate raider by the name of Irwin Jacobs inquired about buying AMF's Hatteras boat division and was nastily spurned.

Jacobs is not a man you want to piss off. He launched a hostile takeover, bought AMF, kept what he wanted, and sold off the rest. AMF succumbed to a hostile takeover after "saving" Harley from a similar fate 25 years earlier.

That's one of the many ironies of Harley-Davidson's first century.

By keeping the old Shovelhead engine in production, H-D had a fallback in case the Evo bombed. At the same time, the company had something to offer both the traditionalist and the hoped-for newer buyers, giving both reasons to believe in the new Harley-Davidson.

To those who wanted modern refinement, Harley would offer the new Evo motor in its newer, rubber-mounted chassis. To the traditionalist, Harley would offer the Shovel motor in its solid-mount, twin-shock FLH and FX chassis.

The Evo was a hit, and that meant curtains for the Shovel. The final batch of Shovels—last-edition FLHXs—supposedly left the line in June 1984, and that was the end for both the grand old Shovelhead engine and for the real—that is, solid-mount, four-speed—Electra Glide.

The venerable Shovelhead retired at the end of 1984.

Chapter 8

THE EVOLUTION ERA

By Greg Field

"When the Evolution engine came out, we wanted the dealers and the buyers to recognize that this, by God, was a new engine!"

—Vaughn Beals, former chairman and CEO

The Evolution engine marked the Motor Company's emergence from the dark ages of the AMF-Shovelhead era into Harley-Davidson's renaissance.

That renaissance officially began in late summer 1983, when Harley introduced another update to its OHV Big Twin engine. This time, the new engine even came with an official name: V^2 Evolution.

True to Vaughn Beals' quote above, when the Evolution came out, the dealers and buyers recognized that this, by God, *was* a new engine. No more 600 miles to the quart of oil. No more parts rattling off. No more breakdowns on every ride. The Evo was reliable and oil-tight and at the same time it was still, by God, a *Harley* engine. Same great sound. Same good vibes. Same indefinable mystique.

From that, the dealers and buyers and even moto-magazine scribes began to recognize that this, by God, was a new *Motor Company*. Before the Evo, Harley-Davidson and its motorcycles were the laughingstock of a niche market; by the end of the Evolution era, Harley-Davidson's methods were studied in business schools and its motorcycles were objects of mainstream lust around the world.

That transformation didn't happen overnight, and Harley-Davidson nearly went under doing it. And it didn't begin in 1983, either.

DAWN OF THE EVO ERA

The first glimmer of a new dawn for the Motor Company came in April 1976, at a management retreat at the Pinehurst Country Club in North Carolina. There, Vaughn Beals, Jeff Bleustein, Willie G., and others put together the plan for Harley's future.

"The basic plan that came out of Pinehurst was, 'Let's ride two horses at once.'" according to Vaughn Beals. "We needed two powertrains. One was the Evolution engine, and the other was a modern water-cooled V-configuration

family of engines, code-named "Nova," that would allow us to compete with everybody else."

At the time, Harley was short on money and engineering might, so why not concentrate on one powerplant? "We all felt the V-twin was our history— that it would have been stupid to abandon it," Beals explained. "That's what Indian did, and it bankrupted the company! And down deep we all hoped that the V-twin would be our future, too, but we were looking at much more sophisticated water-cooled engines from our competitors, so we also felt that having the V-twin as the sole product strategy of the company was too risky at that time."

On their return from the retreat, they fleshed out their plan and calculated the cost. By September of 1976, the plan was ready. "We figured it was gonna

A 1985 Low Glide in two-tone Maroon and Slate Gray.

The Sport was so good, it got noticed outside Harley circles. Magazines loved it, and it lured more than a few riders back from the dark side.

You're looking at Harley's first taste of sweet things to come: the FXRC "Candy Glide."

cost $100 million," Beals remembered, "which was bigger money back then than it is now. I had looked at the prior strategic product plans that had been submitted, and...the numbers were like a third of what we came up with. To go in and tell the boss that the price tag is three times what he thought it was going to be is not something we contemplated with pleasure."

AMF's "Long, Cold Shower"

When Beals presented the new plan to AMF senior management, "It was a long, cold shower for them," he remembered. "AMF never really understood Harley-Davidson. They didn't understand long-lead-time, capital-intensive stuff because it doesn't take five years to develop a new pair of skis or a tennis racket."

AMF wanted a third party to look at the plan Beals presented, so it hired the Boston Consulting Group (BCG). BCG did an extensive study, surveying dealers and customers in depth. "They endorsed our plan and said that what we proposed was a reasonable thing to do," Beals said. With BCG's endorsement and AMF's

money, in early 1977 work began on the planned update of the Big Twin and Sportster engines, the new liquid-cooled engines, and several new chassis.

Building a "First Engineering Department"

The Plan called for reworking the Big Twin engine in-house and contracting out the water-cooled engine, with a planned debut for both engines in the early 1980s, and an updated Sportster engine to follow. Why not do both in-house? "The fundamental problem was that in 1976 we didn't have the first engineering department," Beals explained "We needed to make the Nova engine from scratch. Thinking that we could make one from scratch and simultaneously develop two new engines—I don't think that would have been good judgment."

Only Harley has the heritage to create a new-from-old model like the Heritage Softail, which made its bow in mid-year 1986.

With that, Bleustein began building Harley's "first engineering department" and selecting a firm to design the other engine. One of Bleustein's key acquisitions was a new leader for the Powertrain section, Don Valentine. Valentine's first efforts were focused on improving the Shovelhead, but later he played a key role in designing the Evo. Eventually, Harley-Davidson picked Porsche Design to pen the Nova engine.

HANK HUBBARD AND "THE CONCEPT"

In November 1977, engineer Hank Hubbard began work on an updated Harley engine. The basic assignment? "Redesign the engine from the crankcases up—for state-of-the-art oil control, to increase the bore to get more power, and for cost reduction," Hubbard remembered.

At the time, Hubbard was Harley's main engine "concept man"—the guy who brainstormed the fundamentals of future designs. True to form, Hubbard came up with a design concept by the end of November that remained largely intact as the Evo.

Although Hubbard finished the concept drawing, he said, "Two other guys gave birth to it, Bob Sroka and Dave Webster."

EARLY EVOLUTION

As the whole design evolved over the next two years, the name stayed the same. "We referred to it as 'Evolution' from the start," remembered engineer Bob Sroka. "It's just one of those things that seemed like it was always there."

The Sport version of the FXRS also got fatter 39-millimeter forks in 1987.

Previous spread
The FXRS was designed by a group at the Motor Company who wanted a Harley for spirited peg-scratching. Before long, they discovered that most Harley riders would rather have lower seat heights than world-class ground clearance.

Harley only built 736 copies of the 1987 FXRC.

For 1988, Harley took the Softail one step further back in time with an update of the springer front end that Bill Harley had penned while he was in engineering school.

The Springer may look like an antique, but Harley's engineers labored for years to make it a marvel of modern reliability.

Before long, prototype Evo-powered bikes were tearing up the local roads. "A lot of the durability testing was being done locally when we began, on the streets around Milwaukee," added engineer Dave Webster. "I had a personally assigned prototype for my own use. When we were about halfway through the program, we switched to road and high-speed testing at the track at Talladega [Alabama]."

TEAM EVO

Sroka and Webster completed the foundation design work by 1980, but thousands of additional details still needed to be finalized. "Through the Evolution engine, we wanted to get back the customer base we were losing because of the problems with the Shovelhead," Don Valentine said. "The engine had to be leakfree and relatively trouble free—we were looking for a 100,000-mile engine. And we had to do it on a shoestring budget. Money was very tight—especially in the early 1980s."

With the hardtail look in the rear and the springer up front, the Springer Softail mimicked a 1940s bobber.

Using what money it did have, a whole team of engineers from the powertrain section got to work, under chief Valentine.

Over the next three years of slaving over hot dynos, in front of glowing computer terminals and riding nearly 1,000,000 test miles, the Evo team refined the design for production. "We'd look at problems one at a time and grind them out," Valentine remembered. "Cylinder heads were the biggest challenge. There was a learning curve because the heads were all new. We even had to develop a new casting process for them."

Soon, a host of talented people from throughout the company joined the engineers from Powertrain. "The Evolution project was a collaboration," explained Mark Tuttle, later vice president in charge of Engineering. "It was really the beginning of the program to involve more people in the design and development of our products. Historically, the hand-off from engineering to manufacturing has sort of been, 'Here's the perfect design—now you figure out how to make it,' versus working in collaboration to balance manufacturing needs with functional needs with styling needs and so forth."

With soft bags and a quick-detach shield, the FXRS Convertible could be a cruiser one minute and a sport-tourer another.

THE FINANCIAL SQUEEZE

If the budget had been "shoestring" in the late 1970s, two events during Evo design really screwed the money valve down tight.

The first was Vaughn Beals and a group of other executives buying Harley from AMF (see Chapter 7). Obscenely in debt, and no longer having corporate sugar daddy AMF to cover any shortfalls in revenue, Harley-Davidson could only spend what it made—and it wasn't making much. Sales for 1981 were the lowest in a decade. Despite that, Harley-Davidson put every dollar it could into completing the Evo for 1983 and even raised the bar on the design: "After the buy-back, the decree was given that with the Evolution we would put the Harley engine back to its reputation before AMF took over," Bob Sroka said.

The second event that dried up funding was the bottom dropping out of the motorcycle market in 1982. Motorcycles of all makes were stacked up in

warehouses. In response, Harley laid off nearly half its workforce, cut production by half, slashed salaries, and asked the U.S. government for tariffs. Those cuts put production under levels specified in its loan agreements, meaning the bankers could foreclose at any time. "We were operating at the pleasure of the banks," said Tom Gelb, vice president in charge of Operations.

Ultimately, a supportive banker, Gelb's productivity initiatives, and profits from building practice-bomb casings for the U.S. Air Force kept Harley alive through 1982–1983.

DELAYED EVOLUTION

"I don't think we ever made a tougher decision than when we finally had to delay the Evolution," Beals said. "We had planned to introduce it at the start of model year 1983, but the one vow we took because of the reputation we had was that when the Evolution engine came out, it would be durable, oil-tight, bulletproof.

Fat Boy was the nuclear newcomer for 1990. Its silver-on-silver with rivets styling was evocative of a B-29 Superfortress bomber.

Father of the SOFTAIL

By Greg Field

Think you know your Harleys? Time for a little quiz. What model was the bestseller of Harley-Davidson's first century?

    A: Super Glide

    B: Softail

    C: Electra Glide

    D: Silent Gray Fellow

That's right, it's the Softail, in all its many incarnations.

Now let's see how much you really know, Hog person. Tell me, which of these guys designed it?

    A: William S. Harley

    B: Willie G. Davidson

    C: Vaughn Beals

    D: None of the above.

If you guessed "Willie G.," you would be wrong. The correct answer is "none of the above" because the Motor Company's most successful model was actually designed outside the hallowed halls of Harley.

The hero of this tale is Bill Davis, an avid biker and mechanical engineer from the St. Louis, Missouri, area who started the project with nothing more in mind than to build his own ultimate Hog. "I loved the custom hardtail look," Davis said, "but my interest was in long trips, so I couldn't live with the horrid, uncomfortable ride of the rigid."

To get the classic hardtail look along with the comfort he desired, he began to experiment with several different suspension configurations on his 1972 Super Glide in the mid-1970s. Eventually, he settled on a design with the springs and shocks underneath the seat.

When he was done, he did what came naturally: He rode it all around. Everywhere he went people loved it, so he began to think of building and selling copies. On further reflection, he got an even better idea: Why not show it to Harley?

Davis picked up the phone, dialed Harley's number, and asked for Willie G. "In those days, they'd put you right through," he remembered. Willie G. seemed receptive, so they arranged a meeting and showed the Motor Company his blending of future and past. "They were very impressed," Davis remembered, "but they didn't really make any commitments. I didn't hear from them again until about six months later. I got a letter from Willie G. that said, 'Our engineering plate's full right now, but we are interested.'"

Davis didn't wait around for Willie to call. He developed the design further, ultimately moving the shocks and springs underneath the transmission, allowing him to lower the seat and mount the classic under-seat Harley horseshoe oil tank. The revised design was slick and gorgeous and worked better than even he expected, so he and two partners set up a

Bill Davis, father of the Softail.

business to market it as the "Sub Shock" frame. They even placed an ad in *Easyriders* magazine showing a Sub Shock Wide Glide.

Before the ad even ran, however, Davis and his partners had a falling out. The breakup was so nasty that Davis nearly gave up on his dream of putting the whole Harley world on faux hardtails.

That's when Jeff Bleustein, Harley's vice president in charge of engineering, called. Before long, Bleustein and Davis had struck a deal that would pay Davis a royalty on each unit built, up to what seemed like a generous lifetime cap.

Once the deal was done, however, Davis didn't think much more about his design until one day about 18 months later. "The first time I saw it was when a friend showed me a picture in a magazine," he remembered. When Davis finally saw a Softail in the metal, he was delighted to note how little Harley had changed the design and the look. He was even more delighted when the royalties started rolling in.

So, with his creation thundering down roads all across the fruited plain, did Davis take some of his royalties and buy a new Softail?

No, and he still hasn't. As before, his main interest was in long-distance touring, so when he finally did buy a new machine, it was a 1985 FLHT. He still has it, and still has no regrets. "It suits my needs perfectly and has given me no trouble in the 84,000 miles since I bought it."

As the original Softail eventually branched out into a whole new Harley family tree, those royalties kept coming and coming until the amount reached the lifetime cap. "I didn't like the idea of the cap when we were negotiating the agreement," Davis remembered, "but my patent attorney told me, 'Take it; the royalties will never get there.'" Bad advice.

Nevertheless, Davis is anything but bitter. "Of course, if that cap wasn't there, I wouldn't have to work today," he said, "but Harley's treatment of me was the only shining part of the story."

Davis' frame design became the basis for Harley's most popular line of motorcycles, the Softail series.

Bombs away! Though not an immediate hit, The Fat Boy soon became one of Harley's best-selling models.

"We finally decided that the 1983 model introduction was too risky because we weren't yet confident that it was bulletproof—so we reluctantly decided to delay the introduction until Daytona, which is in March, halfway through the model season. As time went on, we decided to put it off for a whole calendar year. Man, we needed it badly at that time because the market was terrible, which meant that we needed the engine sooner rather than later."

The few engineers who hadn't been laid off used the extra time well, devising fixes for the problems that originally delayed production, and refining the tooling and processes for manufacture. One good thing that came out of the delay was the Evo's ingenious three-piece rocker cover. Once unbolted, the three pieces slide off the heads like cards from a deck, leaving room to remove the heads and cylinders while the engine is still in the frame.

When Beals and company decided the form of the 1984 line-up, they had to decide whether the Shovelhead would go out of production at the end of 1983 in favor of the Evo, or whether both would be built. In the end, Harley-Davidson decided to keep the old engine in production, along with the new one.

New Guts for Old Glory: Debut of the Evolution Engine

When the Evo was finally released in late summer 1983, Harley billed it as "New Guts for Old Glory" in a special brochure that exhorted the faithful and all those who'd been sitting on the fence to come ride it in Harley's Super Ride program.

For those who wanted modern refinement, Harley offered the new Evo motor in its newer, rubber-mounted chassis: the FLT, FLHT, and FXR. For the traditionalist, Harley would offer the Shovel motor in its solid-mount, twin-shock FLH and FX chassis. For those who wanted a little modern and a lot of tradition, Harley offered up an all-new model, the FXST Softail. (See father of the softail sidebar.)

When the magazine test reports came in, they were just the sort of reviews Harley needed. *Cycle* magazine tested an FXRT in the November 1983 issue and raved, "In one 1,000-mile trip, the engine consumed about 12 ounces of oil, and only a slight amount of oil mist weeped from the clutch-actuating arm. It never leaked a drop while in our hands."

Motorcyclist magazine (January 1984) also tested the Evo-powered FXRT and was similarly pleased. "For those who wanted to see if Harley could build a real, honest-to-Davidson 1984 motorcycle, feast your eyes. The '84 season is here—and Harley is right here with it."

That same issue of *Motorcyclist* also named Vaughn Beals as 1983's Motorcyclist of the Year. Because of his handling of the whole tariff issue, plus the astonishing resurgence of Harley-Davidson in late 1983, Beals was the unanimous choice of the magazine's editors for the award. This was just the kind of publicity the company needed in the months following the Evo introduction. Sales continued to rise and even held through the winter months.

After the great reception of the Evos and increased sales, times were better at the Motor Company, but they were still far from good. Needing every sale it could get, Harley released a limited edition model, the FXRDG Disc Glide. The bike's disc rear wheel and chrome engine castings gave a glimpse of Harley's future. The other surprise was a new "wet" clutch. It worked well and had a much lighter pull, courtesy of the diaphragm spring that replaced the coil springs in the old clutch.

Evolution in Blue

With the excellent FXR chassis and the reliable new Evo motor, Harley released the FXRP Pursuit Glide and roared off in high-speed pursuit of the 600-pound gorilla of the police-motorcycle business: the California Highway Patrol (CHP).

Harley convinced the CHP to test the FXRP against the Kawasakis they had been buying since the mid-1970s. After exhaustive testing, the CHP approved the FXRP, and Harley began taking business away from Kawasaki. The CHP bought 152 in 1984. The Chippies liked their new Hogs, so they ordered another 161 in 1985. Other departments did, too, and Harley was once again a major player in the police business.

Long before the 1984 model year ended, Beals and company knew they had a winner. The Evo-powered models were selling at record pace. Everyone loved the Evolution because it looked and sounded like a Harley, but, it didn't leak or burn enough oil to cause concern, didn't need much more maintenance than a car engine, and it didn't rattle itself apart.

Harley started an aggressive licensing program that paid off big time in the years ahead. The first visible product of that effort was Harley-Davidson beer (brewed by Pabst). In later years, Harley licensed everything from basketball shoes to cigarettes.

When all was tallied at the end of the year, Harley's domestic sales were up 31 percent, to 38,741—a phenomenal increase in a year in which the U.S. motorcycle market descended deeper into a sales slump that would continue through the 1980s. Evo-fueled sales increases elevated the Motor Company to third place in the U.S. motorcycle market in the over-850-cc class, behind Honda and Yamaha.

When Harley announced its 1985 Big Twin line, it was all-Evo. The old Electra Glide was gone, but the FX models were back, powered by the Evo engine.

The new Sturgis was a dead ringer for the original.

takeover attempt, AMF, market crash of the 1980s—you've read about them all and how each nearly killed the company.

As damaging as they were, previous crises were nothing compared to the nail-biter of 1985. And, ironically, it was Harley's Evo-powered successes that sparked the new crisis.

During the darkest days of the early 1980s, Citicorp could have pulled the plug any time but didn't because Harley's loan officer, Jack Reilly, was confident Vaughn Beals and company would prevail. But Citicorp also kept supporting Harley because it thought it stood a better chance of recovering the loan by keeping Harley alive than by killing it while it was down.

That all changed in 1984, when Harley began looking like a comeback kid and when Jack Reilly took another job and was replaced by a loan officer who had opposed lending money to Harley in the first place. Citicorp believed another recession was imminent and that Harley would not survive it. Without Reilly to plead Harley's case, Citicorp decided to pull the plug and liquidate Harley before the crash.

Citicorp passed its death sentence in November 1984 by telling Harley the bank would cut off all over-advances in March 1985. "We made money in 1984, but without continuing over-advances, we were dead," Vaughn Beals explained. "We didn't yet have the money to operate and pay off all the loans."

On further reflection, Citicorp figured the best month to liquidate Harley would be the end of November, so in March the bank extended over-advance privileges to carry Harley-Davidson into October. That brief reprieve meant that Harley-Davidson would have to find a new lender and close the deal by December 31, 1985, or file Chapter 11 bankruptcy.

All through the summer, Beals and chief financial officer Rich Teerlink looked for another lender to save the company, but were rejected because all the banks thought there must be a catch. If Harley was making a profit, regaining market share, and getting steadily more efficient, why was Citibank bailing? Try as they might, Beals and Teerlink couldn't convince other bankers that Citibank just wanted out—even if that meant destroying a now-viable Motor Company. With time running out, Beals started preparing to file for Chapter 11 bankruptcy.

When it was just about too late, Rich Teerlink found a couple of new heroes who helped save the company. The first was Steve Deli of Dean Witter Reynolds. Deli introduced Teerlink to the other savior, Bob Koe, a Harley-riding banker at Heller Financial. Koe liked Teerlink's pitch and the idea of helping the Motor Company, so he got the deal rolling and set up a meeting with Heller's chief, Norm Blake.

By the time Heller had investigated Harley's finances and was ready to discuss details, it was late December, leaving no time to find another savior if this deal fell through. Beals, Teerlink, and Operations

The real news for 1985 was in the final drive, because even the five-speed models were fitted with rubber-belt final drive. Vaughn Beals said, "We just wanted something you didn't have to oil or adjust, that didn't spray oil all over you. We got all that, but the belts also lasted much longer and looked better, too." Now, it's difficult to imagine a Harley with any other type of drive.

Sales of the Evo Big Twins were up again for 1985, in a year of massive losses for everyone else in the industry. Harley's share increased to put it in second place, behind only Honda in the over-850-cc class.

A Near-Death Experience

At the end of Harley-Davidson's first century, who can question that the company is a survivor? Ford Model T, Great Depression, World War II, British invasion, Japanese invasion, breakup of the clan, hostile

If you wanted the traditional FLH look with all the toys, the Ultra Classic FLHT was your bike for 1991.

Another limited edition Dyna debuted for 1992. This one commemorated the 50th Anniversary of Daytona bike week.

vice president Tom Gelb made their do-or-die pitch on the morning of December 23. They laid out all the numbers, showing how Harley had improved in every way. Like all the other bankers, though, Blake didn't believe Citicorp wouldn't bail out if things were really that rosy, so he rejected the deal.

Lesser men would have given up then and gone home for the holidays, but not Beals, Teerlink, and Gelb. Instead, they convinced Bob Koe to beg another meeting that afternoon with Blake.

Incredibly, Koe came through, and with Deli as go-between, the Harley executives negotiated terms progressively more advantageous for Heller until Blake finally approved the deal.

Normally, the signing of papers and transferring money to close the deal would have been mere formality. In this case, it was the holiday season, leaving just a few business days to get it all done on the 31st. Naturally, everything that could go wrong did, and the 31st became the longest day of Rich Teerlink's life. Several times that day one of the parties told him it couldn't get its part done in time. Through force of will, he exhorted each to exert themselves on a holiday, completing the last transaction with just minutes left before bankruptcy. If any man deserved a drink that New Year's Eve, it was Rich Teerlink.

"We still operated at the pleasure of the banks," Tom Gelb explained, "but at least we had breathing room and weren't paying this tremendous amount of interest on the over-advances."

With each year, the Ultra got more luxurious. All the baggers were fitted with the barrel-type "Coke machine" locks for 1992.

SOFTAIL CUSTOM AND HERITAGE

While the refinancing drama played out, Harley introduced its 1986 line. The Softail line was updated with a new frame and five-speed transmission, which meant the end of the line for the old four-speed with its kickstarter. "We had a major insurrection over that," Beals remembered, "but the company decided 'to hell with it' and just ignored the complaints."

The Softail line also split to include a glitzier sibling: the Softail Custom. The most notable features of the Softail Custom were its disc-type rear wheel, black-and-chrome engine, and a frame painted to match the tanks and fenders. The high-priced Custom was Harley's best-seller that year.

Mid-year, Harley introduced the FLST Heritage Softail, which flaunted a fat front end styled after those of the 1950s Hydra-Glides. The Heritage was another masterpiece from the styling department and an even

more audacious future-from-the-past trick than they'd pulled off with the original Softail. *Cycle* called it a "machine of arresting simplicity" and "the most elegant Harley-Davidson of its generation." Like the original Softail before it, the Heritage was a hit its first year, and later spawned its own distinct model line.

If you were one of "the few among millions" who wanted your new Harley with a four-speed tranny and a kicker, the Wide Glide was your only choice for 1986. Last of the old-frame Big Twins, the Wide Glide was clearly reaching an evolutionary dead end, but sales had doubled during its first year in Evo form, so the Evo Wide Glide was certainly deserving of one last limited run.

In a final and fond nod to its heritage, the final edition Wide Glide was available with (and without) the flamed tank graphics that had made the original so striking. The new Fog Candy Red flames blazed over the Candy Burgundy of the rest of the bodywork.

To celebrate its 90th anniversary, Harley released anniversary editions of many models. Among them was the FXLR, shown here.

Leader of the Pack
VAUGHN BEALS

By Greg Field

In the darkest days of Motor Company history, when everybody from denizens of the dingiest biker bars to buffed-fingernail executives in the AMF boardroom had written off Harley-Davidson for dead, one man never gave up.

That man was Vaughn L. Beals Jr., leader of the pack at Harley-Davidson from 1975 until he retired in 1989. He's one of the main reasons you're able to buy a new Harley today, and, along with Willie G. Davidson, he's the most compelling figure in the latter half of Harley's first century.

Why does he still matter in 2003 and beyond?

First, because he convinced a cadre of 12 colleagues—sensible businessmen all—to put their life savings on the line and buy the failing Motor Company. He did this at a time when Harley was the laughingstock of the motorcycle industry and the U.S. economy was in a deep recession.

A year later, in 1985, when the bottom really fell out of the motorcycle market, when everyone knew Harley was doomed, Beals kept those guys together and even got two more otherwise-sensible colleagues to buy in. Those two were Rich Teerlink and Tom Gelb,

both of whom played key roles in saving Harley-Davidson. Gelb and Teerlink knew full well that Harley-Davidson was just an "over-advance" away from bankruptcy, yet the two bought in anyway. Why? Because of their confidence in Beals.

"The other guys thought we were nuts," Gelb said. "They just knew they were gonna lose all the money they'd invested in Harley-Davidson. When Rich and I put our money in, we thought we'd never see it again, either, but to do our jobs, we had to buy in. Through it all, Vaughn was the only optimist. He knew we were gonna make it. He just knew!"

How did he know? Was he an expert in motorcycle marketing or one of the old guard at Harley? Did he have a crystal ball?

Actually, as he admits, when he joined AMF as deputy group executive in charge of Harley in December 1975, he "didn't know what a motorcycle was." After getting a master's degree in aeronautical engineering from the Massachusetts Institute of Technology (MIT), Beals had worked for North American Aviation and Cummins as an engineer and executive before running a logging equipment company. AMF hired him as a generic "suit" to preside over the decline of one of its many leisure divisions. Fortunately, he had guts, drive, and integrity—qualities that made him ill-suited for such an ignoble role.

When Beals came in, he worked with the other execs to forge a long-term plan for Harley-Davidson, and then he convinced AMF to invest tens of millions of dollars in implementing it. Then, he shed his suit for leathers and became an enthusiastic rider.

After he took over as group executive in 1977, he forced his own standards of integrity on the Motor Company and exhorted everyone to make a critical stand against the practice of shipping incomplete or nonrunning motorcycles just to make AMF's end-of-the-month quotas. "Vaughn's personal ethics wouldn't allow that," Tom Gelb asserted. AMF didn't fire him, even when he didn't make the numbers, so Harley-Davidson's reputation steadily got better.

Vaughn Beals, the leader of the pack.

From that point, everyone at Harley quickly got notice that the AMF malaise was over, and that rattling, oil-puking, unreliable motorcycles were no longer good enough. It took time to make that attitude reality, but everyone involved quickly sensed that the new guy in charge had the right stuff, and by extension, that the

company did, too. That attitude was the root of Harley-Davidson's resurgence in the 1980s.

By the time Beals turned over the keys to Rich Teerlink in 1989, Harley's sales were limited only by the company's production capacity, and the quality of Harley's motorcycles was the equal of any in the world.

Once the 1,000 or so copies Harley built were all sold, that was it. As for the Wide Glide model, it would rise once again in the 1990s like a phoenix out of the metallic flames on the final edition's tanks.

GOING PUBLIC

Less than six months after Heller Financial's last-second save of the company from bankruptcy, Harley-Davidson confounded all expectations by "going public"—selling its stock on the NASDAQ stock exchange. "When Steve Deli from Dean Witter told us we should go public, we all said, 'You're crazy!'" Tom Gelb remembered. "But he was right. From then on, we controlled our own destiny."

After the sale and paying off bankers, Beals and company were free to run Harley-Davidson without interference from bankers, and they actually had cash on hand for the first time. Deli convinced Harley-Davidson to use the money to diversify, so in December 1986 the Motor Company bought Holiday Rambler, a manufacturer of motor homes. That acquisition doubled the size and earnings base of Harley-Davidson Inc.

As the motorcycle market continued its long crash, Harley-Davidson was the only motorcycle company in the world to increase sales in 1986. Its share of the over-850-cc market was now one-third, neck and neck with Honda.

To celebrate the 10th anniversary of the Low Rider, Willie G. and Louie Netz created a new model for those who wanted the comfort of rubber mounts with all their chrome and polish: the FXLR (Low Rider) Custom.

The Custom featured a 21-inch front wheel and skinny tire, a slim fender, chrome bullet headlamp, chrome triple clamps, a hand-laced leather strap down the center of the tank, and special two-tone paint and striping. Harley was justly proud of the new Custom and featured it in full-size poster form on the flip side of a fold-up brochure. It sold well its first year, but then sales declined steadily until it was canceled at the end of 1994.

Harley scored a public relations coup on March 17, 1987, when it petitioned the ITC (International Trade Commission) to end the tariff on Japanese big bikes, and on May 16, 1987, President Ronald Reagan visited

Harley throws a hell of a birthday party. Here's a scene from the 90th, in 1993.

the York, Pennsylvania, assembly plant and gave a speech praising Harley's fast recovery.

RIDING WALL STREET AND TAKING THE LEAD

By early 1987, Harley-Davidson was healthy enough to qualify for listing on the New York Stock Exchange (NYSE). To celebrate its first day of trading on the NYSE, Vaughn Beals, Rich Teerlink, and Willie G. thundered down Wall Street on July 1, 1987, leading a procession that included a semi and trailer painted in Harley colors.

Newspaper accounts of the landmark event noted that Willie G. even wore a necktie, which some said was the first time since Ronald Reagan visited York. In a possibly related event, Harley began licensing its trademarks to a tie maker.

Year-end tallies gave Harley-Davidson another reason to celebrate: Its 38 percent market share in the over-850-cc category made it the industry leader for the first time in nearly a decade.

By 1988, the tough times were finally becoming good times for the Motor Company. Though the U.S. motorcycle market was down 28 percent, Harley's sales were up by nearly 14 percent, surpassing 40,000 for the first time since the crash of the U.S. motorcycle market in 1982. Celebrity converts began showing up everywhere (even in the 1988 Harley catalog) on their Harleys, raising Harley's profile as an American icon.

And mid-year, Harley released a new icon, the FXSTS Springer Softail, created by bolting up to the

Another of the anniversary models, the FLSTN, featured Holstein fur seat and saddlebag inserts.

The FLSTN was back again for 1994, but with silver-on-white paint and a new name: Heritage Softail Special.

Softail a modernized version of the Harley's old springer front end. "I loved the idea because it gave us a way to attract new customers and screw the Japanese because they didn't have anything like it in their heritage to go back to," Vaughn Beals exclaimed. "The only problem was that making it happen took longer than any of us would like to have seen."

It took longer because at first they couldn't figure out how to get modern durability out of the bearings on the fork rockers. "Remember," said chief engineer Don Valentine, "the old rockers at the bottom of the forks had bushings and grease fittings. No matter what you did, those bushings would wear out and get sloppy real fast."

Eventually, they found a Teflon bearing that could do the job, but new problems surfaced during pilot production. "It was a real bitch to make!" Tom Gelb explained. "With that mechanical setup, there were a million parts, and I mean they were all polished and chromed. It was a very labor-intensive process. At the time, we were just hoping we wouldn't sell too many of them."

Complementing the chrome front end were the slimmer (3.5-gallon) Fat Bob tanks, black paint with red and yellow pinstripes, the blacked-out and chromed engine from the Softail Custom, and 85th anniversary tank graphics. All 1,300 numbered copies of this limited edition classic sold out almost instantly.

BEALS BOWS OUT

In March, leader of the pack Vaughn Beals stepped down and left the Motor Company in the

The Wide Glide look was back for 1993. Shown is a 1994 model.

Nineteen ninety-four was the end of the line for the FXR models. Shown is a 1994 FXLR.

capable hands of Rich Teerlink, the new CEO. Beals stayed on as chairman of the board.

To show how Harley prospered under Beals' leadership, consider these numbers: In 1989 when he left, the overall market for street bikes in the United States was down by 28 percent compared to the previous year, and had dropped by two-thirds compared to 1981 when he led the buyback. Despite that, Harley's sales were up by 17 percent for the year and total production of Big Twins and Sportsters topped 55,000, the highest total in company history.

Another new trend: Sales figures began to reflect Harley-Davidson's production capacity more than the actual demand, and waiting lists became the norm for the most popular models.

Harley released a new Softail for 1990, The FLSTF Fat Boy, a production replica of the custom Heritage Softail ridden to Daytona by Willie G. in 1988.

By design, Fat Boy had the tough look of bolts and rivets and aluminum plate. In fact, the only parts soft and humanistic about it were the pigskin seat with hand-laced detailing on the seat valance and the hand-laced leather tank trim. It was, as the ad said, "a heavy-duty hunk of style."

What's in this name? Well, the atomic bombs dropped on Japan were code named "Fat Man" and

For 1995, Dyna models took over as the sporting Big Twins. Shown is a Dyna Convertible.

The old FLH look returned for 1994 on the Road King. Based on the FLT chassis, the Road King's new fork shrouds and headlight recaptured the look of the 1960 Duo-Glide.

A mix of Fat Boy and Heritage, the Nostalgia model is usually the beauty of every model year.

The next natural progression of regression for the Softail line was to put the Springer front end on the Heritage.

"Little Boy." Some say the Fat Boy name is a combination of the two and the bike's silver-on-silver look was inspired by the sleek silver B-29 Superfortresses that dropped those bombs. And the new Fat Boy insignia on the tank looks suspiciously like a few U.S. Army Air Force unit insignia during the war.

Also in 1990, Harley enthusiasts mourned the passing of the company's best customer and perhaps most flamboyant booster, Malcolm Forbes, who died on February 24.

While the FXR models were darlings of the motor-cycle press, they were never popular among Harley's more conservative fans, because the FXRs looked too "foreign." When the FXR series finally replaced the classic FXs, these guys let Harley know just how unhappy they were. To its credit, Harley listened and put extraordinary effort into correcting the problem by creating a new chassis designed from the start to have the FX look.

After an early brainstorming session with the marketing and styling folks, lead engineer Rit Booth left with a slogan that would carry him through the design process: "What the customer wants is a bike that looks like an FX. And this next part is very precisely worded: If it doesn't vibrate, that's OK." Nothing else mattered as much as making it look like the old FX models—not rubber mounts, not stiffness of the frame, not handling qualities, not comfort, not anything. *But,* if they could get the look *and* still squeeze in rubber mounts, they should go for it.

The look boiled down to long and low, or low and long, because one helps create the illusion of the other.

Nineteen ninety-eight was Harley's 95th anniversary. To celebrate, Harley offered anniversary colors on most models.

For 1999, all models but the Softails and some special-edition FXRs were fitted with the new Twin Cam 88 motor. This is the gorgeous FXR[2].

So Booth and his team stretched and lowered wherever they could. When they were done, almost every part was new, including crankcases, the transmission case, and the primary covers. But in the end, Booth and the other engineers on the team got both the look *and* the rubber mounts.

For 1991, the new bike was released as the limited-edition Dyna Glide Sturgis. Even with all the updates, the new Sturgis looked almost identical to the original Sturgis. As in black on black. Orange highlights on the tank, timer cover, wheels, and elsewhere. Low bars on high risers for the drag-bike look, without the backache. It even got the old-style, dual-strut Sportster front fender, as on the original Sturgis.

It was another in a string of winners. And it was the start of a whole new line of Dyna Glide models that soon replaced all the FXRs.

Nineteen ninety-three marked the company's 90th anniversary and a cause for celebration. Harley released special anniversary editions of most models and invited everyone to join the celebration in Milwaukee in June. Over 100,000 of the faithful made the pilgrimage.

The new FLSTN Heritage Softail Nostalgia anchored the anniversary line. Willie G. based the new machine on the Fat Boy but added fishtail mufflers, "fat gangster whitewalls" on laced wheels, and a seat and bags with black-and-white Holstein-fur inserts. Paintwork carried through the Holstein theme—Birch White with Vivid Black panels on both tanks and fenders, with red and gray pinstriping.

Naturally enough, the Nostalgia took on several appropriate nicknames, including "Moo Glide," "Cow Glide," and "Heritage Holstein." And all 2,700 numbered copies sold out quicker than you could tip a cow.

Harley's factory chopper—the Wide Glide—returned in Dyna guise for 1993. Since the Dyna was designed from the start to mimic the look of the old FX chassis, it was a natural base for an updated Wide Glide.

Just as Harley fans missed the look of the FX models, they also missed the look of the old FLH Electra Glide. Harley first tried to re-create it by stripping the fairing off the FLHT, but the upper fork and headlight area never looked right, and it didn't have the speedo on the tank-mounted dash, where Bill Harley had decreed

Following the FXR[2], Harley released the flaming FXR[3] in 1999. The 2000 FXR[4] was the last Harley to carry the Evolution engine.

it should be. Harley finally got it right for 1994, with the FLHR Electra Glide Road King.

END OF THE FXR LINE

By 1994, Dynas had replaced all the FXR models except the basic FXR Super Glide (the lowest-cost Big Twin) and the FXLR (Low Rider) Custom. At the end of the year, these last two were cut, and the FXR chassis was put out to pasture, but not permanently, as we'll see.

For 1997, Willie G. and Louie N. unveiled their latest rendition of a Harley idea whose time had never really passed: The FLSTS Heritage Softail Springer. Basically, it was another front-end trick. First, they modified the Springer front end and fender to fit a fat 16-inch front wheel and topped it off with a chrome horn just like the original. Then they added a tombstone taillight, whitewall tires, and a big saddle with outsized tooled-leather skirts, chromed dual exhaust with fishtail mufflers, and fringed, tooled-leather bags. The result was an almost spot-on re-creation of the pimped-up bikes the bobber guys of the 1940s and 1950s derided as "garbage wagons."

By the late 1990s, fashion in the custom circles had gone from the tall, slim chopper to the long, fat and low lead sled look. For 1998, Willie G. presented his own rendition of that look—the FLTR Road Glide—simultaneously creating the factory "custom bagger" and a successful new model. The Road Glide's frame-mounted fairing was based on that of the FLT, but it was chopped and lowered and given some attitude, and a very low windscreen.

For 1999, the Twin Cam 88 replaced the Evolution engine in most Big Twin models. The Softails remained the only regular production Harleys still powered by the Evolution powerplant.

The limited-edition FXR^2 and FXR^3 released in 1999 were the only other models that retained the Evolution engine. The FXR^2 and FXR^3 were the first factory "super customs"—chrome-covered beauties that were all-Harley, yet as customized as any bike on the bike show circuit. All that was really missing was a custom exhaust, but the factory couldn't supply that and still remain in good graces with the EPA.

For 2000 came the FXR^4, which was the last of two distinguished breeds: the last of the rubber-mounted FXR models and the last of the Evo-powered Harley Big Twins.

THE EVO'S EPITAPH

Between the production capacity increase Harley gained every year and the continued increase in demand, Harley took the U.S. sales lead during the Evolution Big Twin's last year, and not just in the over-850-cc category. Combined sales of the Big Twins and Sportsters surpassed the U.S. sales of the whole Honda line for the first time since the early 1960s. That's the best possible send-off for the engine that made it all possible to get to this point—the Evolution Big Twin.

The
FEULING TRIPLE

By Chris Maida

After the initial, "What the hell is that!?" most people are intrigued, if not downright mystified by the W³, Jim Feuling's newest engine creation. Motorheads usually follow this up by saying something like, "He just stuck another cylinder onto a Harley-Davidson engine." But as they think of what that entails, a confused look spreads over their faces. After all, there's a lot more to it than *just* bolting on another cylinder, even with a special set of crankcases! The biggest question is how to position the connecting rods in the flywheels. There's no way the traditional knife and fork arrangement is going to work. "How the hell did he do that!?"

However, if that motorhead has a background in aviation, he may have come up with the answer to question number two. Old airplane enthusiasts looking at the W³ should have images of radial engines dancing in their heads. In fact, if you ever get to see the engine of a World War II T-6 trainer up close, you'll find yourself looking at a nine-cylinder version of an H-D engine. Creative dude that he is, Feuling, used a connecting rod arrangement similar to the one

found in old radials to make his three-headed Hydra come to life.

Here's how Feuling did it: The master connecting rod, which holds the middle cylinder's piston, connects to the crank pin between the flywheels. Mounted onto the base of this master rod are two link connecting rods, each one with its own crank pin. These link rods take care of the front and rear pistons. This arrangement allows all three connecting rods to rotate on a single crank pin, just the way the two rods in a conventional H-D engine do.

But enough of the "How was it done" stuff. The big question now is, "How does it run?" Answer: Just the way you would expect a 150-cubic-inch mutha-thumping Harley would! (That's 2,470 cc or 2.5 liters for you metric folk.) This beast pumps out 210 foot-pounds of torque at just 3,000 rpm and backs that up with over 150 horsepower at 5,000 rpm, at the rear wheel. That's more than enough power to shred the 200-millimeter rear tire while lifting the front one, all

with just a twist of your wrist. (If that's not enough, Feuling also offers a 183-cubic-inch stroker version!)

So where, oh sweaty-palmed one, can you get one of these fire-breathers? The Feuling Motor Company is based at 2521 Palma Drive, in sunny Ventura, California. (The zip is 93003, but calling 805.650.3406 or visiting www.feuling.com will, of course, reap quicker results.) Jim sells a W^3 engine for $16,900 or an engine and frame package for $19,500. As for the rest of the bike, which you get to supply, the W^3 requires a Twin Cam tranny and primary system, while the frame will handle most front ends, etc., that can bolt up to a normal American V-twin.

The engine/frame package is the smart way to go for two reasons. Reason number one: Remember that third cylinder? There's no way you're going to shove the W^3 into your existing frame without major work. Reason number two: Even if you could get it in there, the W^3 would probably twist your frame into an unusable—though interesting—shape.

Chapter 9
THE TWIN CAM ERA
By Steve Anderson

Harley-Davidson is about as parsimonious when it comes to doling out new engines as an IRS auditor is about giving rebates. The Sportster powerplant debuted in 1957—but as an overhead-valve adaptation of the KH flathead that appeared in 1952, itself closely related to a non-unit construction motor introduced in 1937. Even that engine was based in an earlier powerplant introduced in 1929. The first of the overhead-valve Big Twins, the EL61—or Knucklehead—was birthed by Bill Harley and others in 1936. In an evolutionary problem-solving process, the Knucklehead led to the Panhead, the Panhead led to the Shovelhead, and, in 1984, the Shovelhead gave way to the Blockhead, or Evolution. But even after all those changes, a reincarnated Bill Harley would still have been able to recognize his handiwork in the Evo Big Twin. He would even recognize some of the parts.

So when the Twin Cam 88 debuted in 1998—the first completely Big Twin since 1936—it was the biggest news the Harley world had heard since the first of Franklin Roosevelt's four terms in office. The motorcycle press hurried to describe the new powerplant, to tell of the improvements and quantify its performance. But in all the talk about power and technology, performance and reliability, camshafts and oil systems, not all that much has been said about the Twin Cam's roots, about how it came to be, or about how this new Big Twin took exactly the form and shape it now has. If you're familiar with Harley's increasingly corporate look, you might expect the beginning of that history to be the result of plans laid out by some buttoned-down product planners and marketing experts in some fluorescent-lit conference room in that old red brick building on Milwaukee's Juneau Avenue. But you'd be wrong.

Try instead Zorba's, a funky family-owned restaurant (Greek, of course), where some mid-level Motor Company managers liked to get together on Saturday

271

Opening page
The Twin Cam 88B introduced in 2000 featured a counterbalancer to take the edge off the vibes on the solid-mounted Softail models.

For 1999, Harley introduced the Twin Cam 88 engine on all the Big Twins except the Softails.

mornings. Bruce Dennert, powertrain design manager, was one of the Harley folks there in the spring of 1992. "There was Bill Schultz, manager of the Softail," Dennert said. "Scott Miller, marketing guy; Hugh Vallely, office of program manager; and myself. The whole idea was to get Scott Miller—the marketing guy—to buy breakfast."

Expensing the breakfast wasn't totally illegitimate, Dennert points out: "We used to talk product. That morning we were talking about the problems and limitations with the Evo. We said you had to do something new or better, and we sketched out on a napkin what we should do to enhance the Big Twin family. Meanwhile there was some long-range planning going on in the company, and one of the goals was to do the traditional product as long as we could legally."

That napkin and the sketch on it set wheels in motion. After further Saturday discussions at Zorba's, the idea of an enhanced, yet traditional, Big Twin gained ground. A meeting was set up at Harley. Miller, Dennert, and Vallely represented the Zorba regulars, along with some new additions. Don Keiffer came from Manufacturing Engineering (he was one of the two technical managers of the Capitol Drive plant who actually built engines), and Willie G. was the representative of Styling and, well, tradition.

According to Keiffer, the first question that came up was: "Do we do a Nova-type project (Harley's never-produced, Porsche-designed water-cooled V-4 from the early 1980s), or do we stick to the tried and true?" Tried-and-true won easily, and with significant urging

The new engine had a big-finned, muscular look.

from Willie G., the group came up with a specification list for what was called "The Classic Engine Project." It was just five items long. Any new engine, they decided, should:

> Be a 45-degree V-twin;
> use air cooling;
> have pushrods rather than overhead cams;
> place its cylinders inline, rather than offset;
> look like an Evo from 25-feet away.

Keiffer remembers some polarization. "(Engine designer) Dennert pushed for more innovation, while Willie G. said, 'Do anything you want as long as we have that spec list.'"

Dennert, reasonably enough, wanted more: "A new Big Twin had to be better than an Evo, it had to give our customers a reason to buy a new one, to relight the passion that was already there."

In additional meetings, the Classic Engine Project was further defined. Mark Tuttle, vice president in charge of Engineering, presented the project to Motor Company executives at a strategy planning retreat

called Pinehurst II in North Carolina. The location carried historical weight, because the decision to go with traditional powerplants instead of the Nova water-cooled V-4 had been made at Pinehurst, more than a decade earlier. The meeting produced a preliminary go-ahead for the Classic Engine. Dennert, then acting chief of Powerplants, started with five engineers to flesh out the specifications. In the spring and summer of 1992, Keiffer remembered, the project came together. "We wanted to strengthen the whole lower end; people with hot rods were breaking crankcases. The idea was to leave the Evo top end alone, and slide new cases under it." In many ways, the project at that time was seen simply as an evolution of the Evo, another incremental step on the path that began with the Knucklehead.

Keiffer also remembered that at that point it was a "traditional engineering project"—proceeding with too little regard for the concerns of manufacturing, the people who actually had to build the engine. Dick Click, the other technical manager at Capitol Drive, called Keiffer in August 1992. "Here we go again," Click sighed. Keiffer suggested getting a meeting together about the program.

Following pages
The FXDX Dyna Glide Sport featured taller and better forks and shocks than the standard models.

From the primary side, the Twin Cam engine looked nearly identical to the Evo.

Some call the Twin Cam engine the "Fathead," but most enthusiasts call it "Twin Cam" or "Twinkie."

Click and Keiffer attended the meeting, as did Dennert, Leroy Zindars, and Bruce Wells, the man who had birthed the Evo on the assembly line. Zindars and Wells represented Manufacturing. For 45 minutes, remembered Keiffer, "We bitched about 'What *they* were doing to us.'" And then a new thought came up. "Why don't the five of us take the program over and make sure *they* don't do it to us.' We appointed ourselves to be the program board—five people who were going to do whatever it took to make this a success. It allowed us to cross the functional lines between departments."

The plan made sense to Dennert: "We became the tactical managers for the project, because we had all the people who were going to do the job."

The group of five went to Harley management and asked permission; they were more than a little surprised when the answer came back, "Cool. Go ahead." Shortly thereafter, the group went back to management, asking whom it wanted in overall charge of the program. Again, a shock: *"Who* do you want to run it?" was the reply. After some conferring, the five chose Keiffer.

Keiffer, tall and closely bearded, looks back to that period with some amazement, recalling his trepidation.

276

There was a history of ambitious projects within Harley that came to dark ends, and not so ambitious programs that ran years behind schedule. He remembered discussing the Classic Engine Project with Harley's upper management: "Every executive I talked to had a different idea about what they wanted from it. I was convinced that we could do it, but we had to nail down the scope. I had to get a mandate from the executives."

So during those days of 1992, the definition of the new engine was top priority. According to Dennert, "We had put together a list of features of what this engine could have, hundreds of features. A lot of these—twin-overhead cam, multicylinder—got dropped. During 1992, we sorted through this entire list of items for manufacturability and reliability."

Dennert said some of the items were pretty simple: "Some of the criteria for a good engine were things like any single cover should be held on with bolts of one length, so a mechanic wouldn't have to worry about which bolt went where." Other things were done for noise reasons, such as setting the criteria "that covers can't carry any bushings or bearings," because those transmit mechanical noise to the cover.

"During 1992, we had active projects going on, testing ideas that might go into a new engine," Dennert explained. "There were a number of enabling technologies we were running, such as the straight crankpin and modified Evos with a single chain-driven cam. We presented Styling with sketches of the single cam and various twin cams with different pushrod configurations. Styling liked the twin-cam concept. We actually built a twin cam in 1992 with gear-driven cams. We found that the chain-driven single cam gave us the best noise reduction, but the twin-cam was the most pleasing visually. So we combined the two."

The definition phase accelerated in mid-December, as Harley hired Bob Kobylarz from Kohler to be head of Powertrain Engineering. Keiffer remembered the strangeness of the situation: "It was my project and *his* engine." But the two quickly sorted out responsibilities. Keiffer would run the program and make sure it was on budget, on time, and had the resources required, while Kobylarz's group would be responsible for the design and engineering of the engine. With a top-level product planning review coming up at Keiffer's request in January, Kobylarz took his top engineers off-site for a week and narrowed down the choices.

"We came up with three options," Dennert remembered. "One was a minor upgrade to the Evo. The second was a significant change, but not as far as option three. Option three had a one-piece crank and automotive rods." The second option included both a new oiling system and the twin cams, while the first did not. Each of the three came with a complete list of features and an estimate on how long it would take to get each version into production.

In January 1993, those were the options presented to Harley's Product Planning Committee, a select

group of top executives and department heads who had to give the thumbs up or down on any major new program. The presenters made their pitch, and then were asked to wait outside. Keiffer remembers the wait being an hour, while Dennert is sure it was just 15 minutes. In either case, it seemed forever. Finally, the Planning Committee called them back in to say it had chosen option two: an all-new bottom end, carrying a largely carryover Evo top end. "At that time," Keiffer said, "it did not include revised displacement or the Revised Rear Interface [the new gearbox mounting]."

But the best part was the commitment that had been won from Harley-Davidson CEO Jeff Bleustein: "This is it. We won't alter the scope of the program unless you ask for it." This was one program that wouldn't grow out of control as executives piled on features midstream.

"That was day one," Keiffer said, "of the P-22 project," the name he gave to the engine that would eventually become the Twin Cam, and the only name by which anyone within Harley-Davidson would use for the next five years. What did it mean? "Guys would guess," Keiffer said, "two cams and two cylinders, or something like that." Keiffer smiled and shook his head. They didn't have a clue, his body language was saying.

"It was after Catch-22. You know, 'Anyone sane enough to ask for a psychological discharge from World War II bomber duty was obviously not crazy enough to get it,' or something to that effect. This was Project-22, and it had its own catch: 'The only way for this project to be successful is if we understand the depth of our failures to this time.'"

And on that cheery note, Keiffer and the others set Harley-Davidson on the road to the Twin Cam 88.

"The plan we had brought to the Product Planning Committee estimated we could build the first running engine in 10 months: December 3 was the day," Bruce Dennert recalled, the man who led the engine mechanical design group. "The first engine ran on December 2."

Even with its late-1990s engine, the Road King kept the look of the mid-1960s Electra Glide.

Nearly 25 years after the original Low Rider, that model's style still graces the Dyna Glide line.

What made that possible was the preliminary decision making that had emerged in the past year. "We had a nice definition of what we wanted to do; we didn't have to try something and show it," says Bruce Leppanen, design lead for the P-22's bottom end. The bottom end was where all the action was; initially the idea had been that the top end would only be lightly modified Evo components. "Forty-five-degree, air-cooled, in-line cylinders; vertically split crankcase; twin cam with chain drive—those had all been decided," Leppanen said, who had earlier been the lead engine designer on the five-speed Sportster. "Then we gave ourselves a lot of soft definitions: commonized fasteners, no leaks, easy-to-work-on without a lot of specialty tools, easy-to-assemble."

"We started with a crank and deck height and cylinder-angle and cam positions, and started piecing it together," Leppanen remembered. "We had done some previous work with Jeff Coughlin on a straight crankpin," so that was incorporated. Once basic locations were nailed down, the next question presented itself: "'What do you do for an oil pump?'" Leppanen answered that: "We had a lot of options. Internal oil pump, gerotor type, on the crankshaft made more sense. Once that decision was made, making the models and designs of the oil pump was just a task." Leppanen is similarly nonchalant about the design of the cams and their drives; once using twin cams had been decided, he considers that the rest was just detail design and execution.

Dyna Super Glides were the cheapest ticket to the Big Twin leagues.

None of these design decisions took place in a vacuum; the very air around Harley engineering percolated with ideas that had yet to find a home in a production engine. Bruce Dennert, in a Saturday morning bull session at Zorba's, had proposed an internal oil pump for the new Big Twin, with a cam-carrying "spider" plate serving to route oil, eliminating numerous drilled passages from cases or covers that were truly manufacturing headaches. And gerotor pumps driven directly by the crank weren't new ideas at Harley either; the first VR-1000 layouts back in 1988 had proposed such a design, which eliminated a shaft, a gear pair, and the associated bearings, and thus reduced both cost and noise—a particular concern with Harley

Engineering. Only the reality of 50-degree lean angles in road racing and the need for ground clearance had prevented the VR from having a similar pump sticking off the end of its crank.

"The engine size wasn't fast and hard," Leppanen said. "Bruce Dennert's performance prediction programs helped develop the size we needed."

Dennert remembered, "We changed to 1,450 very early in the year as we were doing the vehicle performance predictions. We started the design road at 1,350 with the option of 1,450, perhaps eventually going to 1,550. We quickly changed that when Marketing wanted a clear improvement in performance over the Evo." The actual bore and stroke were chosen so that the shaking

The most noticeable difference between the Twinkie FLHT in the foreground and the Evo-powered version in the background is the Twinkie's oval air cleaner.

force, and thus vibration, "would be no greater than a 1,340, which meant bigger on bore and down on stroke." So by early 1993, the P-22 was nailed down as a 1,450, with the 1,550-cc option available for later production or for parts and accessories kits.

"Part of the engine definition," recalled Leppanen, "was that you have to prepare it for upgrades. The idea was you shouldn't have to buy a crankcase to build a hot rod. We made a lot of the bearings oversized. Even the cylinder stud spacing took this into account. We asked, 'How big can you go out on the stud pattern and still get the head gasket to seal?' We built a lot of growth potential into the engine. Even

the cam lifter was designed to work with high-performance cams without modifications."

A lot of the bottom end strength was simply in the detail design of the crankcases. By then the problems with Evo cases—which in hot-rodded engines would crack in predictable locations—were very well understood. Skip Metz talks about the testing that had been done: "Under a high-speed camera, you could really see Evo cases moving around; it almost looked like breathing. We knew where the weak spots were." Leppanen filled those in with good basic engineering design practices, doing the obvious like "putting all the load bearing walls in line, and not putting notches in them." He

In fact, the Twinkie was Harley's first all-new Big Twin engine since the 1936 Knucklehead.

then passed his CAD models to Harley's Analytical Engineering Group. There the engineers used computerized Finite Element Analysis (FEA) to predict stresses long before a casting was made, and Leppanen refined his design based on those predictions.

Dennert noted that Harley went so far as to buy a prototype die to get the high-pressure die-casting process down. "That development die cost a quarter-million dollars, and was intended to be thrown away." But it allowed the actual crankcase design made with the actual production process to be tested early in the program. "There were lab tests," Metz said, "of loading and cycling of the first prototypes to see if they duplicated what the FEA models predicted before they were ever put into an engine."

The testing paid off; the parts that would change the least during P-22 development were the crankcases and the flywheels, the two parts that had been most thoroughly studied early on. According to Metz, the only serious problem ever to show up on the crankcases was with some cracking on the front left motor mount, a problem that quickly yielded to a slight increase in the fillet on the mount.

The most notable improvement for 2000 was the adoption of new brakes across most of Harley's motorcycle line-up.

According to Dennert, "The design team was really rocking and rolling in 1993. No one was going to stand in the way of that engine running in December. By August, all major pieces and patterns were being made. For the cylinder heads, we used old Evo tooling and modified that."

If you could look back at the engine that came together for the December 2 run, it would have been recognizably a Twin Cam 88. The bore and stroke were 3.75 inches by 4.00 inches, the same as the production engine. The cams were in their current locations, driven by similar chains. The gerotor oil pump was there. The crankcases were identical to the 1999 production cases in all details except the passages connecting cam case to crankcase. Visually, though, the top end looked like an Evo, with the same finning, and the various covers were clearly prototypes, not the final styled pieces. And there were all the hoses and instrumentation wires

For 2000, the FXDX was even more monochromatic.

attached that clearly identified the engine as an engineering prototype.

But it fired up on December 2, 1993, and, boy, did it run. According to Dennert: "Fortunately or unfortunately, that first engine ran for 300 hours on life support"—referring to the huge external scavenge pump that vacuumed the bottom end of the prototype. "We thought it was going to be a cakewalk...and then the later engines went to hell. It was a long time before we got another that lasted as well as the first one."

As soon as engines were run without "life support," it was clear that the first attempt at an oiling system wasn't going to be the last. The problems took years to solve and delayed the release of the engine. Before the difficulties were over, the weary P-22 program leaders began joking about digging up and reviving Bill Harley, the designer of the Knucklehead, and getting his advice on how to do an oiling system.

The actual solutions came from a young engineer named Paul Troxler, brought in from the outside to specifically solve the oil system problems. According to Skip Metz, Harley first went to the Southwest

Research Institute, a well-respected engineering consultancy, simply to help the Motor Company on testing; "We didn't have enough dyno capacity," Metz, said "and we went down to see if they could run our engines. We eventually signed a contract and started to send our engines there."

After that, it was a small step to a second contract with Southwest to specifically look at the P-22's oiling and breathing system. "We needed someone," Metz said, "who could sort out the technical issues. We were working with Dr. Ping Sui to do a computer model of flow. Paul Troxler was a design engineer at Southwest and was assigned to work with Dr. Sui on this project.

"Paul is a very analytical engineer. He's the kind of guy in a college engineering class you always wanted to strangle, 10 pages ahead of the instructor. We hired him away from Southwest to understand how the test engine related to Dr. Sui's model. He spent his next two years on the motoring dyno, and if it hadn't been for him, we'd still be in trouble."

The problem with the P-22 oiling system was easy to explain: Oil was where it shouldn't be, most specifically

coming out the breather and oozing from gasketed joints. According to Troxler, "The general layout of what you see today was in the original oil system design. There are subtle differences but not major differences. Initially there was an attempt to drain the cam case into the crankcase and have a single scavenge pickup. But the velocity of the air coming into the cam case, through ports in the crankcase wall, was keeping the oil from draining. The scavenge system was the problem."

The beginning of the solution was to abandon the single oil pick-up and go to a "split-kidney" dual-passage scavenge, as had recently been tried for the Sportster. The separate scavenge paths for the crankcase and cam case started the process of getting the oil under control.

But the cam case and crankcase were still connected by a high port, and there were still high levels of oil carryover in the crankcase. The excessive oil from the crankcase would come in the cam case through that port as mist, and then get carried up through the breather. No P-22 would ever see production until it kept its oil inside the engine. Troxler essentially moved into the one test cell on Juneau that was set up

with a motoring dyno, one that used an electric motor to spin a noncombusting P-22. The engines were fitted with Plexiglas covers and windows to allow direct observation of oil flow.

"It was long days, and weekends, and Saturdays," Troxler said. "Often I would have the test cell running two shifts a day. I'd have two engines. One would run shifts one and two while the other engine was being reconfigured. The third shift would swap engines. That scenario went on two months straight while we were working on the crankcase scavenge pump. Everybody and their brother had an idea, and we tried just about every one of them."

Another engineer, Mark Hoffman, thought that reducing the velocity of air in the pushrod tubes—which provided the breathing path between cam case and cylinder head—would give the oil more time to settle back and thus reduce carryover. It did, but the big pushrod tubes that were required weren't an acceptable solution to Styling.

Troxler had saved his personal idea for last—totally sealing the crankcase from the cam case. Eliminate the

The balanced Twinkie motor made the solid-mounted Softails as smooth as their rubber-mounted counterparts, or even smoother.

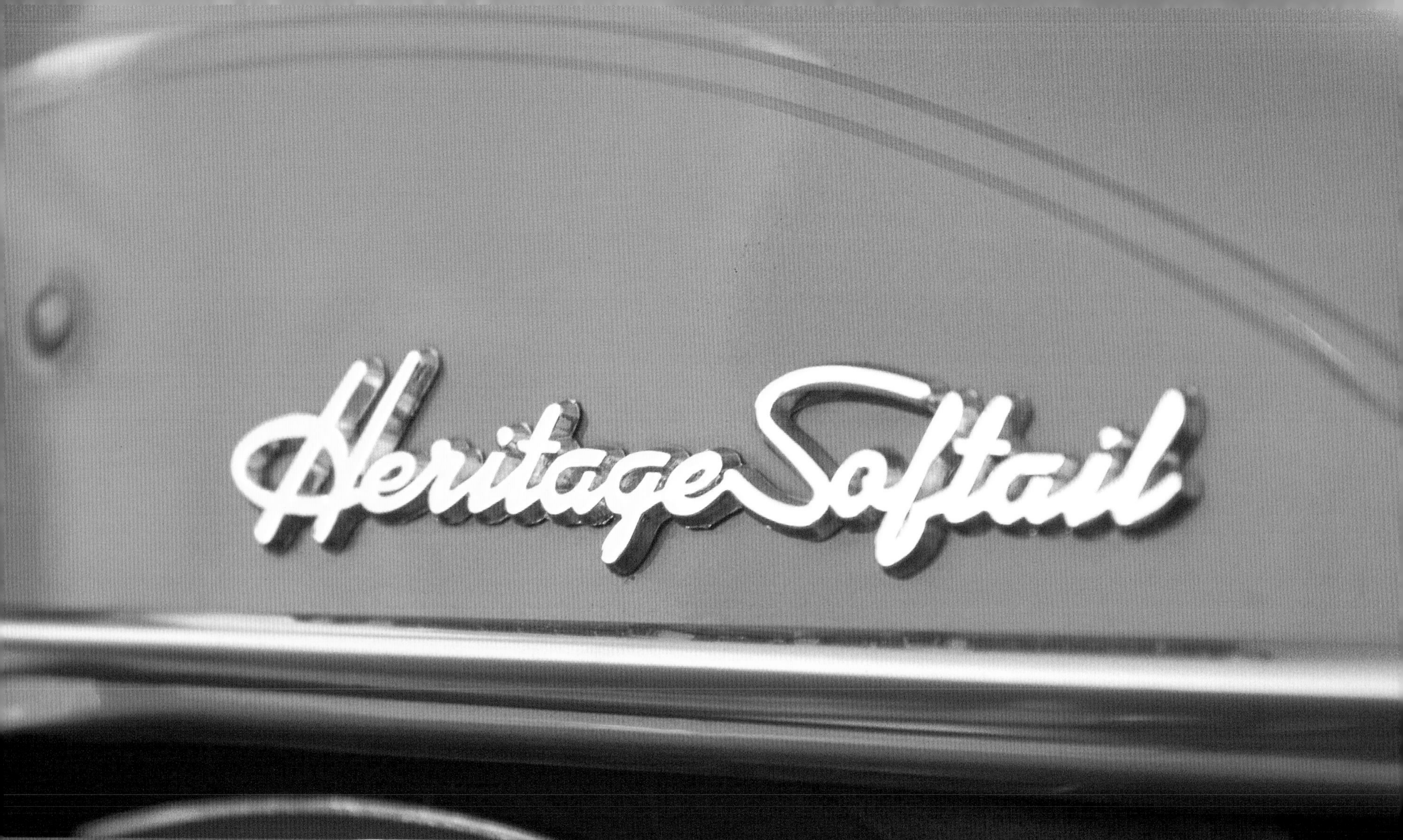
Heritage Softail

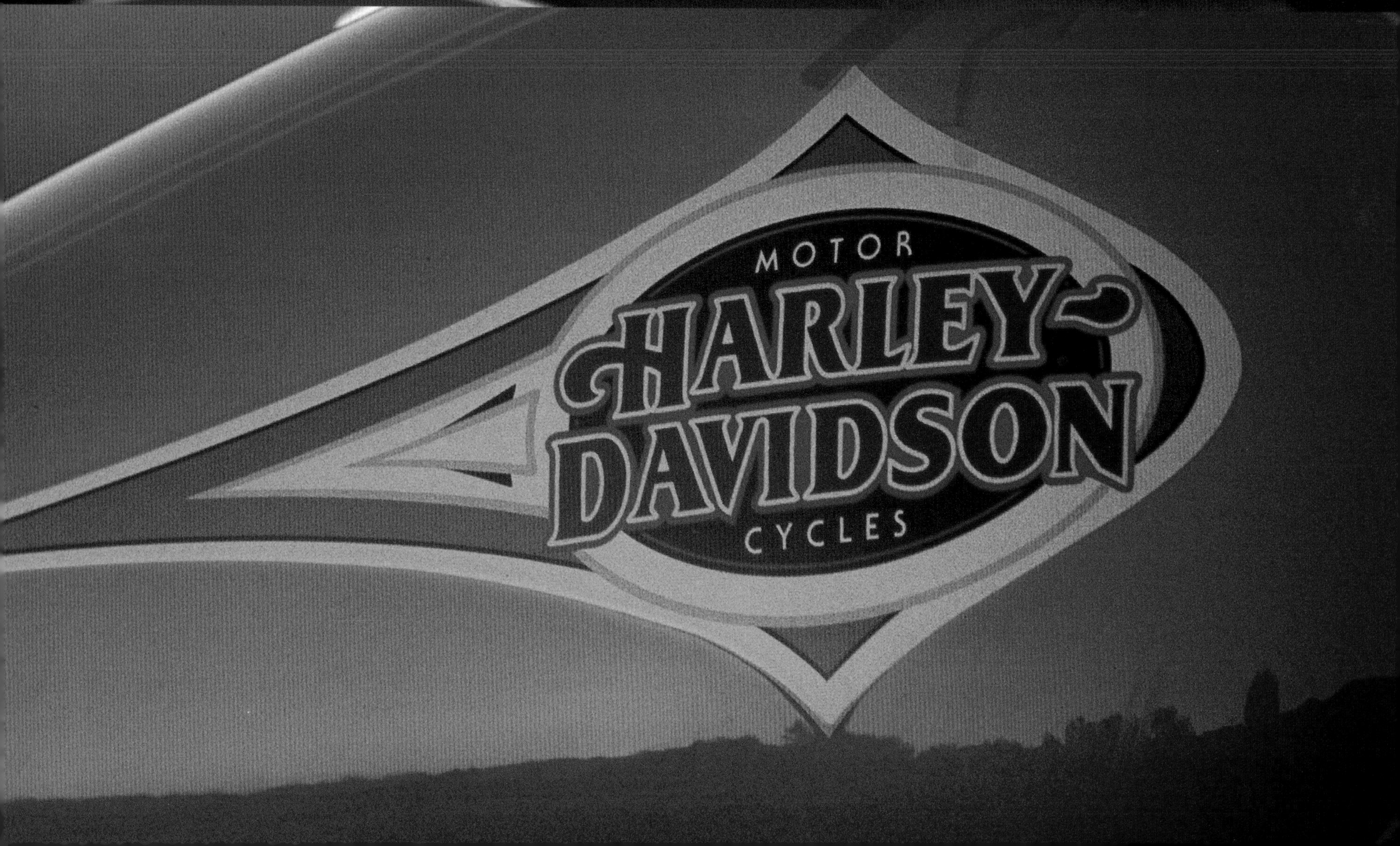
MOTOR
HARLEY-DAVIDSON
CYCLES

The FLHTCU Ultra was still the king of the highway in the Twin Cam era.

passages between the two chambers, and "Lo, and behold," Troxler said, "the carryover dropped." With that change, and with the addition of both a coalescing air/oil separator and a tortuous path separator in the cylinder head, the test bikes at Talladega no longer generated oil carryover unless the engine had other problems.

But the oil system gremlins weren't finished. With the crankcase newly sealed, less oil made it up from the cam case to the cylinder heads and the breather, but crankcase scavenging actually worsened. Oil would build up excessively in the crankcase at 1,500 to 2,500 rpm, just the type of speed Big Twins are frequently run. The solution to that took months, and

was almost bizarre. "The fix was to restrict the inlet to the scavenge line," Troxler said. The scavenge passage was a longish 7/16-inch line connecting crankcase to oil pump. "It was an acoustic phenomenon," Troxler said. "The passage was pressurizing when the piston came back down, filling with air, and—when the passage was depressurizing with the crankcase—the air was coming back out, preventing oil from coming into the passage. We found it out experimentally, and only then modeled it on the computer to show how the restriction worked."

Of course, anyone looking at a Twin Cam crankcase is going to wonder why there's a roughly 3/16-inch hole leading to a 7/16-inch passage. "Yeah," Troxler said, "and they're going to assume more is better and drill this passage out, and, boy, are they going to be sorry."

The more than two years spent chasing down the oil system issues as well as other problems guaranteed that the P-22 would miss its original 1997 model year production target by at least a year. To some extent, Harley, which had not done an all-new engine in decades, didn't know what it was getting into when it started the project. But it quickly sought out the expertise it needed, and added new skills and abilities along with new personnel to its engineering staff.

When Troxler looks back, he said "Much of what was done with the scavenge and breather system was done by blacksmithing and the traditional approach of just getting in and trying things. Someday, new tools of computational fluid dynamics will speed up development. I'm trying new tools now, using the Twin Cam 88 for my test case."

Bob Kobylarz, former head of Engine Engineering, summed it up: "We're not intimidated by oil systems on Big Twins anymore. We didn't understand how it worked; now we do."

By 1996, test bikes were running with prototype Twin Cam engines, Harley's dynos were fully occupied with Twin Cams hammering away, and the development was in full flurry. But not all was going well, and the problems went beyond the oil system difficulties that had already pushed the release of the engine a year beyond its original 1997 schedule.

The most reliable Harley-Davidson engine ever: that was the goal for the Twin Cam 88. Early testing, though, revealed some obstacles to achieving that

With the T-Sport, Harley went after the sport-touring crowd for 2001.

goal. With the increased displacement and power, the Twin Cam generated more heat than the Evo, and that heat was translating into higher piston temperatures.

That was a problem for aluminum pistons. In almost every way, aluminum serves well in pistons. It's strong, with a strength-to-weight ratio similar to steel. It's castable, so complex piston shapes can be molded, rather than expensively machined. It conducts heat exceptionally well, so combustion heat can be pulled from the piston crown out to the cylinder walls, preventing hot spots. Unfortunately, though, aluminum quickly gets weak in the knees as temperatures rise past 400 degrees. According to Nicolae Glaja, the Romanian-born development engineer who was involved with many of the temperature control issues on the P-22, "We had to drop the piston temperature to ensure that there would be no degradation all the way to 100,000 miles."

The chosen approach was one found on many diesels, and many high-performance, imported motorcycle engines: oil jets spraying up from the crankcase on the bottom of the piston crowns. Once the oil system and the crankcases were modified to include the jets, they did exactly what they were supposed to do: they pulled the piston temperatures down to acceptable levels. But there was a not entirely unexpected cost: heat from the pistons was pulled into the engine oil, and now oil temperatures were too high.

"In early 1996," said Skip Metz, engineering project leader for the P-22 program, "we got permission from the styling department to start working on an oil cooling system. We came up with a nice oil cooler that mounted down low on the chassis." The oil cooler, according to those who saw it, was a particularly attractive unit, much nicer than most aftermarket versions, and it dropped oil temperatures to acceptable levels. But within the company it brought up bad memories of pre-Evo engines that ran too hot, and the oil coolers that had been affixed to them. It wasn't a particularly elegant solution.

But time was running short. According to Metz, "In late 1996, we were running the QRL (Quality Reliability Longevity) test on bikes fitted with the oil cooler at the VW Volvo proving grounds near Phoenix. (Passing this test was essential for production approval for the 1998 model year.) The results were pretty good, and the durability was pretty good. We still had some problems with noisy cam drives, and that side of the engine. There were about five specific problems we identified on that test that we didn't like, but we thought we could address those problems in time for 1998. But we came to a roadblock: Styling said there was no way they could see an oil cooler on this engine. Oil coolers were seen as a Band-Aid for the basic design of the engine."

chief) had known Jim from his past life at GM [General Motors], and thought he could help us. Jim has a list of patents as long as your arm on things he has done on engines, many things that aren't obvious. He had a lot of ideas we tried. Some of them worked and some of them didn't—but he got us to open up our minds and not to think we couldn't do something in a specific length of time. You can have a conversation with him, and he'll have something fabricated and running on a dyno in a couple of days."

During that period, parts were being developed and tested before they were ever designed. "We contacted Volvo to see if we could use their test track near Phoenix, and set up shop in their development lab for four to six weeks in March and April of 1997," Metz recalled. "We had motorcycles and engines at Jim's place in Ventura, California, and used his facility

Following page
The Deuce was still the ultimate custom as Harley began its second century.

Harley put the new counterbalanced engine in the Softail Deuce, a new custom Softail with a stretched tank and custom rear end.

The members of the QRL committee soon were meeting with the members of the Product Planning Committee, reviewing the oil cooler issue and the decision for 1998 production. "Their consensus," Metz said of a December 16, 1996 meeting, "was that the oil cooler was a bad thing, and that we couldn't go into production with it." The P-22 program had just crashed into a wall over the oil cooler; a very significant redesign of the engine would be required to dispense with it.

Production in 1998 was history. To make the 1999 model year, "we had from Christmas until April 1, 1997, to solve the problem," Metz said. "That four-month period was the roughest period of the whole program."

Doug Grant, an engineer from the applied mechanics group at Harley, had been assigned to track and fix engine leaks and seeps. He was reassigned to help develop a mathematical model of the engine that predicted heat flows and temperatures. The thermal model showed that increased finning, as everyone suspected, would help. The Twin Cam, at that time, still had Evo-sized fins. But the big-fin concept had to be proven before a million dollars of already-ordered production tooling was scrapped.

Harley engineering began running on war mode in the winter of 1997. "One of the things that really helped us during this period was working with Jim Feuling," Metz remembered. "Earl Werner (Harley engineering

At the end of the Motor Company's first century, the Road Glide still anchored the custom bagger end of the Harley line.

as a resource for prototypes. We'd fly parts over to the Phoenix airport and test them for a day or two. We were working from sketches and phone calls and just trying things, new oil pan baffles, finning, etc. Volvo's 2-mile test track was right next to its lab, and we could go do parade laps or high-speed laps. It was a little skunk works, to look at oil temperatures and get things done without the usual bureaucracy."

Development engineer Glaja was in Phoenix, and he remembered how hard the battle was. "To shave 10 degrees Fahrenheit out of the oil is a big thing; you have to fight for each degree." Big, welded-on fins

were helping, as was oil flow changes in the oil tank that increased cooling, as was Feuling's patented exhaust valve and exhaust port, but those changes in and of themselves didn't add to the kind of drop in oil temperatures required to get rid of the cooler.

The big win would come from an insight from Milwaukee. Ben Vandenhoeven took time from his work on the counterbalanced Twin Cam Beta engine, and went down to a dyno cell and began a test program that restricted oil flow to various parts of the engine. The objective was to find out exactly where the engine oil was picking up most of its heat. The results were staggering;

while other changes to the engine were cutting a degree here, two degrees there, shutting down the oil flow to the cylinder head and the rocker shafts dropped oil temperatures by 30 to 35 degrees.

"We were trying to cool the cylinder heads with excess oil flow," recollected Bruce Dennert, the man who led the initial mechanical design of the Twin Cam, "without doing a very good job." The situation was this: the biggest heat flow from the cylinder heads was to the atmosphere through the finning. The Twin Cam had been designed with heavy oil flow to the heads, far in excess of mechanical needs, with the undeveloped idea that it might help cooling. However, so much heat flowed through the heads that even the heavy oil flow couldn't significantly drop cylinder head temperatures. Yet, at the same time, the amount of heat picked up by the oil in the heads was huge from the point of view of the oil system, which was dealing with much smaller heat flows overall than the heads. "We rebalanced the oil flow," Dennert said, "and cut the oil flow to the heads to one-quarter to one-sixth of what we had previously. That was adequate for lubrication."

"Oil temperatures of 260 and 280 degrees were pretty common before the oil flow change," Metz said, "and that's pretty close to where oil starts to oxidize. Our target oil temperature was 230, and on the dyno, the (temperature-controlled) oil coolers were on more than they were off. After the oil flow change, the oil cooler never came on and the oil temperature was pretty much in the 215 to 220 degree range."

So by the end of April 1997, solutions to the temperature problem were known. The problem was to get them incorporated into design-intent bikes by August to allow sufficient time for testing for 1999 production. Brian Thate, senior project designer, was given the task of turning the concepts into production-ready designs. "Nick [Glaja] and Feuling took existing heads and welded on pieces near the exhaust ports. Then they gave the pieces to Willie G. and the styling guys. We had to take the final welded-up parts and get them into production. You couldn't do conventional drawings—there wasn't time. We made tooling off the 3-D models. Harley had guys flying over to Germany [where the tooling vendor was located] with SLA [Stereo Lithography, essentially a 3-D plastic printing technique from a CAD file] models to set tooling. We had design-intent cylinders and heads by August, but there were a lot of sleepless nights."

Of course, the big fins of the Twin Cam have since become its visual trademark. But they wouldn't have happened if the oil temperature problems hadn't reared their head. Because the P-22 program started as a bottom-end redesign, Styling had been told early on that it couldn't change the Evo finning. And by the time the problems emerged, Engineering had assumed that Styling was married to the look of the Evo-style top end. In the meantime, no one in upper manage-

ment was volunteering the millions of dollars that it eventually took to give the Twin Cam its big fins. But the oil temperature problem broke the log jam, and while it delayed the Twin Cam a year, it's hard to do anything but applaud the big-finned, cool-running, macho-appearing final result.

The rubber-mounted Twin Cams entered production with the 1999 model year, to be followed a year later by the solidly mounted counterbalanced "Beta" version of the new engine in the new Softails. While minor problems cropped up in cam bearings and cam sprocket retention, the new engine was all Harley could have asked for, offering vastly improved performance and reliability, and leading to new sales records.

Sturgis
FREAK SHOW LITE

By Darwin Holmstrom

Each August, thousands of miles of High Plains high-ways, normally desolate stretches of empty road hosting more coyotes and jack rabbits than motor vehicles, fill with the roar of hundreds of thousands of Harley-Davidson motorcycles. These bikes carry riders about to experience an event vaguely referred to as "Sturgis." Sturgis is a small town in the Black Hills of South Dakota, home of the Sturgis Rally and Races, but it's also something more esoteric. It's a chance to wear clothes we can't (and proba-bly shouldn't) wear anyplace else. It's 100,000 bikers trying to look bad on Main Street while bumping into each other and saying, "Excuse me."

Over the past 20 years, the rally has transformed from a drunken, hallucinogenic orgy into a relatively tame family affair. Many rally goers lament this

While Sturgis is mostly rally today, there is still plenty of racing.

The late, great, Karl "Big Daddy Rat" Smith, founder of the Rat's Hole Custom Motorcycle Show, one of Sturgis' main attractions.

The guy was a little scary, but the dog was actually quite friendly.

transformation, but it accurately reflects the changes that have taken place in motorcyclists ourselves. Face it—as a group, we've grown older, fatter, calmer, and more responsible than we were back in our hedonistic glory days. Even if The Man would tolerate us getting stoned out of our heads and drag racing naked down Main Street, our bodies wouldn't. Those who tried to keep living the old ways are dead, in jail, or too broke to afford motorcycles, which probably explains why fewer and fewer of the old-time bikers show up at the rally each year.

For a couple of weeks each August, motorcycles scour the normally deserted highways of the High Plains. Many people ride to Sturgis to share the camaraderie of the road with a half-million other motorcyclists. Still others trailer in pristine show bikes whose innards have yet to be soiled with petroleum products.

Pull in to any gas station in the High Plains during the rally, and more often than not you'll find other motorcyclists refueling. It doesn't matter what you're riding or where you come from—the fact that you're out sharing the same highways guarantees you'll have enough in common to carry on a conversation.

Camping is another key component of the true Sturgis experience. Stay in any campground in the Black Hills during the rally and you'll be serenaded all night long by unmuffled Harleys rolling by your tent. Loud pipes may save lives, but at 3 A.M. they might make you want to go out and take a few.

Minneapolis resident Al Burke, former flat track racer and 1996 National Motorcycle Museum Hall of Fame inductee, has attended every rally since 1949. Al was the guy your parents pointed out when they needed an example of the bad end you would come to if you bought that motorcycle. Al rode to Sturgis for the first time at the age of 15 and Pappy Hoel, founder of the Sturgis Rally and Races, awarded him a prize for being the youngest rider to attend the rally on his own machine. Thus began a friendship that lasted the rest of Hoel's life.

"I've watched Sturgis grow up," Al says. "Back in the '70s, when people still camped out in City Park, it was out of hand. We had busses parked on the side of the highway, filled with people getting blow jobs."

Although most people come for the party, there's plenty of racing at Sturgis, too. There's an AMA Grand National at the Rapid City Speedway, vintage flat track races, an AMA hillclimb, and the All Harley Drag Racing Association finals. None should be missed, but the drag races are perhaps the most extraordinary. Watching the racers straddle their freaky machines as they rocket down the eighth-mile track at over 150 miles per hour, the noise, the smell of burning nitro, the sheer power of the spectacle can only be compared to a religious epiphany or a Led Zeppelin concert.

There's a different crowd at Sturgis' these days. Cigar smoke has replaced the hashish haze that used to hover over the vendor booths. Strains of Lee Greenwood and Brittany Spears waft from juke boxes that once belted out Canned Heat and Bob Dylan. Main Street now hosts a much more suburban, middle-class collection of bikers than it once did. The stereo-typical one-percenters are much less evident today.

Some people miss the old-time bikers, those seri-ous nonconformists and rebels, which was what you had to be to ride a Harley in the old AMF days. Spending six grand on a machine guaranteed to leave you stranded sooner or later, a machine that vibrated like a Soviet diesel-powered marital aid, was a political statement.

These days conformity rules on Main Street. At any given moment during the rally, Sturgis is filled with at least 100,000 bikers, all riding bikes that differ only in the number and placement of chrome "Live to Ride, Ride to Live" badges. Hang out with the old timers, and you'll hear a lot of grumbling about the new breed of Harley riders with their $20,000 motor-cycles and preweathered leathers. But these folks have every bit as much right to enjoy motorcycling as those of us who have been riding all of our lives.

The people at Sturgis may change, but one thing that remains constant is the lack of good food. The High Plains offer much to a motorcyclist, but good food is not part of the package. Out there, mayonnaise is considered a spice, and food with flavor violates the Calvinistic principles that drove people to settle in such desolate country in the first place. But it doesn't really matter. It's easy to forget frivolous things like food when you get caught up in the spectacle that is Sturgis. The rally is another planet, a place where motorcyclists forget about their daily grinds and revel in the presence of a half-million of our own kind.

Sturgis is a place where people wear clothes they can't (and shouldn't) wear anywhere else.

Chapter 10

BUELL

By Steve Anderson

The most important thing to know about Buell motorcycles is this: They are not Harley-Davidsons, they have never been Harley-Davidsons, and—if Erik Buell and Harley Chairman and CEO Jeff Bleustein have anything to say about it—they never will be Harley-Davidsons.

Harley financially dominates the American motorcycle market, selling more over-750-cc street bikes in the United States than all four Japanese motorcycle companies combined, but its success remains bounded by its image. Bleustein learned this from bitter experience in 1993 when he bought a 49 percent interest in a new company, Buell Motorcycles. If Harley attempted to build its own sportbikes, explained Bleustein at the time, "We would be faced with the problem in the marketplace that we've encountered many times when we've tried to do anything different than a classical Harley-Davidson. Starting with the XLCR Cafe Racer, continuing with the FXRT—probably even with the FLT—every time we've made something a little different from what a Harley-Davidson should look like, it gets spit out by the marketplace. It gets rejected."

So acceptance of new product types was the key goal of the Buell-Harley joint venture—a mission fundamentally different from that of previous Harley-Davidson acquisitions, such as Italian Aermacchi in 1960. Back then, Harley simply wanted to repackage Italian lightweights as Harleys, filling out the range to better compete with the newly popular Japanese lightweight motorcycles. The new joint venture with Buell was not meant to produce Buell machines carrying H-D decals. Instead the goal was to create a new company with its own identity, its own culture, its own brand, and—most importantly—its own unique customers.

Both sides were getting something valuable from the joint venture. Bleustein was once again getting the

services of an engineer whose work he respected—Erik Buell had reported directly to Bleustein in the late 1970s and 1980s, when Bleustein headed Harley Engineering, and Buell worked on projects like the FXRT. (See Buell biography sidebar.) Buell later had proven his entrepreneurial oats by starting Buell Motors in 1987, the tiny company that was consumed in this transaction. For its five-plus years of existence, Buell Motors had been getting international press, and had a far greater presence in the minds of motorcyclists than perhaps the 420-odd Harley-powered sportbikes it had sold between 1987 and 1992 warranted. Bleustein was also getting a bargain, buying an experimental Harley corporate diversification for a relatively piddling amount, something that could be done by a CEO without having to get the approval of his board of directors.

Fully faired in fiberglass, the Buell was the most streamlined bike of the era.

Opening page

In 1985, former Harley engineer Erik Buell built a showpiece racer-replica around the Harley XR1000 engine. Enthusiasts and the press loved it, so Buell started his own company.

For Erik Buell, the rewards were different. The creation of Buell Motorcycle Company wasn't about personal wealth; instead it was about the chance to build American sport motorcycles the way he wanted to build them. At the under-capitalized Buell Motor Corporation, more often than not the struggle had been to simply stay afloat, with payroll being met only because a dealer took another bike that week. Buell Motor Corporation operated with 10 employees out of a Mukwanago, Wisconsin, garage, a building that looked as if might soon settle back into the earth it sat on. When asked to describe the financial condition of Buell Motors in 1993, Buell had replied with a laugh: "Desperate. It was always marginal, and we were juggling everything. I used to read about privateer road race teams that had more money than we did to run our whole business. It was pretty crazy." It was also frustrating. Looking back at his earlier designs, Buell can point out any number of painful features that were dictated by limited resources, from the Harley-Davidson Sportster instrumentation to the drooping muffler—a supplier mistake that would have cost too much to retool. The new company, backed by Harley, would bring the resources to do it right.

Hidden beneath the sleek bodywork was the Sportster-based engine for the ill-fated XR1000.

Of course, there were doubters within Harley; someone in the marketing department in 1993 suggested there might be a demand worldwide for about 300 Buell motorcycles annually. But for Erik Buell and his team, and for Bleustein, the opportunity was huge. Said the Harley CEO in 1993, "We're not interested in selling a few hundred Buells a year; we want to sell thousands."

The key to that was to build a good product. When Buell Motorcycles was formed, Erik Buell and Harley-Davidson knew that they needed a new machine, and needed it quickly. They set the direction for the new bike, the motorcycle that would become the Thunderbolt S2, in late March 1993. According to

Buell himself, the goal for the Thunderbolt was to build a machine "that was both more Harley, and more Buell."

But because Buell was given a small budget and even less time—the new bike was to be shown to dealers in just five months—the Thunderbolt remained firmly rooted in former Buell Motor Corporation designs. The first Harley-powered Erik Buell creation had been a showbike designed around the limited-production Harley-Davidson XR1000 in 1985 (See Buell biography sidebar). That first Buell Battle Twin was intended only as a centerpiece at motorcycle shows, a publicity missile that would demonstrate what a competitive Harley superbike might look like. But public

In late 1993, Harley-Davidson bought 49 percent of Buell's enterprise, and Buell used the money to bring to market an exciting series of models in the following years.

reaction to it had been so strong that the original Buell Motor Corporation had been brought to life in 1987 to put the RR1000 Battle Twin into production. With some assistance from friends at Harley, who had arranged for the Milwaukee company to supply engines, Buell had begun building the extravagantly streamlined RR1000, derived directly from that first show bike.

The original Buell Motor Corporation, struggling with limited funds—it was never to have more than $200,000 in capital—eventually built 50 of the RR1000s, and then moved on to the RR1200, a similar machine powered by the 1200 Sportster engine. That first RR prototype had been built with the hope of being at least potentially competitive in Superbike racing, so all RRs shared some characteristics—characteristics that live on to this day in the latest Buell Firebolt. To keep the Sportster engine from shaking apart the light-weight frame, the first RRs used rubber engine

mounting—essentially the same design as used on the Harley-Davidson FXRS. A pushrod Sportster engine was never going to put out as much power as a 16-valve, four-cylinder 750, so aerodynamics and handling were primary concerns in the RR design. The engine was carried high for ground clearance, and the wheels were positioned as closely together as the long engine allowed for quick turning ability. The stiff, multitube Buell frame resisted bending and twist-ing like that of few other motorcycles. The bodywork was bulbous and large—and very slippery, shaped by the lessons taught inside Harley's wind tunnel during the development of early XR750 road-racers.

In many ways, the RR proved too radical for the American sport bike market, and its racer-replica posi-tioning out of synch with its 60-horsepower engine. The market and Buell Motor Company dealers eventually demanded movement away from the RR's road-racing purism. In 1990 Buell introduced the dual-seat RS to the line, and a year later saw the single seat RSS. Both were fundamentally RR models with less bodywork and a slightly revised riding position with more forward pegs and higher bars.

The Thunderbolt was directly derived from those earlier Buells, with time taken to fix the annoyances that had been unfixable before. To show off the Sportster-based engine, most of the bodywork was left off; only a small, frame-mounted quarter fairing remained. To make it more comfortable, the riding position was modified considerably. All previous Buells were based on the RR seating position, which itself was taken from a mid-1980s Honda RS500 GP bike. A fairly rearward seat placement on older Buells forced a rider to fold over to reach the handgrips. Not so the Thunderbolt, which positioned its rider closer to the bars.

But minor modifications cascaded into an avalanche of change. The new riding position required a shorter gas tank—but the RR's frame would have then occupied space required for the rider's knees. So the Thunderbolt would get a new yet similar frame, narrower under the gas tank, and simpler for easier (and less expensive) production. Because the Thunderbolt was a road machine and not a racer, a low-maintenance toothed belt was judged more appropriate than a chain for final drive—but that meant the motor had to be moved to the left to make room for a 170-mm-wide rear tire. For the first time ever, Buell had the money and resources to design a machine with relatively minimal compromises—all too often in the past, finances had ruthlessly dictated design. But now design features such as a rotomolded plastic fuel tank tucked neatly under a lightweight cover were within reach, a long-held idea that had awaited the availability of money for expensive tooling.

The new relationship with Harley-Davidson brought other benefits as well. While Harley in the past had been a more than somewhat grudging supplier of standard Sportster engines to Buell Motor, now it was willing to more closely tailor an engine to sister-company Buell Motorcycle's needs. More power was a necessity, but how to find it in the few months available before production was to begin? The answer was in the Sportster's restrictive intake and exhaust systems.

Traditional Harley styling demanded tiny mufflers for a Sportster, while engineers always knew that the bigger the muffler, the better they could balance airflow requirements and silencing demands. Fortunately, Harley styling constraints weren't constraints for Erik Buell. He instructed Harley's engineering department to "build a muffler that works, no matter how big, and I'll find a way to package it." What resulted was a huge, free-flowing oval can that tucked directly under the engine—a controversial looking item that became a Buell characteristic. But the tractor-like muffler allowed the Thunderbolt's engine to meet 80-decibel noise regulations while running an air filter with mini-

mal restriction. The Thunderbolt made almost as much power as it would have had with open exhaust pipes and an uncovered carburetor: 76 horsepower at the crankshaft on Harley's dyno, 20 percent more than a Sportster.

When Buell Motorcycles was formed, Harley-Davidson management agreed that Buell would be entirely responsible for its own motorcycle design; Harley's styling department wouldn't be involved. The Thunderbolt's bodywork was the product of Erik Buell and industrial designer Mike Samarzja, a Buell employee. Erik Buell said of the Thunderbolt, "The style and look took a great deal of effort; the Thunderbolt was styled as a whole. This is the first motorcycle we really got right."

Whether or not they "got it right" is a question of personal taste, but the finished bike certainly had a unique presence, and the quality of the paint and bodywork was undeniable. Earlier Buells used fiberglass body parts manufactured by a Wisconsin maker of limited-production, glass-bodied replicars, and neither the chopper-gun-sprayed glasswork nor the easily chipped paint befitted a $14,000 motorcycle. The Thunderbolt began to remedy that. While earlier Buells had a plethora of body parts, the Thunderbolt had only three: a small, frame-mounted quarter fairing; the gas tank cover; and the tailpiece. Buell made all three in two-sided molds by the resin transfer process, and

The first of the new models built with Harley's help was the S2 Thunderbolt, which arrived in late 1994.

Following pages
No other brand had as much in common with Buell as the Italian marque Bimota. Both companies built boutique sportbikes around engines supplied by other manufacturers.

The Lightning had Screaming Eagle cams and higher compression for a useful bump in power and torque.

combined strength, light weight, and a smooth finish inside and out.

When it finally made production late in 1994 (as a 1995 model), the Thunderbolt impressed both motorcycle magazines and show room browsers. Buell was to sell 1,500 Thunderbolts in its first year of production, a 15-fold improvement over Buell Motors' best year ever. The growth of Buell motorcycles had started.

That growth accelerated in the 1996 model year with the introduction of the S1 Lightning, a derivative of the S2. According to Erik Buell the S1 wasn't intended to be a standard, a dumbed-down and compromised machine designed to appeal to the broadest audience at the lowest price. It was to be "a pure sportbike for more forms of the motorcycling sport" than any racer-replica. It just didn't happen to have bodywork.

That first Lightning captured the stripped-down streetfighter look. It was an extreme machine in a number of ways. It kept the high-quality suspension and chassis components of the Thunderbolt, but packaged them with a tiny gas tank and the thinnest, stubbiest seat fitted to anything this side of a trials bike. It also carried a further development of Harley's Sportster engine, the most powerful yet. The power increases came from the obvious: longer duration camshafts, the Screaming Eagle cams from Harley's accessory catalog; a higher compression ratio; and less flow restriction in the intake ports, with the use of

In 1996 came the S1 Lightning, a hooligan bike guaranteed to peg the fun-o-meter. Shown is the 1998 version.

shorter valve guides. With the standard exhaust system, the Lightning also packed its power high in its rev range, with a noticeable soft spot at 3,000 rpm.

But the radical Lightning was an instant hit, and led to further Buell derivatives. Nineteen ninety-seven brought the S3 Thunderbolt, an update of the S2 that got the Lightning engine tune. More importantly, though, it was moved further from the Buell heritage of a few guys piecing together one bike per week in a garage. According to Erik Buell, it was "a bike designed to be made by industrial processes instead of by hand." This was perhaps best exemplified in the new plastic fuel tank that replaced the rotomolded tank and fiberglass tank cover of the S2—the fiberglass bodywork of the S2 had proved to be ridiculously expensive to make in volume while maintaining quality. The M2 Cyclone, a civilian version of the hard-ass S1 Lightning, joined the S3 that year. According to Buell, the Cyclone was intended to be "a wonderful sportbike that can be your everyday bike." The Cyclone was built around a slightly modified S1 frame, with a new rear subframe carrying a seat long enough for comfortable two-up riding, and one that swept out to a 9.5-inch width—2.5 inches wider than the skinny S1 unit.

With standard Sportster cams running in conjunction with high-compression Lightning heads, the Cyclone's engine made slightly less peak power than the Lightning, but with much stronger off-idle torque.

Buell's innovative suspension features a shock absorber under the engine, similar to the design used on the Harley Scat of 1963.

In 1997, Buell added a two-up tail section to an S1 to create the M2 Cyclone.

Erik
BUELL

By Steve Anderson

In the dot-com era, it seemed every newly hatched MBA with a bit of gall and a medium bad idea was able to raise millions of dollars, start a company, and then cash in at the IPO and secure his luxurious retirement. Now you can find those same MBAs dining at too-trendy restaurants, explaining how their company's failure wasn't their fault—they were just too far ahead of the market. It's almost enough to give the term "entrepreneur" a bad name. Fortunately, there is the counterexample of Erik Buell.

Buell harkens back to an earlier era of engineers—company creators who were driven not by the desire to own yachts and business jets, but who just wanted to make better products. Buell's goal was and is simple: make an American motorcycle that qualifies as one of the world's best sportbikes. He's known how to do it for a long time, but, along the way, he also discovered he'd have to build a company to get the chance.

Buell grew up in Gibsonia, Pennsylvania, near Pittsburgh. He came by his workaholic tendencies naturally. His dad was a patent attorney who also ran a farm on evenings and weekends, when he wasn't busy writing briefs. Erik used to go with him after school and do farm chores under artificial lights.

Motorcycles were part of the local culture as well. "My first ride was on a step-through 50 when I was 13," Buell recounts. "When I was 14 got a Parilla moped." He had to wait until the ripe old age of 15 to get a real motorcycle, a Panhead hardtail that he put together from pieces that came in a number of cardboard boxes. "Yeah, it sat next to all the 305 scramblers in my high school parking lot and leaked oil," Buell says.

Erik describes his college experience, as "kind of like a rock skipping—I bounced a few times before it sank in. I had the highest board scores of anyone getting into the engineering school and was the first to drop out." The problem? "I was doing all the things I thought girls liked: playing bass in a rock band and working in motorcycle shops. There are only two methods that work with girls: cute and bad. And I couldn't do cute."

But Buell's interest in bikes got him back into engineering school. "It had a lot to do with finding out that I enjoyed working on them and designing

Erik Buell in front of the factory that bears his name.

them," Buell says. His racing had started back in 1973. "I started doing some motocross initially," he remembers. "Then I had a bad accident, a head-on with another motocrosser, and ended up with a lot of plates in me." While he healed, he helped build a road racer for another rider, a mongrel machine with a Kawasaki 350 Single engine in an H1R frame. "I ended up buying his half of the bike, and won some races on it, running against 350 Yamahas in 1973—1974."

The next year, Buell moved up to AMA Pro racing, and got his Pro Novice license. He borrowed a 250 Yamaha and rode it with some success. Then came a 250 Aermacchi/Harley that "was the end of my career for a couple of years. Gary Scott won Loudon on one, and I thought the bikes they sold were like his—when maybe they shared a triple clamp bolt."

His riding career came back strong in 1977 and 1978 with rides on a Ducati 900SS in the new Superbike class, and on a Yamaha TZ750D in Formula 750. "The big Yamaha was one of my favorite motorcycles. For the era, they were very reliable, and they handled well—it was the engine that was really violent. I was a rookie expert at Daytona in 1978, and qualified as fastest rookie. I was running 10th when the ignition went bad, about two-thirds of the way through the race. I was running fifth in the Superbike race, right behind Baldwin on the Guzzi and ahead of Dave Emde on the Yosh Suzuki," remembers Buell, before problems ended that ride as well.

While he was racing, Buell worked on his engineering degree. Upon graduation in 1979, he went to work for Harley instead of Pratt & Whitney, which had been actively recruiting him. Why? "I wanted to design motorcycles." His racing, though, took a setback at Daytona that year. "I was going to ride Baldwin's Superbike Guzzi for Reno Leoni in 1979," remembered Buell. "At Daytona, I was running times quick enough on my TZ750 to qualify in the top 10 for the 200, but during practice, I ran into Randy Mamola going into the chicane, and I missed the Superbike final because of the trip to the hospital. Reno got mad at me and fired me."

But work was beginning to take first priority. "It was really insanely busy at Harley. I didn't have time to race, and my TZ was destroyed. I didn't race much in 1979 at all. I got the bike fixed and ran a few races in 1980. I couldn't take off two or three days and go to the races; I had a 60-hour week at Harley. Harley was suffering then, and I started feeling guilty about owning a Yamaha and a Ducati. I sold them and started the Barton project."

He had been gaining invaluable experience at Harley, starting with his first position as a junior test engineer. "The major thing I did there was a whole lot of chassis development work, a lot of testing. A tire development program, a lot of tests for chassis stiffness, rain groove testing, a lot of chassis related stuff. We had a 14-channel information gathering system, which was really cool back then." At test tracks from Talladega to the EG&G track in Texas to the old Bendix proving grounds in South Bend, Indiana, Buell rode motorcycles and analyzed their handling. "It was one of the ultimate chances to experience a lot of conditions on a bunch of different motorcycles with good test data," he said. "It really gave me a lot of sensitivity to design variables."

Buell rose rapidly within Harley's engineering department, and was soon running a major program. "The FXRT was mine from concept to production. It was myself and a designer, one other guy." He notes that there was very little money during those hard years for the Motor Company. The FXRT, for example, was pieced together from existing components, its fairing originally intended for the never-produced Nova. Though the FXRT was never a big seller, Buell said, "It got Harley a lot of PR, and got them into a little different market."

In his spare time, Buell was trying to go racing with his Barton. The "Barton project" was almost an insanely large program for one man to take on. Buell bought one of the under-developed English square-four two-strokes to run in the AMA's Formula 1 class, and found that all the detail engineering was left to the customer. But unlike any other customer, he was up to the task, manufacturing his own crankshafts, redesigning any engine component that needed it, designing his own chassis, testing the bike in club races. When Barton declared bankruptcy, Buell bought the tooling for the square-four engine. After giving the matter long and hard thought, he decided to leave Harley and start a business making race bikes. It was not a decision an MBA would have made.

Buell eventually sold one RW750 (for *Road Warrior*). Before he could sell another, the AMA killed the Formula 1 class, leaving no place to race a big two-stroke, and leaving Buell with no compensation for the travail of trying to build a sophisticated race bike in his garage. Only a little bit of engineering consulting and selling a few racing oriented products such as Dymag wheels were keeping macaroni and cheese on the Buell family table.

But from that conflagration came the Buell Motor Corporation. "Before I left Harley, I told Jeff (Bleustein), I really want to do a rubber-mounted sport-bike around a Sportster engine," remembers Buell, suggesting that the rejection of that project contributed to his decision to leave. "Then the opportunity came when the guy from Vetter (Rex Marsee) approached me in 1985 and told me he had a spot in the Great American Show for a Vetter Show Bike. They wanted a very modern looking future bike to put next to the replica Daimler wooden bike." All Vetter had in mind was an RW750 with lights. But not Buell: "I said, 'Why don't I build a very modern bike with a Harley engine?'" That was fine with Vetter, as long as it could be done for $6,000.

That first Battle Twin was in many ways a classic Buell effort, over-delivering on promises in an impossibly short time. "It didn't have to run, but I built the first RR1000 as a runner, with everything working," recalls Buell. "I started it in September, 1985, and it was a done, running bike in December. I didn't sleep for about three months."

After the show, Buell bought the bike back from Vetter for the same $6,000. "I needed it—I didn't have drawings," he explained. "In 1986, I built two more chassis. One went to Harley for Lucifer's Hammer II; the other was sold to a Harley engineer who wanted to go racing." By the spring of 1987, Buell had managed to raise a tiny amount of capital, and placed the RR1000 in limited production, creating a motorcycle company with his name on it through little more than the sheer force of his will. Five years later, Harley would join his efforts, and the rest is history.

Without a tach and with a conventional Showa fork replacing the Lightning's expensive White Power unit, the Cyclone was priced attractively.

Thundering into the Buell line-up a year later, for 1998, was the X1W White Lightning, a hot-rod version of the standard Lightning. In classic parts bin engineering, the large gas tank from the S3 and the slightly longer solo seat fitted to European-export Lightnings gave the White Lightning visual distinction from a standard S1. But more importantly, its engine distinguished it. With new, free-flowing big-valve heads, the Firestorm engine bumped a Buell into the more-than-100-horse-power club. The White Lightning was fast for an air-cooled Twin in stock form, and with the factory race exhaust and air filter fitted, it wheelied almost too easily. The White Lightning was the perfect definition of a hooligan bike, and riding one was almost to put your license at risk.

Buell motorcycle sales grew throughout this period. Big changes continued with its relationship with Harley-Davidson as well. In February of 1998, Harley exercised its option and bought an additional 49 percent of Buell Motorcycles, raising its interest to 98 percent. Erik Buell retained the other 2 percent, along with his chairman and chief technical officer titles. Jerry Wilkie, formerly vice president in charge of sales at Harley, continued in his position as Buell CEO.

With the increasing involvement of Harley-Davidson came increasing resources for new motorcycle models. This was demonstrated with the 2000 model year X1 Lightning, and even more so a year later with the Blast, a 500-cc single powered by Harley's first designed-for-Buell engine.

The X1 Lightning replaced both the S1 and S1W Lightnings, and attempted to add refinement to the raw appeal of its predecessors. It started with a similar state of engine tune as the White Lightning, but tamed it with a new, unique-to-Buell fuel-injection system. Its matte aluminum subframe and one-piece cast-aluminum swingarm added to the bike's visual appeal, and were clearly higher quality pieces than anything that been on a Buell before.

Another newcomer for 1997 was the S3T, the bags and fairing of which turned the Buell into a sport tourer.

The S3T combined sportbike performance with long-haul comfort.

Erik Buell described the reasons for the new Lightning at its first press introduction: "We had a lot of people who loved the naked raw look of the S1; we had other people who thought it was just too crude. The potential customers we weren't getting were telling us, 'Damn, this is cool, but...' They wanted a higher level of sophistication."

In contrast to the X1, the Blast was aimed at a new customer type altogether: new riders. A team of Harley powerplant engineers working in a trailer behind the Buell design facility created the new engine, a one-cylinder, short-stroke derivative of the existing Buell V-twin, with many enhancements for both reliability and production efficiency. (Many of its features that marked it as a new generation of Milwaukee power-plant—including engine cases incorporating swingarm mounts and the new small oil filter—would later be seen on the Buell Firebolt engine.) Instead of being tuned for high peak power, it was tuned for a broad torque curve, making it easier to ride. The Blast was a small bike built around 16-inch wheels, a bike with a very low seat height. It was introduced with a $4,395 sticker price, and it quickly became Buell's best-selling model. (See *Marketing the Blast* sidebar).

But the really big project within Buell wouldn't be seen until the summer of 2001, with the introduction of the SB9 Firebolt, the machine that would let Erik

Buell take several solid steps closer to his dream of the totally uncompromised American sportbike. For the first time ever, Buell would be able to design engine and chassis together, to come up with the combination that would work best on the street.

The intent of the Firebolt project, according to Erik Buell, was to build "the best backroad bike of all time." His idea was to package a big four-stroke engine in a tiny motorcycle, to stuff 1,000 cc into a bike the size of a 250-cc Grand Prix machine. Most of the Firebolt's

innovative features, such as the frame that doubled as a gas tank and the swingarm that served as an oil tank, were there to simply allow everything to fit within the desired 52-inch wheelbase.

The Firebolt engine was new, but shared its architecture with the Sportster. It remained a 45-degree, air-cooled V-twin with nonoffset cylinders; kept the Sportster-style knife-and-fork connecting rods; and still used pushrods pushed by four individual camshafts down on the right side of the engine. But other than

The new X1 Lightning replaced the S1 models for 1999. Its engine used Buell's own fuel injection.

Along with all the power, the X1 features top-flight suspension.

The huge Buell muffler looks as if it belongs on a semitruck more than on a sleek sportbike, but it does keep things quiet while allowing lots of power.

the gears in the gearbox and a small handful of other parts, almost every aspect of the short-stroke power-plant was new. It redlined at 7,500 rpm, had shed more than 30 pounds, took less room, shifted better, and had been designed to be stronger and more reliable. Perhaps the best way to think of the Firebolt powerplant is as simply the next generation air-cooled Buell engine, dif-ferent but still designed to be built on similar tooling as its predecessors. It incorporates both lessons learned by Buell from the Blast engine and Pro-Thunder racing, and lessons learned by Harley engineering in the Twin Cam 88 program.

But while the Firebolt's engine may have taken the Sportster engine back to its sportiest roots, and ensured one of the longest-running powerplants around another decade of production, the Firebolt chassis scored innovation points against any motorcy-cle chassis produced on any continent. The Firebolt's aluminum frame mounted the new engine in a deriva-tive of the traditional Buell rubber-mounting system; this time one rubber biscuit hung between the engine and frame just in front of the front cylinder head, while a second, Dyna Glide-style laminated steel/rub-ber mount supported the rear of the engine.

The new frame and swingarm were beautiful examples of aluminum craftsmanship, and combined, according to Buell, to make an "obscenely stiff" structure. The Firebolt frame is fabricated by Italian framemaker Verlicchi, and carries 3.7 gallons of gasoline and a fuel pump inside it. The gasoline fills the space immediately behind the steering head, in the side beams, and in a large cross-member behind the rear cylinder. According to Buell chassis engineer Vance Strader, the current Firebolt actually resulted from the third design attempt. The earlier two designs utilized tube frames. In Strader's words, "Two-thirds of those bikes were really cool, but there was always one part with no room—either the gas tank, or the shock, or the airbox." Combining the frame and gas tank was the only option that allowed the original intent of the big-engine/light-tiny-bike combination to be achieved.

The Firebolt's ZTL (Zero Torsion Load) front brake was as distinctive as the frame. As on every other Buell, a single front disc was used, but on the Firebolt, that disc mounted on its outer diameter to bosses on the spokes just prior to the rim. With a single 375-mm disc grabbed from the inside by a six-piston caliper, the ZTL brake provided sufficient stopping performance even on a tight racetrack and, by removing the brake torsional load from the spokes, Buell engineers could make the front wheel phenomenally light. Weighing just 9 pounds, it scaled less than some magnesium racing wheels.

The Firebolt clearly catapulted Buell into a new level of performance and refinement. The 984-cc machine offers performance that is essentially equivalent to a White Lightning, the quickest prior Buell, with a smoothness and slickness that can't be touched by any of its predecessors. In handling, too, the Firebolt sets world standards, and not just for an American sportbike. While niggling reliability faults and recalls tarnished the image of early Buell bikes, the Blast and the Firebolt were engineered and tested from the beginning to meet and exceed world-class standards of reliability and durability.

The Firebolt's brakes are nearly as unusual as its fluid reservoirs. The front disk mounts to the wheel rim rather than to carriers on the hub.

No word describes Buell's unorthodox XB9R, introduced in 2002, better than "unusual." Perhaps the most unusual part of the design is the frame that doubles as a fuel tank and the swingarm that doubles as an oil tank for the dry-sump engine.

Marketing
THE BLAST!

By Steve Anderson

Selling entry-level motorcycles in the 1990s had been difficult. Most motorcycles designed to attract first-time buyers pinioned between non-motorcyclists' fear and inertia, high expectations, and the low prices of used bikes. No motorcycles targeted at beginners had made the best-seller lists.

Harley wanted to change that with the Blast. The new low-cost bike didn't exist to pump up the corporate bottom line—not immediately. It was to be a magnet designed to pull a fence-sitters into motorcycling and help build a new generation of riders who could eventually be sold more expensive Harleys or Buells. Back when the Blast still went by its internal code name of "Thor," Buell and Harley worked hard to understand who these potential customers were. The marketers divided them into two classes: people in close proximity to motorcycles and motorcyclists (friends and family) and people who weren't involved even in the periphery of motorcycling. In their opinion, the first group would largely sell themselves, but reaching the second group would require real effort. Of that second group, Buell concentrated on the relative youngsters (34 and under) who shared similar values and lifestyles with current riders. Lisa Forthofer, manager of special products planning, explained that the following adjectives described current riders and potential riders equally well: adventurous, challenge-driven, discovery-seeking, energetic, experimental, physical, outdoorsy, spontaneous, and committed to physical freedom.

According to Forthofer, both groups were into "exercise, instant gratification, sophisticated design, sports, and unique styling." In general, both riders and those identified as potential riders, Forthofer continued, "love all forms of physical activity and prefer outdoor activity. Right now these people don't have motorcycling on their radar." The intent was for these potential riders to conclude, "Motorcycling is a fun activity that has some utilitarian positives with it."

So Buell engineers designed the Blast to make that point. Again and again in focus group studies of potential riders, the perceived dangers of biking were mentioned. Responding to that concern, Buell styled the Blast to look sporty and fun—but not aggressive. Pure sportbikes were seen as too dangerous. Pure performance was less important for the Blast than simplicity and ease of use. Accordingly, the engineers designed an engine that made about 30 horsepower with a fat torque curve and required almost no maintenance,—very different characteristics than those of an engine aimed at jaded long-time riders.

But the biggest and most important step Buell and Harley took for the Blast was to help remove the barriers that prevented potential motorcyclists from joining the club. Specifically, this meant removing the rider training requirements for licensing now in effect in many states. Harley joined the Motorcycle Safety Foundation before the Blast's release and created a program of basic and advanced rider training called "Rider's Edge." The program is offered through participating Harley-Davidson and Buell dealerships. These dealerships supply Blasts to riders who take Rider's Edge classes.

The Blast's first year also saw Buell use a program that had proven overwhelmingly successful for the original 883 Sportster—the guaranteed, full-price trade-in. While the program was in effect, anyone who bought a Blast could trade it in during his or her first year of ownership for a larger Buell or Harley, and receive full credit for the original purchase price of the Blast. However, as Blast sales have more than met expectations (doubling Buell's overall sales), this is one promotion that is no longer needed—or offered.

That was surely one of the reasons that Buell decided in late 2001 to discontinue the older tube-framed Twins, including the X1 Lightning and the M2 Cyclone. Instead, the future would belong to the Firebolt, which would spin off a family range as broad as that of the first S2.

So Buell continues to grow, and to produce sportbikes that could never come from Milwaukee. Why? Culture is everything. The V-Rod, for example, high-tech new engine or not, was largely conceived by Willie G. and Louie Netz in Harley's styling department.

It was designed to look good first, with the engineers constrained to make it work well within the tough parameters laid down by styling. The Firebolt, in contrast, was designed by engineers who moved heaven and earth to produce a machine with the performance they wanted—and only then worked with stylists to define the look that went with that design. Two different approaches, two different customer bases—may Buell and Harley long thrive by being different things to different people.

The wheel located between the exhaust pipe and the brake lever keeps constant tension on the final drive belt, eliminating the need for belt adjustment.

Chapter 11
RACING

By Allan Girdler

Ora ne word defines Harley-Davidson: tradition. Racing is one of Harley's oldest traditions. From its earliest years, the Motor Company's reputation for quality and value was largely based on sport and competition. Since the current AMA Grand National championship began in 1954, Harley riders have won the number one plate 38 times in 49 years. The manufacturer's title race began in 1972, and H-D has won it all but eight seasons. That's a record no other maker can match.

Yet racing is something the folks who run the show have never really wanted to talk about. Pull into a gas station anywhere in the United States with a vintage track bike in your truck and someone is sure to exclaim, "A Harley? When did Harley get into racing?"

"About 1908," is the correct answer. In fact, Harleys were taking part in sports events before that.

There are reasons for the company's shyness about its racing successes that go back to the very beginning of the sport of motorcycling. Early Harley-Davidson ads mentioned almost in passing that Harley owners had won this race or that rally, noting that the factory hadn't spent any money or even helped in any way.

Then came 1908. Walter Davidson, a natural athlete, entered a stock—albeit carefully prepared—single-cylinder Model 4 in an enduro on New York's Long Island. Davidson didn't just win; he won with a perfect score. The feat collected headlines coast to coast. The next year, Davidson and his pals rode four stock machines in an endurance run from Cleveland to Indianapolis. They turned in a set of perfect scores and took home the team prize.

Impressive stuff, but the day came when reliability was no longer an issue, and road bikes didn't make the news. Indian and others now forgotten, like Merkel and Thor, fielded professional racing teams on purebred racers. Their racers earned acclaim, and prior to World War I Indian topped the sales charts, worldwide.

Dodge City race, 1916.

BOARDS AND BAKED DIRT, 1914–1931

On July 4, 1914, at Dodge City, Kansas, Harley-Davidson fielded the firm's first factory team, six top stars of the day riding stripped and tuned versions of production street twins. Spectators watched four Harleys fail to finish the 300-mile race, and the two that finished were back behind the pack.

H-D hired an engineer with racing experience, and the team's results improved. In 1915, H-D fielded souped-up F-head machines and some overhead-valve racers with four valves per cylinder. This was the first of a series of golden ages. Back then, cities closed streets so motorcycles could race on real roads. They raced on fairgrounds ovals, usually half-mile or mile tracks used for horse racing, or they raced at speeds of 120 miles per hour on fearsome banked ovals made of splintery boards. Racing was a popular form of entertainment before World War I, and motorcycle races drew huge crowds.

Harley Davidson offered racing models for sale to private racers, further increasing the sport's popularity.

Perhaps "offered" should be in quotes. In 1915, Excelsior advertised its Model 16-S.C., winner of the American National Championship, as "The fastest motorcycle ever built." It came with a full-race 61-cubic inch V-twin, and sold for $250. In 1916, Indian advertised its Model H, a racer with a 61-cubic inch overhead-valve engine, available with four valves per cylinder, priced at $350. The 1916 Harley catalog features the "Twin Cylinder Model 17," with a 61-cubic inch eight-valve engine, but with all the specifications vague or optional. The price was $1,500. The outrageous price guaranteed that no average racer would be able to purchase this exotic racing machine.

Instead, the factory assembled a pro team nicknamed "The Wrecking Crew." Harley built only enough bikes to fill the team's needs, plus a handful for selected dealers and tuners, including some from overseas.

Harley's F-head twins developed into the dominant racing engines of their generation.

The first 61s used shortened spindly frames and direct drive, had no brakes or suspension, and used tires no thicker than your thumb.

Harley's men in charge, chief engineer William Harley and racing engineer William Ottaway, knew enough to know they didn't know everything. When the new Harley engines didn't equal rival Indian's 61 twins, H-D hired English wizard Harry Ricardo and kept him under contract until the Harley 61 cranked out 55 horsepower. When Merkel went broke, Harley hired its best man, Maldwyn Jones, who arrived at the Motor Company with a machine he'd had Merkel build to his specs. The Harley shop fitted the bike with a Harley engine. Jones said the Merkel's forks worked better, so for several years, the Harley team used Merkel forks.

The racing was almost too good, in the sense that speeds were incredible. There were injuries and even deaths, including spectators struck by out-of-control machines, which led to the board tracks being sensationalized in the press as "Murder Dromes." In 1921, Otto Walker won the Fresno board mile on a Harley 61 at an average speed on 101.4 miles per hour, making Walker the first motorcycle racer in the world to finish a race with an average speed faster than 100 miles per hour.

Just how fierce were the machines of this era? In 1922 the lap record for the dirt mile was 39.6 seconds. The modern record? The late Ricky Graham did one lap of the Springfield, Illinois, mile in 34.548 seconds. So in nearly 80 years, we've shortened the time for the mile by five seconds. Those old guys were fast.

In 1921, the Harley Wrecking Crew won all the national titles. The next year, the Harley factory pulled the plug on its racing team, and either sold or gave away the machines.

Light, loud, elemental, and fast, the early Harley twin-cylinder racers earned the Motor Company a reputation as a serious competitor in the teens and a perennial winner in the 1920s.

Irving Janke (left) won the race at Dodge City in 1916 aboard a Harley Eight-Valve.

PRODUCTION RACING RETURNS: 1931–1952

The Great Depression nearly killed the sport of motorcycling. How salvation arrived is a story so unusual and improbable that it must be true, mostly because it's too unlikely to be believable fiction.

As racing evolved, the various sanctioning bodies developed three levels of competition. Class A allowed pure-race machines, with displacement the only limit. Class B was professional, and required production-based engines modified for racing. Class C was for amateurs, typically owners who raced the machines they rode to the event. They stripped the street gear, such as lights and even brakes, and after they had competed, they bolted the gear back on and rode home. The idea was to give the ordinary enthusiast a fair way to compete with his peers, which was why the bikes

During the board-track era, gladiators blasted around tracks built of splintery wood at 100 miles per hour on skinny little tires, in a 1920s equivalent of Rollerball. Carnage was an expected part of the spectacle.

Sidecar race, July 4, 1921.

The San Jose (California) Velodrome, 1937

The invitation was accepted. The top event at the Isle of Man was the Tourist Trophy, quickly shorted to TT.

One Sunday afternoon, Pink went into the country, borrowed some land and laid out a course in the dirt, over hills so steep you could jump into the air. It seemed (to him, anyway) like a miniature replica of those Isle of Man laps, so he called the event the TT.

An Indian executive and top guy in the AMA came to watch Pink's TT. He was intrigued and wrote an article for the AMA magazine explaining the new event and its rules. Presto! TT became a uniquely American offroad event.

At the time, the AMA's competition committee realized that the pure racing classes were dying out. The crowds weren't big enough to pay the kind of prize money that would allow professional racers to buy or maintain their machines. As a potential cure, the AMA devised a national championship for Class C.

In the early 1930s, both Harley-Davidson and Indian made 750-cc side-valve V-twins that were marketed as sport bikes, so the rules for the new Class C events required the motorcycles to be side-valve 750s. Because Pink was a valued member of the AMA and his customers' sporting mounts were overhead-valve 500-cc singles, such machines were also allowed in Class C. At the time, this equivalency formula was one of inclusion, rather than exclusion, and it provided fair competition (as well as heaps of politicking, as we'll see in due course) for nearly 30 years.

The first Class C Nationals were held in 1934. Harley-Davidson had the only factory Class A team. That team consisted of one rider, Joe Petrali, and Petrali won every Class A title in the 1935 season, which turned out to be the last year of Class A racing.

In 1934, Harley built a competition version of its basic 45-cubic-inch model, and marketed the bike to people who wanted to race. Many riders bought the racer, rode to the races, stripped the road gear, and raced against riders mounted on Indian Scouts. The new Class C regulations were a success. Class C did in fact save the sport of motorcycling in the United States. New talent showed up, and guys (along with some women, notably Dot Robinson, a top enduro rider) bought what they raced, and raced what they bought. Class C was truly the national class by 1939.

In addition to the 45-inch class, Class C featured an open class that allowed any engine size. It turned out that the Model E, the legendary Knucklehead introduced in 1936, did very well in TT events. Owners began modifying the Big Twins, removing the front fenders, moving the back fender to the front, and raising the bars so the rider could stand up over the jumps.

There were kits to raise the engine in the frame, for more ground clearance, and the exhaust pipes ran

Later, Harley switched to flathead engines for both street and track, and the board tracks gave way to dirt tracks.

were strictly production, as delivered by the factory. The rules even required the rider to be the owner, with papers to prove it.

Back in the early 1930s there was only one notable dealer who sold imported (read: English) motorcycles. Reg Pink had a dealership in the Bronx, and he knew that the most important thing a dealer could supply was something for his customers to do with their motorcycles. Pink knew that early in the twentieth century, when the spoilsport English government banned racing on public roads, the tourist-friendly chaps on the Isle of Man invited racers to compete on their lovely island.

Harley's WR models became dirt- track legends.

down the side of the bike, at exhaust port level, to keep the pipes from being crushed on jumps or drowned in water crossings .

Backyard mechanics made TT modifications to their bikes, and eventually these modifications led to bob jobs, or bobbers, which later evolved into choppers. Choppers evolved into customs, which evolved into today's cruisers. The current Softail Deuce can trace the origins of its stylish good looks straight back to Depression-era TT racing. The fashions of the 1970s, which became the sales force of the 1990s, began as the production racer of the 1930s.

THE WR

Class C revived racing and many new events sprang up, most notably the road races at Daytona Beach, Florida.

This was another of those happy accidents. Daytona's beach—actually the event began at Ormond Beach, the next town to the north—was a God-given, hard-packed surface used for speed runs. When race cars got too fast, the locals came up with a race for stock cars. The cars raced up the beach and down the narrow asphalt road parallel to the beach, for 200 miles. The first race didn't make 200 miles, however, because race organizers hadn't reckoned on the tide coming in.

When the motorcycle road races at Savannah, Georgia, were canceled, the AMA was invited to race at Daytona Beach. This event had serious sales potential.

Harley and Indian both tested the limits of the Class C principle, Indian by the straightforward production of a limited number—50, according to the official records—of racing machines known as "Big-Base" Scouts because of their strengthened crankcases. Harley-Davidson was subtler. In 1941, the same year the Scouts arrived for Daytona, H-D introduced the WR.

There were two models. The WR and WRTT. According to Motor Company press releases, the WR models were simply Ws without lights, mufflers, brakes, and all the other gear the racers removed. Why make the customer pay for stuff he'll throw away?

In reality, the WR and the WRTT both were a lot more different from the W or WLD, or even each other, than they looked.

The WR, made for flat ovals, came with what was known as the "light" frame, made of stronger steel than the WL's frame. The WR had no brakes, and a WR was at least 100 pounds lighter than the WLDR.

The WRTT was intended for heavier TT duty, which included jumps and deep ruts. It used a trimmed version of the WL frame with extra bracing, although in 1948, the factory switched to a braced version of the light WR frame.

The WR engine had the same bore and stroke and outward appearance, but inside the flywheels were steel instead of iron. The camshafts were radically timed and a magneto handled ignition chores rather than points and coil. The cylinders also differed, with the valves closer to the bore, and with the valves tipped toward the piston, to aid combustion chamber flow. The area between valves and piston was sculpted and massaged, also for better flow.

Willard "Red" Bryan on Two-Cam-OHV, circa 1929.

Al "Squibb" Henrich at St. Louis hill climb, 1932.

Hollister, California, 1937. Len Andres, Al Torres and Jerry McKay collecting their trophys.

The WR proved fierce competition for the Indian Scout until the KR replaced it in the 1950s.

The ownership rule was still in effect, but somehow WR cases often left the factory without numbers, to be added later, or in multiples, so the "owner" (actually a dealer or tuner) could have several engines but only one title.

Both models were available with numerous options. The standard WR and WRTT used saddle tanks slung over the frame's top tube, gas and oil side by side. But for the longer road and dirt events, there was an optional pair of gas-only tanks, with an added oil tank beneath the seat. There was a long list of sprocket and gear choices, and the rear hubs could be fitted with two sprockets, so if the inside of the tire wore, the wheel could be flipped for a fresh section of tread.

The factory revived the racing department and hired a racing engineer, but didn't hire riders. Instead, the engineer worked with the engineers in the production division, and with the dealers who sponsored teams and with the outside tuners, several of whom knew as much as the factory.

There was sort of a pyramid—the sponsored rider with backing, equipped with a WR and a WRTT and all the options, had an edge on the WR rider with one machine, who, in turn, had an advantage over the guy who had stripped his WLDR.

But there were riders whose talent put them ahead of the riders with equipment, and the Harley faction was pretty much equal during this time to the Indian backers and the Norton, Matchless, and Triumph contingents, who won at least their share, considering they were always outnumbered.

The bottom line is that the sport of motorcycle racing survived the Depression. There was a pause during World War II, of course, but after the war, when prosperity came roaring back, racing picked right back up, with hardly a pause. With the WR, Harley-Davidson had made another in its history of smart moves.

Harley's flatheads also carved out their own legend on the salt of Bonneville. This 1951 WR set the record for its class at 123.52 miles per hour.

Harley-Davidson and
THE AMA

By Ed Youngblood

Prior to 1966, Harley-Davidson motorcycles won 14 of the 24 races staged at Daytona. To dethrone the Harleys, Triumph spent a lot of money in 1966 and 1967, pushing the rule book to the limit and upping the ante for factory involvement in AMA competition. Factory racing had always existed in America, but after the Depression it frequently came in the form of parts, technical advice, and small amounts of money channeled to privateers through motorcycle dealers. But Triumph's 1966 assault was a direct factory effort, with salaried riders and special machines built in England especially for Daytona.

Following Triumph's victories in 1966 and 1967, Harley-Davidson responded with a vengeance in 1968, fielding new motorcycles and a seven-rider Wrecking Crew. Arguably, Daytona 1968 was the beginning of the modern era of road racing in America, and it was Harley-Davidson that was responsible for raising the stakes to a higher level. The team Harleys had all new body work, designed by Dean Wixom. They featured a wide, rump-hugging seat that helped the rider's body become part of the streamlining, and a beautifully sculpted gas tank with recesses where the rider's arms could be tucked in out of the air stream. The fairing and windscreen took the dimensional limits of the rule book to the absolute limit. The whole package, gel-coated in lustrous black and orange with white trim, was wind-tunnel developed, leaving no reminder whatsoever of the dirt track heritage of the side-valve KR power plant hidden inside.

Cal Rayborn, Mert Lawwill, Fred Nix, Bart Markel, Dan Haaby, Roger Reiman, and Walt Fulton were chosen to pilot this fleet of Harleys, and rather than the usual hodgepodge of personally designed leathers, Harley-Davidson provided team leathers in a standard livery of black, orange, and white. Others, such as Yamaha, turned up with larger and better appointed teams, but none so impressive and over-powering in size and appearance as the Harley squad. *Cycle News* publisher Chuck Clayton noted that something had changed in American road racing. Clayton wrote, "The new look at Daytona this year is factory team riders in bright leather uniforms and identical looking bikes." Harley-Davidson's massive effort delivered Daytona victories by Cal Rayborn in both 1968 and 1969, followed up with brilliant seasons. In 1968, Harleys won all four road races on the national circuit (Rayborn at Daytona, Loudon, and Indianapolis, and Fulton at Heidelberg), and in 1969 they won four of five (Rayborn at Daytona, Heidelberg, and Indianapolis, and Fred Nix at Loudon).

Then a rule change for the 1970 season made obsolete the 18-year-old KR engines. Engine capacity was set at 750 cc, regardless of valve-train technology, opening the door for modern, large capacity, multi-cylinder machines. Harley-Davidson bravely threw together its overhead-valve cast-iron XR for the 1970 season, but it had little hope of matching the fast multi-cylinder motorcycles produced overseas. Honda fielded a four-bike team at Daytona in 1970 and imported three of its riders from England. The fourth rider was race winner Dick Mann. Honda came, saw, conquered, and—having proven a point—disappeared from factory road racing. All of the XR-powered machines broke. The best-finishing Harley rider in the field was Walt Fulton, riding one of the old side-valve KR-powered bikes.

BSA and Triumph fielded five-rider teams on superbly constructed triples. Gene Romero earned second at Daytona with a Triumph in 1970, and Dick Mann won on a BSA in 1971, but the days of glory for the British marques were numbered. Like the shooting star on the side of a BSA gas tank, they went out in a blaze of glory, spending money as if they had it, while their market share—like Harley-Davidson's—declined under the onslaught of Japanese imports. All of the manufacturers—including Suzuki, Yamaha, and Kawasaki—fielded teams, many with imported riders, and most spent money that would have made Harley-Davidson's 1968–1969 budget look like cab fare.

The XR-powered Harleys failed to win a single race in 1970. Mark Brelsford won Loudon in 1971 and Rayborn pulled out wins in 1972 at Indianapolis and Laguna Seca. Then it was over. Except for secondary races like the Battle of the Twins and Twinsport classes in the 1980s and 1990s, Harley-Davidson has never won another national road race. By the time its new alloy XR

was developed and running, rapidly advancing two-stroke technology had rendered any push-rod four-stroke engine hopelessly obsolete.

When Harley-Davidson reentered the fray in the 1990s with its VR program, it seemed as if the Motor Company just didn't get it. It appeared to have no idea how quickly cutting-edge technology must be developed in the world of modern road racing, and how much money must be spent to be competitive and win. Today the machines, riders, and supporting programs must each be budgeted in seven figures. Harley-Davidson apparently was not prepared to spend that kind of money on the VR effort. It is ironic that the model for this kind of over-dog spending and rampant development can be traced back to the Wrecking Crew fielded by Harley-Davidson in 1968.

Harley-Davidson's 1968 factory race team

Al Nelson (kneeling), Daytona
Beach, 1940.

TT Race water crossing,
Minnesota, 1949.

THE KR: FORWARD...AND BACKWARD

As soon as the Allies' victory became a matter of when and not if, Harley executives began planning for the future. In their usual cautious manner, H-D introduced the little Model S, the 125-cc two-stroke single aimed at the youth and entry markets, but the really new bikes didn't arrive until 1952. Even then, new was relative. The new street machine was the Model K, a unit engine with unit-construction crankcase and gearbox, hand clutch, foot shirt. and rear suspension, that kept pace with the wildly expanded import market.

With the K came the KR and the KRTT. These were nearly direct descendents of the W, the WR and the WRTT. At first glance, the KR and KRTT looked like the street-going K minus road gear.

Again, not so. While the flathead K engine shared its bore, stroke, and 750-cc displacement with the KR, the R version used low-friction ball and roller bearings.

The K had needle bearings and bushings. The KR's valves were tipped toward the bore, like the WR's, and the camshaft timing was radically different. The ignition was magneto rather than the K's generator.

The KR frame featured no rear suspension. The KRTT used a swing arm that pivoted at the rear engine mount and had shock absorbers bolted to the swing arm at the bottom and the rear of the frame at the top.

There was a third model in the competition department book, albeit seldom seen in the showroom or in real life. This was the KRM, designed for racing in the western deserts. The KRM had a skimpy muffler and front fender and used roller main bearings, which lived longer, but otherwise was like the KRTT.

The AMA's national championship rules changed in 1954. Previously the AMA awarded the Number One plate to the winner at the Springfield, Illinois, mile. For 1954, the AMA devised a series that included

Brad Andres and Joe Leonard sparring at Daytona.

short track, half-mile, mile, TT, and road-course events, with points awarded at each event and the championship awarded to the rider with the most points.

By the early 1960s, imports had made major inroads and the AMA again changed the rules, with short track nationals contested by 250-cc production-based engines, modified and placed in special frames.

In another of those happy accidents, Harley-Davidson had replaced the home-grown two-stroke singles, the Hummers and kin, with four-strokes from Aermacchi, an Italian maker absorbed into H-D.

The Aermacchis—named Sprints for the U.S. market—provided the engines for the CRTT and CRS racers. The road-racing CRTT featured a tuned engine in a lightened stock frame modified with rearset controls, clip-on handlebars, and a choice of tanks and brakes. In 1963, the AMA allowed full fairings in the road-racing classes. The CR, the short track model, featured a lighter and lower frame, and lacked brakes and lights.

An Era Ends

There's no question these machines, the KR and KRTT especially, were successful racers. But racing doesn't stand any stiller than life, and as the 1960s closed, there was more and more proof that the old side-valve KR and the production-based C-series Sprints were on their way out.

Gary Nixon won the AMA title for Triumph in 1967 and 1968. Mert Lawwill restored the Number One plate to the Harley camp in 1969, but Gene Romero won for Triumph in 1970 and Dick Mann for BSA in 1971. Then came the two-strokes. Yamaha had a 350-cc two-stroke twin that was perfect for modification, and the little 350 became a match on the road courses for the big 750 side-valves and 500 overhead-valve singles. The AMA's competition committee, comprising racers and promoters as well as factory reps, was aware of all this and in 1968, they changed the Class C and AMA championship rules.

The production requirement remained, with 200 examples needed, although the machines need not be street legal. And there was simply a 750-cc limit, with valve location and number of cylinders free choice. The new rules were to apply to dirt track in 1969, and road racing in 1970. This set in motion a series of circumstances that led to the side-valve KR's last great achievements. The rule change came at a bad time for Harley-Davidson. The Motor Company was in deep financial trouble, about to be taken into the American Machine and Foundry conglomerate. In the long run, AMF kept H-D alive, but in the short run there was no money for a new, or at least up-to-date, racing program. When the 1969 season opened, Triumph and Gary Nixon came loaded for Milwaukee's Finest, with a Triumph twin and a triple, both of which were 750-cc overhead-valve engines producing more power than the side-valve KR ever dreamed.

When the Sportster was introduced in 1957, it was a hot drag racer, even in stock form. But stock wasn't good enough for many of the Sporty guys.

After the K models replaced the W, the KR, a racing model, replaced the WR. KRs competed and won on the dirt tracks and on the tarmac.

Nixon lost the National to H-D's Fred Nix, on a KR, and Harley's Cal Rayborn—arguably the best road racing talent of his or any era—won the 1968 Daytona 200 on a KRTT Lowboy, so called because the KRTT frame was lowered and wrapped around the engine, all tucked inside a full fairing.

But in 1969, the final version of the KRTT, featuring two carbs, a full fairing, and huge brakes, was inexplicably slower in qualifying than it had been the year before.

On race day, it rained. One week later, having used the providential time to sort out the two carbs, Rayborn won again. He won by outlasting the Yamahas, which were much faster. It doesn't say "Lucky Break" on the trophy, but something clearly had to be done.

THE NEW ERA BEGINS...BADLY

When the new rules were announced, team boss Dick O'Brien and engineer Peter Zylstra knew they were in for a tough time. There wasn't much time and there was less money to come up with a competitive race bike. For inspiration, they went back to 1958, when the new XL Sportster got an unpublicized teammate, the XLR. This was mostly an XL top end, but with hotter camshafts and bigger valves, atop KR cases with the ball and roller bearings from that racing engine. The XLR was built for national TT races, which at the time allowed overhead valves.

The XLR was a competitive TT mount, so when the racing department needed a new 750-cc racer, the engineers shortened the XLR's stroke, revised the camshafts to suit the displacement and timing, and put the engine in a mildly reworked version of the KRTT frame. The new model was named the XR-750. It was a beautiful motorcycle, as clean and crisp as any racer

Following pages

Underneath that late-1960s fiberglass beats the heart of Bill Harley's 1929 flathead design. Only AMA rules that allowed flatheads a 50 percent displacement advantage over their overhead-valve counterparts kept the flatheads competitive.

The great Cal Rayborn at the Imola 200 in Italy, 1973

The AMA changed Class C rules in 1969 to eliminate the displacement advantage long held by flatheads, so Harley went the overhead-valve route, too, with the original XR-750. Unfortunately, the cast-iron iteration of the XR was not successful.

Below and right
For 1972, Harley reworked the XR750, using aluminum alloy in place of cast-iron. The resulting motorcycle was the winner you see here. With few changes, this model still dominates flat-track racing today.

ever made. And it was a disaster. The XL engine used cast-iron for the cylinders and heads, while the big Harley twins had used aluminum heads since 1948. The XLR raced TT, which required short bursts of power followed by braking and turning, while the mile and half-mile courses kept the power on all the time. The iron retained heat and the engine melted, earning the XR-750 the nickname "The Waffle Iron."

As the rules required, the factory assembled 200 XR-750s and offered them for sale. There was a separate run of XR-750s for road racing, with revised Lowboy frames and bodywork. The equipment appeared in the 1970 catalog as the "Road Race Group."

The road racers debuted at Daytona and promptly blew up. The 1970 season was a debacle. The team and racing department did some incredible and extensive work on the ironhead XR, all to no avail. Factory records show approximately 100, 1970 XR-750s sold, with the leftovers dismantled and put back in the parts department, or spirited out of the factory.

Here's what the XR is all about: nose-to-tail, crossed-up, dirt-slinging competition.

Harley even raced Aermacchi-built two-stroke road racers. Shown is an RR-250.

The iron XR had one heroic occasion. Late in 1971, the H-D team was invited to a series of road races in England. The team's alloy XRs weren't ready and the brass didn't want to look bad, but Cal Rayborn wanted to go. Walt Faulk, an H-D employee, had built his own iron XR engine, so he and Rayborn went off to England.

They're still a legend there. Faulk somehow kept the fragile engine alive just long enough to finish each race—the cold English weather didn't hurt—and Rayborn rode the wheels off the bike. He won three of the six races and came in second in the other three. Say "XR" to an English fan to this day, and he'll say, "like Calvin rode."

THE ALLOY XR

If there was a good side to the Waffle Iron's failure, it's that O'Brien and Zylstra and the team had a chance to do a lot of research. It paid off. For the 1972 season, with AMF willing to invest in the product, the team introduced another XR-750. This time it was done right, with alloy heads and barrels, twin carburetors, and an absolutely up-to-date racing engine, still in the classic 45-degree V-twin.

The alloy XR began with as much power as the hand-grenade iron XR had in its final form. Then, the alloy XR got better. Also thanks to AMF, the team could hire riders, the top men. In the dirt, the alloy XR was king. Mark Brelsford won the AMA title in 1972.

The RR-250 and RR-350 gave
Harley-Davidson its only
world titles.

Then the racing world changed. Yamaha's 350 two-stroke twins were competitive and its 650 four-stroke street conversion was almost as good as an XR-750 in the dirt. For road courses, Yamaha built the TZ700, a full-race 700-cc two-stroke with all the brakes and streamlining that it needed. Yamaha shipped enough of them to the United States to qualify for Class C racing, and Kenny Roberts Sr. won the AMA championship in 1973 and 1974.

The four-stroke twins built by the Yanks and the Brits weren't competitive with the two-stroke fours from Yamaha or the two-stroke triples from Kawasaki. Harley-Davidson's road-racing XRTT faded away. The team used the model for several seasons and took part in some European races, but Harley's team was never again a factor in AMA road racing.

THE NEW LIGHTWEIGHTS

Aermacchi had been involved in racing long before H-D absorbed the company. The Italians went through the same painful learning experience at the

hands of Yamaha, and responded with two-stroke twins of their own, in 250-cc and 350-cc versions.

The machines attracted top talent, notably Walter Villa, who rode the water-cooled twins to the world 250 title in 1974, 1975, and 1976. Villa also won the 350 title in 1974. The 1974 championship was Harley-Davidson's first world title.

The AMA had a road-race class for 250s, so Harley homologated the Aermacchi as the RR-250. In its debut, the RR-250 piloted by Gary Scott beat Yamaha's national and later world champion Kenny Roberts. But it never happened again, and because the 250 class was the junior class and didn't count toward the national championship, the RR-250 faded away.

Aermacchi and Harley tried the Yamaha approach, doubling the 250 twin into a 500-cc four, but it was too complex and too far from what H-D was actually selling to customers to justify the expense.

Next came a 500-cc twin, a radically enlarged version of the RR-250, and designated (what else?) the RR-500. The RR-500 had lots of power. Gary Scott,

For a time in the 1970s, Harley even got serious about motocross and built a pretty fair competitor in the MX-250. This one's been lowered for flat-track racing.

In an attempt to give racing back to the common man, Harley sponsored a special series of races for the 883 Sportsters.

who won the AMA Number One plate for Harley in 1975, rode the RR-500 in Europe but spun out in the rain. The Harley team went to the AMA national at Laguna Seca and was in the hunt when a clamp loosened. Scott retired and the Harley never raced RR-500 again. Why not? Scott and O'Brien agreed that the RR-500 wasn't competitive, and that the money and time needed to make it so would be better spent on the XR-750. Which it was.

THE XR RULES

By the late 1970s, the XR-750 was the best motorcycle in dirt track racing (which evolved into a separate series from road racing), so much so that the English teams withdrew. The alloy XR-750 was truly a production motorcycle, for racing if not for road use. The first 200 sold out, so in 1975 the factory built another 100 dirt models. There were also 50 frames

The
VR-1000

By Allan Girdler

When Harley-Davidson announced the closing and dismantling of the VR-1000 Superbike program late in the 2001 racing season, there couldn't have been a Harley racing fan who didn't feel equal parts chagrin and relief.

The VR-1000 program was the worst and most puzzling failure in H-D's long racing history, all the more so perhaps because the wound was self-inflicted. No outsider is privy to the record, so we don't know who made the calls or what motivated the decisions, but in the late 1980s, someone at H-D decided to field a team for the AMA's Superbike series. Harley had been out of American road racing's premiere class for years.

In 1994, the VR-1000 appeared, ready to race. The basic concept made sense: a 60-degree V-twin with overhead camshafts, four valves per cylinder, water cooling, fuel injection, and electronically pro-

The ill-fated VR-1000 road racer.

grammed ignition. The VR was state of the art, which means it was more or less the same as the competition.

During the VR-1000's seven years on the track, the VR led two races, was on the pole once, qualified on the front row at Daytona once, and was on the podium twice, (one second place and one third). Yet it failed to win a single race, in spite of being ridden by some of the finest racers ever to ride on American race tracks. The roster of VR-1000 riders includes AMA national dirt track champ Chris Carr as well as Superbike champions Doug Chandler and Scott Russell, the latter a multi-time Daytona 200 winner and World Superbike champion. Miguel DuHamel, who has won every class there is on a Honda, fought his way into the leading pack at the 1994 Daytona 200 aboard a VR-1000, but lost the race when his pit crew couldn't manage to change the rear tire. An international audience watched the whole debacle on live television.

What the hell went wrong? The answer depends on whom you ask. Perhaps the VR-1000 was a loser because it didn't deserve to win. When the VR program was begun, Harley-Davidson had a winning racing team and competition department, with engineers, managers, tuners, and expediters. They were all shut out. Literally. From Eric Buell to Peter Zylstra to Bill Werner to Dick O'Brien, all the men who'd built winning motorcycles, who drove Yamaha and Triumph from the field, who'd designed an engine Honda had to copy, all those guys were deemed not smart enough, worthy enough, or educated enough. The execs banned the racing guys from the lab. They hired an outsider to design the chassis, let the H-D engineering department do the lower end of the VR engine, and farmed the top end—the heads and induction and exhausts—out to some car guys. In selecting a company to design the top end, the powers that be could have chosen between John Britten, who'd created a winning motorcycle in his own garage, or Cosworth Engineering, most notable for building a failed motorcycle engine for the street. They hired Cosworth.

It got worse. Chris Carr and Kenny Tolbert had won the AMA dirt title. Carr hoped to expand his career, following the examples of Kenny Roberts and Bubba Shobert, who went from dirt to road racing. Carr and Tolbert switched to the road-race team. These were two guys who knew how to win races, but every time Carr and Tolbert had an idea about how to improve the bike, every time they asked to change this or move that, they were turned down. So Carr and Tolbert went back to their dirt-track roots, and since then have won the GNC (Grand National Championship) twice.

Next, the V-Rod was introduced. As detailed elsewhere, the V-Rod is Harley's new radical and impressive road warrior. It's water-cooled, powered by a 1,000-cc, 60-degree V-twin. That aside, it has nothing in common, not one part or piece, with the VR-1000.

As soon as V-Rod was announced, the VR-1000 was killed. The program was disbanded, and Pascal Picotte, the rider who'd done the most and worked the hardest, was out of a job. Thus ends the sad story of the VR-1000.

In the early 1990s, Harley tried to compete in Superbike racing with its VR-1000. Despite spending lots of money and hiring top-shelf riders, Superbike competition was Harley's only unsuccessful endeavor in the 1990s.

made for road racing in 1972, with lower steering heads and frame backbones wrapped around the engine. There was another run in 1976–1977, and 200 more came off the production line in 1980. Since then there have been other production runs at the foundry.

Nature fills vacuums, and Honda and Yamaha returned to Grand National Championship (GNC, as the AMA shorthands it) in 1981, both with stupendously reworked versions of their road-going V-twins.

Neither worked. But while Yamaha quit losers and retired from the battle, Honda bought an XR-750, took it home, dismantled it and asked themselves, "What would Harley-Davidson have done, if Harley-Davidson had our money?" Then, they did it. The RS750 featured an overhead-cam engine with four valves per cylinder. Honda had built a better Harley. Honda went on to win the AMA title with Ricky Graham in 1984, and with Bubba Shobert in 1985, 1986, and 1987.

The AMA decided that because there were a couple hundred Harleys and a handful of Hondas and the Honda had the better engine, the racing wasn't fair. So the Honda engines were restricted, evening out the power difference. Harley's Scott Parker won the GNC title in 1988.

Honda withdrew from dirt track and the XR-750 has been the winning machine ever since.

ON THE ROAD RACE...AGAIN

When Yamaha's two-stroke four took over the road races on the AMA circuit, the fans lost interest. In 1983, race promoters tried to revive fan interest by inventing a new series: The Battle of the Twins. At that

Harley hired Cosworth to help design the VR-1000 engine.

On the dirt, Harley-Davidson could not have been more successful in the 1990s, nor could this guy, Scott Parker.

same time, H-D introduced the XR-1000, a Sportster with a version of the XR-750's two-carb top end. O'Brien and the racing shop took some old XRTT parts, converted an XR-750 engine into an XR-1000, put Jay Springsteen on board and won the race going away. Those who were there still remember the look on the leading Ducati rider's face when Springsteen caught him in the corner, pulled even, then motored away.

The team handed the equipment over to a factory-backed privateer, Harley dealer Don Tilley, and with help from the Harley Owner's Group, Tilley and rider Gene Church ruled The Battle of the Twins series for

the next three years. It wasn't exactly a major series, nor was the machine—named *Lucifer's Hammer* by O'Brien, a Harley racer in the tradition of the WR or the KR—but it did make the H-D fans happy and it did fill the grandstand at Daytona.

Meanwhile, there were changes inside the GNC and out. The AMA dropped the 250-cc limit for short track and mandated 500-cc singles for that class as well as the TT class. Harley-Davidson didn't make a big single, but there was no problem. H-D simply arranged for Rotax, the Austrian engine maker, to sell racing engines through Harley dealers.

These views show what Parker's fans saw.

Following page
And this shows the view Parker's competitors saw, until he retired while still on top.

363

LUCIFER'S HAMMER AND A NEW ERA

By 1986, the AMA had made another set of changes. In response to public taste, the Superbike class had been expanded, eventually eclipsing the two-stroke class, known as Formula One. The Japanese focused on road racing, and AMA's GNC was left to Harley-Davidson.

As a result, the GNC became a battle of riders and tuners, everyone beginning with the same parts and rules, and the XR-750, like the Offenhauser Indy engine and the Cosworth V-8 in Formula One, dominated its class for a generation. Still, there was plenty of competition, even if the XR-750 was the only competitive

mount, and there was constant improvement to the engine. But times are changing. For the 2002 season, the AMA admits certain motorcycles with 1,000-cc overhead-cam engines and the 1,200-cc overhead-valve engines into the GNC, provided they are fitted with devices to restrict their power output.

This means the 1,200-cc Buells and Suzuki's TL1000, which features a 1,000-cc V-twin engine, equal the mighty XR-750 in power output. If the XR-750 won't do the job against the new competition, there will be a racing Buell (or a new XL engine) that will.

Walter Davidson wouldn't have had it any other way.

Racers use Rotax-powered Harleys on short tracks.

Epilogue

THE FUTURE

By Steve Anderson

arley has had a kickass first century. It rode the first motorcycle boom, survived the Model T, defined the American motorcycle with its Knucklehead, became part of a huge conglomerate, produced tens of thousands of machines of questionable quality in the seventies, escaped the huge conglomerate and teetered on extinction in the early eighties, designed and introduced much-improved-yet-still-classic products, and went on to almost unimaginable success going into its hundredth birthday. So what comes next?

Predicting the future is a fool's game, and never more so than when those speculations are about technology and products. Think back to all those predictions from the mid-twentieth century of a gyrocopter in every garage, of a world of flying cars and Ma Bell picture phones. Instead, we got tank-like SUVs and spam e-mail. In 1980, the future was tiny diesel cars and six-cylinder motorcycles. The V-twin was written off as a dead configuration and the smart money bet was that Harley would not survive to see its 100th anniversary.

So before making any rash long-range predictions, it's worthwhile to take a look back at Harley's most recent effort, the V-Rod. What does it tell us about the Motor Company's future?

THE V-ROD

The 2002 V-Rod broke away from Harley's Big Twin heritage. A Porsche-designed engine—an engine with twin cams instead of pushrods, four-valves in each cylinder, fuel-injection, and water-cooling—powered the aluminum-skinned bike. It redlined at 9,000 rpm and easily pumped 115 horsepower or more at the crankshaft. It was not your father's Harley.

But the V-Rod, regardless of its innovations, was still solidly rooted in Harley's past—its recent past, that is. As Harley-Davidson Powertrain Engineer Joe Schafter noted of the V-Rod's Revolution engine, "We

367

Opening page

The V-Rod's styling took its cues from Harley's Softail Deuce, especially with its custom-looking rear fender.

noise reduction was the most compelling reason for Harley to have a new design for the Revolution. Noise laws worldwide have been getting stricter. As a 21st-century engine, the Revolution had to make meeting 21st-century regulations easier.

The need for a new design around a known architecture drove the second important aspect of the V-Rod project: the hiring of Porsche to handle the details. "We were pretty busy with the Twin Cam when this project started," said Coughlin—so busy that an engineering shortage prevented Harley from doing the engine in-house. Porsche Engineering, the car company's consulting division, had worked closely with Harley before, including designing the never-produced V-Four Nova in the last days of AMF ownership. Now Harley turned to Porsche again, enlisting the Germans and just a small team of Milwaukee engineers to help transform the VR concept into a new engine. The emphasis would be on strength, produceability, and quiet running, rather than the performance-at-any-cost or at-any-noise-level goals of the VR.

It's not hard to find Porsche's influence inside the Revolution. The five-speed gearbox comes from German supplier Gertag (manufacturer of BMW motorcycle gearsets). As in most Porsche engines, the Revolution's connecting rods are forged in one piece with end caps cracked away after the big end is machined for perfect alignment.

But if the V-Rod's engine was a joint project, the rest of the machine was all Milwaukee, the manifestation of a vision of Willie G. Davidson and his colleagues in Harley's styling department. They began playing with a racing VR engine years ago, trying out such things as building a VR-powered Softail—or "learning what not to do," in Willie G's words. The proportions of a modern racing engine like the VR are completely different from classic Harley powerplants. The shrink-wrapped cases and small primary drives and gearboxes of modern engines have none of the visual mass of a Big Twin, and one simply can't take the place of the other. So Willie G. and company began looking for a different type of vehicle to house the engine.

The idea of a drag-racing-influenced machine was a natural. It fit with the high-performance goals of the new engine, and it fit with Willie's vision. Motorcycle drag racers had long swingarms to minimize wheelies; a long swingarm would look right coupled to the Revolution's short gearbox. They were long and low, and Willie liked that look. He also wanted the raked-out front ends that drag racers traditionally had. But that part of the vision initially ran into engineering resistance. "They told us it wouldn't work," he said. "And styling told engineering, 'you can't say no until you've tried it'." So soon after, a Sportster test bike was given a new 34-degree steering head, with the forks kicked out another 4 degrees via offset triple clamps— a trick that Harley has been using for years on FL's.

kept the VR's (the VR1000, Harley's Superbike racer) architecture." Both the Revolution and the racing-only VR (a project started in the late eighties) share some basic features not found on other Harley engines. Start with the 60-degree V-angle, 15 degrees wider than that of Harley's air-cooled engines.

At the VR's introduction, Jeff Coughlin, Harley's project leader for the V-Rod, commented on even more similarities between the two. "The balance shaft of the VR has stayed, and in relatively the same position." A 21st-century motorcycle can't vibrate annoyingly— with the rapid acceptance of the counterbalanced Softails, Harley customers had already signaled that they were ready for the low-vibration future.

In a trend that will shape every Harley-Davidson engine design in the future, the quest for mechanical

Prior to the introduction of the V-Rod, the Super Glide Sport was Harley's hottest Big Twin.

That test Sportster handled well, so the V-Rod was granted its signature raked-out look.

On other parts of the machine, the stylists gave ground from the beginning. On Big Twins and Sportsters, they had for decades insisted on tiny, traditional mufflers—the shortie duals of a Big Twin have less than a liter of volume apiece, and simply can't be quiet and non-restrictive at the same time. For the V-Rod, the mufflers and airbox would have to be huge to achieve the expected stock performance. Harley styling director Louie Netz says, "We knew we could solve the exhaust system—we knew we could make it a part of the look. The air cleaner, though—well, we knew we weren't going to hang it from the side. We'd already seen that on Buells." That left only one place for the airbox to go, above the engine in the normal gas tank location. The gas tank would have to go under the seat, which in turn dictated twin shocks—there was no room for both gasoline and a single shock in front of the back tire.

Willie G. and company also had a clear picture of what they wanted the V-Rod's frame to look like—they wanted it to literally frame the engine, like a picture frame, and "to hang the engine in space." Unlike most other Harley's—other than the FXRs—the V-Rod frame would be prominent on the outside of the bike, so it was vital it should look good. From the engineering point of view, it was equally vital that it be stiff for good handling. With these needs, styling and engineering began an iterative collaboration that ended with the design of the V-Rod frame you see today. Big tubes were good, because they could give adequate strength with ungussetted joints—a clean look that scored high with styling. The big tubes scored high with engineering for stiffness. Manufacturing processes

The First
PORSCHE-HARLEY

By Greg Field

As the V-Rod proves, great things can come when Porsche and Harley-Davidson collaborate on a project. What many people don't realize is that there was an earlier and even more elaborate collaboration between the two companies, but only one piece of it ever saw the light of day.

It all came out of the same golfing retreat that spawned the Evolution. In addition to developing a next-generation Harley V-twin (the Evo), Vaughn Beals and the others involved decided Harley needed to develop a series of high-tech, water-cooled, overhead-cam "modular" engines. "It was to be a family—a V-twin, a V-4, and a V-6," explained Don Valentine, Harley's former chief of powertrains.

At the time, though, AMF had more money than Harley had engineers, so they decided to develop the Evo in-house and farm out the water-cooled projects. After reviewing proposals from a number of companies, Harley selected Porsche Design to pen and develop the bikes that would be called Nova. Why Nova? "Nova is latin for new," Beals explained. "Mike (Hillman, project lead for the Nova) probably named it; he was better educated than most of us."

The only Novas built were V-4s. "It was a typical German-engineered product—very nice!" Valentine remembered. "They built like 10 bikes for testing. It was a different breed of motorcycle. First off, it was water-cooled, and it had huge air horns on what would be the side of the fuel tank for ducting air to the radiator and induction system." The radiator was behind the engine and the real fuel tank was underneath the seat, with a car-type fuel filler on the side of the tailpiece. The "gas tank" over the engine was a fake; it was really just a shroud over the induction system.

Based on the remaining NOVA bikes in Harley's collection, at least three versions were planned, and they all looked good.

One was a muscular street rod that looks very similar to the later Yamaha V-Max (and some at the Motor Company insist that Yamaha stole the look). One difference was that the scoops on the sides of the fake gas tank were real and functional on the Nova, while they are fakes on the V-Max.

Another was a sleek sport-tourer, and one piece of it actually made it to production. Ever wonder why the FXRT fairing looked awkward and out of place on a Big Twin and why it had those cheek scoops? That fairing was plucked from the sport-touring Nova, and the scoops were to duct air to the Nova's tank-side scoops. That fairing looks graceful and natural on the Nova.

Another was a full-boat tourer with the FLT fairing. Even that fairing looked good and natural on the Nova.

Harley developed the bike and brought in a group of dealers and fast riders to test it out against the competing fast multis from Europe and Japan. "We were all pleased with it," Vaughn Beals said. "It was a great engine and a great chassis. I'm not the world's greatest rider, but I can sure tell the difference between a motorcycle that works with you and one that works against you. The Nova worked with you. By comparison, I rode I think it was a Honda V-4. I thought the goddamned thing was gonna put me in the bull rushes. You had to damn near throw it into the turn. It did nothing, that I could see, willingly."

By some estimates, AMF put $10 million into the Nova. Once Harley was on its own, there was no money to finish development and retool to build it, though Harley tried. The MoCo even tried jacking loan guarantees out of the Japanese by offering to ask that the tariffs be lifted in exchange.

Harley never did find a financier for the Nova, which may have been a blessing. By the time it had the money to build it on its own, the need had passed.

Though even its fairing is now out of production, some bits of the Nova may live on in Porsche's design for the V-Rod engine, but no one's saying.

were stressed to the limit for strength and appearance. All the joints are robotically welded to produce crisp, well-finished welds. The top frame tubes swoop in complex curves that couldn't have been made at all a few years ago; now they're produced by hydroforming the tubes in hard dies that are capable of producing the three-dimensional shapes agreed upon by stylists and engineers.

Similarly, both engineers and stylists sweated the details on the radiator and oil coolers. There was no way that Willie G. was going to let the V-Rod ship with some black-painted boxy radiator on it, like some Japanese and European bikes. "It had to be an integral part of the design," he said. "Black paint doesn't make the radiator invisible." The solution emerged when both engineers and stylists were working together doing wind tunnel testing. It became clear that the space immediately behind the front tire was dead to airflow, and you might as well block the front of the radiator there. The next logical step was to make side scoops that caught clean air and directed it into the radiator. When those scoops were made of the same signature aluminum that covers the rest of the bike, Willie had the shape of his styling-integrated cooling system.

That aluminum was, in and of itself, another internal battle inside Harley-Davidson. No one doubted it was cool, and the engineers had no problems with the strong and light material. Instead, Manufacturing questioned whether the aluminum parts could be produced at a reasonable price. The fenders, air box cover, and radiator shrouds would all be anodized aluminum protected by only a thin clear coat. Anyone who's spent anytime around a factory might question how such parts could make it through the manufacturing and assembly process without scratches, and how closely the color match could be held from one batch to another. As manufacturing experimented and hesitated to commit—after all, they would have to build it—Willie G. bombarded the manager of the Kansas City plant with e-mails, each containing a single word: "ALUMINUM." Whether it was this barrage or the completion of trials and experiments, manufacturing conceded: The V-Rod would gleam in the metal just like a thirties DC-3, and look just as ready to take wing.

When you see a V-Rod in the metal, you're first struck by that gleaming silver, and by its size: It's long and very low. You can sit on it with your feet flat on the ground. While the spec sheet tells you that the V-Rod

With its brushed aluminum body work, tubular frame, and disc wheels, the V-Rod looked like no other motorcycle ever built. Brushed aluminum bodywork requires special cleaning supplies, but it makes the V-Rod stand out in a crowd.

Though limited ground clearance hinders handling at racetrack speeds, the V-Rod can claim Harley's VR1000 Superbike racer as its ancestor. The liquid-cooled 60-degree V-twin engine, with its four-valves-per-cylinder top end, provided the basic architecture for the V-Rod engine. But as advanced as the VR engine is, not even the great Miguel DuHamel (shown), the winningest rider in AMA history, could put it at the top of the superbike podium.

weighs in at over 600 pounds wet, that's not what your senses tell you. The machine feels small, narrow, and light, more Sportster than Big Twin in weight. Credit that to a low center of gravity, to a bike that carries its engine low and puts a featherweight airbox up high and its 24 pounds of gasoline well below the seat.

The traditional Harley round ignition key fits just below the right side of that seat. Turn it to the "on" position, and red warning lights wake up on the big speedometer dial, and the electronically controlled speedo, fuel-gauge, and tach needles sweep from zero to maximum and back again, just letting you know they're working. Push the starter button, and, almost before you know it's spinning, the cold V-Rod is idling at 1,500 rpm. There's none of the long loping pauses that add drama to the idle of Big Twins; you know just by listening to it the V-Rod isn't going to die if you go back into the house to get your gloves while it's warming up. The engine is smooth, too—there's just the faintest quiver that you can feel at the end of the bars.

Pull out onto the street, and you quickly realize that the while the V-Rod feels light, it also feels nothing like a Sportster. First, the seat is lower, and you sit more down into the V-Rod than on top of it. Second, it's roomy, with the pegs and controls a comfortable stretch away, rivaling if not bettering Softails for legroom.

Run the V-Rod out to 5,000 rpm, and you're in the heart of a meaty midrange, the revs climbing quickly. From there it's just a blink to the 9,000 rpm red line; it's all too easy to bang against the rev limiter, which momentarily kills the engine. But if you're attentive and click into second quickly, you're rewarded with a further forward lunge, and yet another through third. You can be at 100 miles per hour in just seconds, with the V-Rod still pulling hard. Tuck in like Scottie Parker and hold on tight, and you'll soon be rewarded with a top speed never before seen on a production Harley: 140 miles per hour.

What is truly exceptional is how smoothly, readily, and precisely the V-Rod gives you this performance. The injection provides seamless mixture control, so that power delivered exactly matches what your throttle hand requests. Vibration is almost—but not quite—non-existent: There's just enough reaching you past the counterbalancer's efforts and through the rubber mounts to know that there's a V-twin powering this machine, and not an electric motor.

In handling, the V-Rod sets its own course. Its long wheelbase and raked-out steering make for a machine that feels slightly ungainly at parking lot speeds, but fortunately its low seating position and low center of gravity keep rider confidence high. At any road speed, the V-Rod stabilizes wonderfully, and its stout 48-mm fork tubes ensure a solid connection between handlebars and tire. Turn the bars, and—particularly at 30 miles per hour or less—the V-Rod almost seems to have power steering, falling into turns eagerly.

All-in-all, the V-Rod was functionally and visually the winner that Harley was looking for, leading to the all-too-usual waiting lists and dealer price gouging. Once again, Harley's formula of creating a style-driven motorcycle backed by serious function and reliability had proved its worth.

THE FUTURE: THE V-ROD

So what does the V-Rod tell us about Harley's future? For instance, will the V-Rod replace any existing Harley motorcycle? Ask that of any Harley official, and all you'll hear back is an emphatic, "No!" The V-Rod extends rather than replaces any of Harley's

offerings. In the very near future you can expect even more extension, as Harley branches further with a family of Revolution-powered machines.

Expect these new Revolution bikes to express their diversity much as various Dynas do, in both appearance and function. Harley has tooled its frame manufacturing lines so the steering head angle can be easily altered, and it's a safe bet that some of the new Revolution machines won't have the extreme front end rake of the V-Rod. Also, as the V-Rod has been intended to expand Harley's European presence, some of the variations will almost certainly offer the V-Rod's power in a better handling package. A street-fighter variant would seem likely, a larger machine with greater emphasis on power than comparable Buells, as well as a custom-sport-touring machine. But do keep in mind that Harley's entire marketing drive in the last two decades has been to be where there competitors aren't—so perhaps Willie G. will surprise us with the next Revolution.

THE FUTURE: SPORTSTERS

So if the V-Rod isn't going to replace the Sportster, what will? A Sportster, of course. As this is written in the Spring of 2002, rumors flow freely that

The V-Rod's engine is one of the strongest V-twin powerplants on the market.

The V-Rod's complex frame required entirely new manufacturing techniques.

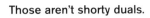

Those aren't shorty duals.

The custom styling touches on the V-Rod extended to the comprehensive instrument pod.

Also expect vibration to be dealt with, either through engine counterbalancers or through rubber-mounting. Why? Listen to Program Manager Dave Rank at the Twin Cam Softail Beta introduction in 2000: "The time was right to reduce vibration. There's always the hard-core that says 'You take the vibration out of the Softail and we're not going to like it very much.' But we've been listening to our customers and people at demo rides. Tastes change and we needed to stop beating people up." The Softail no longer shakes, so don't expect the next Sportster to do so either. Do expect a much slicker, more refined machine that retains the Sportster look while adding a lot of the V-Rod's smooth and seamless operation.

THE FUTURE: THE BIG TWIN

In the short run, the Twin Cam is the Big Twin, period. Expect it to eventually grow in size, and to thus utilize some of the strength and room that Harley engineering gave the engine from the beginning. Production 103-cubic-inch machines (about 1,700 cc) may well be seen in the next years, using both the 3-and-7/8-inch bore and the 4-and-3/4-inch stroke of the Screaming Eagle big-bore and stroker kits, respectively.

As far as chassis changes over the next few years, all you have to do is to look at what custom builders are doing to get some idea of what Harley will offer in the near future. Eight-inch-wide, low-profile radial rear tires are showing up on more and more customs;

Disc wheels added an even tricker look to this unique machine.

Porsche helped design the V-Rod's 60-degree liquid-cooled V-twin powerplant.

new Sportsters will be released for the centennial model year. And a preview of the new Sportster's heart has likely already been seen in the Buell Firebolt powerplant, which is in many ways a second evolution of the Evo Sportster motor. Redesigned for reliability, ease of manufacture, and more power, the Firebolt motor mounts its swingarm on the back of its cases and reverses the direction of cam rotation. Oil jets cool the pistons and larger cylinder and head finning provide more cooling. For the Firebolt, as on the Buell Blast, plastic tunnels cover the pushrods, something that Louie Netz and Willie G. are unlikely to approve for a Sportster. Expect any new Sportster to have chromed round pushrod tubes and to look like a Sportster.

expect more Big Twins to move the belt-line out to make room for such fittings. Bridge-stiff male-slider front forks are showing up on a number of customs; that would be another natural for a new Harley Big Twin model, perhaps in a Dyna chassis. As far as bits of technology making their transition to Milwaukee motorcycles, surely anti-lock brakes will one day be seen, as well as things like microprocessor-controlled suspension components. Indeed, you can imagine sometime in the near future, where those two technologies are almost uniformly used on all motor vehicles.

Also, a new FL chassis is long overdue, and new Electra Glides and Road Kings will eventually have to make an appearance. Any such revision will likely be evolutionary, preserving the traditional look of such classic machines while adding function. Any new chassis, for example, will be much, much stiffer to offer better handling and stability margins than the current chassis. Taking a cue from the V-Rod, such a new machine might offer an aluminum swingarm for both functional and aesthetic reasons. But which engine will power it: the regular Twin Cam or the counterbalanced Twin Cam Beta? For these machines, it wouldn't be surprising to see the Beta engine mounted in reduced-travel rubber mounts, allowing tighter engine-to-frame packaging with new levels of smoothness. All speculative, of course, but surely something must be in the works.

In the longer term, technical change, whether you like it or not, will likely accelerate. While the Shovelhead lasted a couple of decades, and the Evolution endured 15 years, the Twin Cam will likely be replaced sooner than that, perhaps in just 10 years or so. Why? Partly because of intensifying competition from other motorcycle builders, partly because Harley will have the engineering capabilities to come out with superior new engines.

So what might a Big Twin circa 2010 to 2015 look like? Assume that for tradition's sake it retains an air-cooled, 45-degree V-twin configuration. But remove any cam mechanism from the engine, and replace it with the sort of electro-hydraulic valve actuation that's under development at automobile companies around the world. So pushrods would be gone, and the cylinder head becomes a simple finned piece, something like that you might find on a flathead, but interrupted by a couple of aluminum top hats for the valve actuators. Fuel injection would be direct into the cylinders, and the engine would be capable of extremely lean air-fuel ratio operation under part throttle cruising. That combined with the variable valve timing would allow an extremely broad and torquey power band, and allow gearing to be set so tall that the engine would loaf along at 1,500-1,800 rpm or so on the highway, while still maintaining stout roll-on capability.

But note what stays the same in such an advanced powerplant: the narrow-angle V-twin configuration and air-cooling. There's every indication that, with

very careful engineering, air-cooled engines will be able to meet noise and emission laws into the foreseeable future. And as long as that is true, expect Big Twins to stay air-cooled and true to their heritage.

Also expect some surprises from the very energized and expanding Motor Company. Harley now has the resources to do both the traditional and the unexpected, so there may be mid-size water-cooled hot-rods or low-cost singles that emerge in the future, or even a range topper custom that comes in above the Big Twin—anything is possible. The main thing is to expect Harley to continue to listen closely to its customers, to continue to have people who ride and love motorcycles plan the next products, to continue to give us motorcyclists the machines we want. And if it can continue to do that, the Motor Company should have a wild ride through another century.

Happy 100th anniversary Harley-Davidson.

Man of the
HARLEY CENTURY

By Greg Field

Time gets to pick a Man of the Year every year. We're not so greedy. All we want is Harley-Davidson's Man of the Century.

Here's my list of the best candidates, in no particular order:

William S. Harley, founder and first chief engineer.

Arthur Davidson, founder, secretary, and general sales manager.

Walter Davidson, founder, first president, and general manager.

William A. Davidson, founder, vice president and works manager.

William H. Davidson, second president.

William G. Davidson, member of the buy-back team, vice president in charge of styling, and creator of classic Harley designs.

Vaughn Beals, former CEO and leader of the buy-back and resurrection of Harley-Davidson.

Jeff Bleustein, member of the buy-back team, rebuilder of Harley's engineering department, and current CEO.

Tom Gelb, vice president in charge of operations, and initiator of all the productivity and quality improvements that kept Harley alive during the early 1980s and allowed it to grow into the success it is today.

Rich Teerlink, former CEO and the man who saved the day in refinancing the Citicorp debt.

Envelope, please!

And the winner is...sorry, I can't pick just one.

All of them (and many others) made huge contributions to Harley's first century. All of them deserve an award and our thanks, but none stands that clearly above the others.

I think I can narrow it down to four, though, so I propose something different: Instead of a Man of the Century, how about a Wisconsin version of Mount Rushmore? You could call it Mount Hogmore or something like that.

Anchoring one end, I'd put the smiling face of William S. Harley, for getting the whole thing rolling and designing so many great motorcycles.

Beaming next to Harley would be his childhood chum, Arthur Davidson, for being half of the dynamic duo that sparked the whole thing and for his tireless efforts in setting up the dealer network that helped the company grow in the early years and kept it alive through the Depression.

In the middle of this Harley group hug, I'd sculpt the bald-eagle visage of Vaughn Beals, the man who pulled the company out of the gutter, cleaned it up, and set it back on the road to greatness.

Framing the other end, I'd put the bearded, grinning face of Willie G., the man who showed Harley who its best customers were, gave the company back its style, and served as the Motor Company's affable human face for the last 30 years.

Harley, Davidson, Beals, and Davidson—it's the true portrait of Harley's first century.

H-D founders (left to right) William A. Davidson, Walter Davidson, Arthur Davidson, William S. Harley.

ABOUT THE AUTHORS AND PHOTOGRAPHERS

Steve Anderson A former editor of *Cycle* magazine, Steve Anderson now writes for *Cycle World*. He is a long-time friend of Erik Buell's, and a life-long fan of the motorcycles built by Harley-Davidson.

Kevin Cameron Kevin Cameron is one of today's most respected authorities on motorcycle technology. His *Cycle* magazine column "TDC" proved so popular that after the demise of *Cycle*, the column lived on in the pages of *Cycle World*. He is the author of *Sportbike Performance Handbook* (Motorbooks: 1998) and is currently finishing his next project for Motorbooks International, *Superbikes*, a history of performance motorcycles.

Peter Egan Each month, hundreds of thousands of fans read the work of *Cycle World* columnist Peter Egan, and through that column know of his passion for Harley-Davidson motorcycles. Motorbooks International recently published *Leanings*, an anthology of Egan's columns and articles from *Cycle World*.

Greg Field Greg Field has written a number of books on the subject of motorcycles, including several volumes dealing with Harley-Davidson, including the critically acclaimed *Harley-Davidson Evolution* (Motorbooks International: 2001). His latest book is *Original Harley-Davidson Panhead* (Motorbooks International: 2002).

Allan Girdler Allan Girdler has been a key figure in motorcycle journalism since the dawn of the genre as we know it. A former editor for *Cycle* magazine, Girdler is now an editor for *Cycle World*. His latest book is *Harley-Davidson in the 1960s* (Motorbooks International: 2001).

Jerry Hatfield Respected historian Jerry Hatfield has written a number of books on early motorcycles, including *Harley-Davidson Flatheads* (Motorbooks International: 1999). His latest book, *Indian Scout*, was published by Motorbooks International in 2001.

Darwin Holmstrom Darwin Holmstrom has written for a variety of motorcycle magazines and is the author of *The Complete Idiot's Guide to Motorcycles*. His latest book, *BMW Motorcycles*, was published in 2002 by Motorbooks International.

Chris Maida Chris Maida is the editor of *American Iron* magazine, and is currently working on his next book, *101 Harley-Davidson Twin Cam Performance Projects* (Motorbooks International: 2003).

Mike Seate When not toiling at his day job as a columnist for the Pittsburg Tribune-Review, Mike Seate writes books on his favorite topic: motorcycling. He is currently finishing his latest volume for Motorbooks International, *Choppers*, a history of custom motorcycles.

Hunter S. Thompson When the names of great American writers are compiled for future literary canons, Hunter S. Thompson will join the select group—Hemingway, Dickinson, Fitzgerald, Whitman, Twain, Poe—who make the short list for all-time greatest. His first book (*Hell's Angels: A Strange and Terrible Saga*, from which the excerpt here is adapted) redefined journalism.

Herbert Wagner Herbert Wagner is the preeminent expert on the early years of Harley-Davidson. His books include Motorbooks International's *Classic Harley-Davidson 1903-1941*.

Brock Yates Brock Yates is one of the most respected journalists in all of motor sports. Author of *Outlaw Machine*, an in-depth look at the culture of Harley-Davidson, Yates is also the madman responsible for the infamous Cannonball Sea-to-Shining-Sea Memorial Trophy Dash, an illegal cross-country race chronicled in Yates' latest book, *Cannonball!* (Motorbooks International: 2002).

Ed Youngblood In 1970 Ed Youngblood began a 28-year career with the American Motorcyclist Association, including a 19-year stint as President and CEO. He has written a number of excellent books, including *A Century of Indian*, published in 2001 by Motorbooks International.

Nick Cedar For years Nick Cedar's Harley-Davidson collages have added a unique narrative perspective to Motorbooks International's Harley-Davidson calendars.

David Dewhurst David Dewhurst's brilliant photography has appeared in motorcycle and automotive enthusiast magazines for over two decades. This is his first book for Motorbooks International.

Jeff Hackett Jeff Hackett is a social deviant whose photographic talent is of such a high caliber that we continue to bail him out of jail each time he is arrested for engaging in an unnatural act. Hackett's photography has appeared in a number of other Motorbooks International titles, including Allan Girdler's *Harley-Davidson in the 1960s*. He's a very sick man, but we love him anyway.

Michael Lichter After a short stint of playing drums in a BeBop jazz band, Michael Lichter decided he was a better photographer than a drummer and hung up the sticks. It was during this time that he started riding his 1971 Harley Davidson (which he still owns) and photographing bikers. An exhibition of his photography at the Gallery of Photography in Dublin, Ireland was boycotted by the League of Decency. He is currently working on an art book of Sturgis photography to be published by Motorbooks International.

PHOTO CREDITS

Nick Cedar: 13, 47, 69, 99, 131, 157, 158-159, 166, 170, 171, 191, 226, 229, 271, 305, 329, 367

Rick Connor Collection: 22 (bottom), 42 (top), 55, 74 (bottom), 87 (right)

Cycle World: 172 (top and bottom), 358

David Dewhurst: 8, 62 (top), 144, 145, 146-147, 151, 152, 156, 176 (left), 176-177, 178-179, 180 (top and bottom), 181, 182 (top and bottom), 183 (top and bottom), 184, 185 (top and bottom), 188-189, 228, 230, 231 (bottom), 234-235, 236-237, 238 (left), 238-239, 240 (top and bottom), 243, 245 (top and bottom), 246, 254, 256, 257, 258-259, 259, 260 (top and bottom), 264, 266-267, 273, 274-275, 276 (top and bottom), 277, 288, 289, 290, 291, 293, 294 (top and bottom), 295 (left), 316 (bottom), 317 (top and bottom), 321 (top left), 322, 323 (left, top right, and bottom right), 328, 360-361, 362 (bottom), 363, 364, 365, 368, 371, 374 (left and right), 375 (top and bottom), 378 (left and right)

Greg Field: 233

Greg Field Collection: 242, 243, 253

Allan Girdler Collection: 337 (top and bottom), 338 (top left and bottom left), 344, 345, 349

Jeff Hackett: 6, 10, 12, 14, 15 (bottom), 16-17, 18, 19, 20 (bottom), 21, 22 (top), 23, 24 (right), 25, 26, 28-29, 30 (top and bottom), 31, 35 (top and bottom), 36-37, 37 (right), 38, 39 (top, middle, bottom), 40-41, 44, 45, 46, 49 (bottom), 50, 51 (top), 52, 54 (top and bottom), 56 (top and bottom), 57 (top and bottom), 58-59, 60 (left), 63 (left and right), 68, 70, 71 (top and bottom), 72, 73 (top and bottom), 74 (top), 75, 76 (top and bottom), 77, 78, 80, 81, 82 (left), 82-83, 84, 85 (bottom left), 88-89, 90 (top and bottom), 91, 92-93, 93 (top and bottom), 94, 96, 97 (top and bottom), 98, 100-101, 102, 103, 104, 105 (top and bottom), 106, 107 bottom, 108 (left), 108-109, 110, 111, 112, 113 (top and bottom), 114-115, 116, 117 (top and bottom), 118-119, 119 (right), 122, 123 (top and bottom), 124, 125 (bottom), 126-127, 128, 129 (left and right), 134, 162 (left), 162-163, 164, 165, 167, 168-169, 169, 173, 174, 175, 186, 187, 189 (right), 190, 192-193, 194, 195, 196, 199, 200 (top and bottom), 201, 202 (left), 202-203, 204, 205 (top and bottom), 207, 208, 209, 210 (left), 210-211, 212, 213 (top and bottom), 214-215, 216 (top and bottom), 217, 218-219, 220, 221, 222-223, 223 (right), 227, 231, 232, 237, 241, 244, 247, 248 (left), 248-249, 250, 251, 255, 256, 257, 261 (top and bottom), 262-263, 265 (top and bottom), 270, 272, 278 (left), 278-279, 280-281, 281 (right), 282, 283, 284, 285, 286-287, 292 (top and bottom), 295 (right), 296-297, 298, 299 (right), 304, 306-307, 307 (right), 308 (top and bottom), 309, 310, 311, 312, 313, 314 (top and bottom), 315, 316 (top), 321 (top right and bottom), 324-325, 325 (right), 327, 331 (top left and top right), 332, 333, 335, 336, 338-339, 340-341, 341 (bottom right), 346-347, 348, 350-351, 352 (top left and bottom left), 352-353, 354, 355, 356, 357 (top and bottom), 360 (left), 362 (top), 366, 369 (top and bottom), 372-373, 376-377, 379

Jerry Hatfield: 48, 64, 65 (top and bottom), 67, 86-87

Jerry Hatfield Collection: 32, 33

Darwin Holmstrom: 300, 301, 302, 303, 318

Randy Leffingwell: 11, 142, 198

Michael Lichter: 130, 133 (top and bottom), 135, 136-137, 138, 139, 148-149, 150, 153

Chris Maida Collection: 268 (top and bottom), 269

Mike Seate Collection: 120, 121 (top and bottom), 140, 141

Herbert Wagner Collection: 15 (top), 20 (top), 24 (left), 27 (top and bottom), 34, 42 (bottom), 43, 49 (top), 51 (bottom), 53, 60-61, 62 (bottom), 66, 75 (top), 79, 85 (top left, right), 95, 107, 116 (bottom), 125, 132-133, 143, 144, 151 (bottom), 152 (bottom), 155, 160, 330, 331 (bottom), 334 (top and bottom), 344, 380

Ed Youngblood Collection: 343

MOTORCYCLE OWNERS

2000 Springfield mile, Scott Parker/Nicky Hayden, 354; 90th Annual H/D Parade, 255; Algreo, Barry, 51 (top photo); Argersinger, Phil, 63; Battlefield H/D (Gettysburg, PA), 366, 376, 377, 379; Beitler, Tim, 124; Bergan, Jeff, 97, 123; Bielefeldt, Harlen, 45; Biker Billy & Cruising Rider, 272, 278, 279, 321; Bishop, Bob, 73, 340-341; Bordigioni Dean (Golden Gate H/D), 106, 204-205, 208; Buell, 310, 311, 312, 313; Buell/American Iron, 322-323; Carlton, Dave, 164; Carr, Chris (VR 1000), 360-361; Chasteen, Don, 161, 186; Connecticut State Police, 125; Culver, Jeff, 232; D'Angelo, Dennis, 116; Danbury H/D & Rod Pink, 324, 325, 327; Davidson, Chalmer, 19; Daya, Tony, 346-347; Delgado, Nancy, 357; Dillingham, Jake, 96; Dron, Bob (Oakland, CA H/D), 280-281; Dugan, Brent, 112; DuHamel, Miguel (VR-1000 race team H/D), 372-373; Duley, John (Connecticut State Police), 10; Eggers, Bill & Walt Ritchie, 12, 14; Eggers, Bill, 22; Errico, Bob, 213; Esposito, Pat, 68, 77, 82, 82-83, 90, 91, 114-115, 118-119, 199; Esposito, Pete, 90, 105, 118-119; Fatland, Arlen, 92, 93, 94; Friedman, L., 35; Fronk, Carl, 304, 306, 307, 308, 309; Funk, Don, 162, 162-163, 187; Fusiak, Dave, 24, 25, 56, 57; Gagne, Bob, 76; Georgeanni, Dave, 6; Gilbert, Jeff, 20, 26; Glasserow, Jeff / Rusty Lowry / Jon Schultz / Keith Campbell, 350; Glazner, Jim, 194-195; Gonzalez, Louis, 97, 196, 332-333; Gourlay, John (American Iron & Buell), 314, 315, 316; Grindle, Jerri, 168-169; H/D VR 1000 Race Team, 360; Hansen, Maureen, 64; Hilberger, Al, 39, 49; Hollingsworth, Mike, 248-249; Holsinger, Lynn, 247; Hundertfund, Fred, 113; Jacobs, Scott & Gene; Thompson, 281, 292; Jacobs, Scott (Oceanside H/D), 264, 270; Jacobs, Scott, 284, 285, 286, 287; Janiszewski, David, 54; Jones, R.L., 331; Junker, Rolf, 119, 122, 123; Kiesow, Dave (Illinois H/D, Berwyn, IL), 52, 58-59; Knezevic, Joe (America Iron / H/D), 369; Lange, Michael, 44, 333; Lewandowski, Gayle / Pete Orlando, 110; Lindsay, Bruce, 15, 16-17, 18; Livertella, Charles, 200, 201, 202; Mahar, Tom, 126-127; Maida, Chris (American Iron), 298-299; Miller, Don (Metro M/C Clothing), 221; Miller, Raymond, 54, 57; Monahan, Dave, 86-87, 88-89, 105, 111, 134; Mussman, Kyle, 21, 28-29, 30, 75; Myrhe, Arvid, 78; Nester, Tim, 107; Oldigies, Jim, 355-356; Otten, P.J., 265; Paryzek, David, 129; Paul, Dino (HP Cycles), 202-203; Peale, Mallard, 98, 102, 108, 109; Pipech, Ben, 231; Prickett, Walt Sr., 237; Riggs, Scott, 84, 85; Ruffino, Mike, 80, 103, 104; San Diego H/D, 207; Schaeffer, Walt, 348; Schaub, Fred, 38, 39; Scheffer, Dave, 167; Schneider, Roy, 60; Smith, Ray, 70, 71, 73, 100-101, 261; Smith, Ron, 214-215, 216; Smith, Russell, 40, 41; Spencer, Mark (Spencer Cycles, NJ), 174-175; Steel, John, 352-353, 357; Steele, Abby (Benjy's H/D), 250-251; Steele, Amanda (Benjy's H/D), 190, 222, 223, 227; Steele, Benjy (Benjy's H/D, Huntington, WV), 23, 72, 113, 217, 218, 219, 220, 241, 244, 282, 296-297; Steele, Jacob (Benjy's H/D), 261, 262-263; Szulewski, Trish (American Iron), 2-3; Thompson, Gene and Scott Jacobs, 283, 295; Thompson, Mike, 209, 210, 211, 212; Tine, Ted (Essex Motorsports, Chester, CT), 30, 36-37, 50, 81, 128, 129, 173; Tortorici, Ed, 192-193; Tsunis, George, 117; Turski, Ray, 65; Unknown, 31, 35, 46, 74, 335; Vespa, Frank (Classic Cycles), 352; Walksler, Dale (Wheels Through Time), 336; Zimmerman, Mark, 189; Zrubek, Dick, 338-339

Index

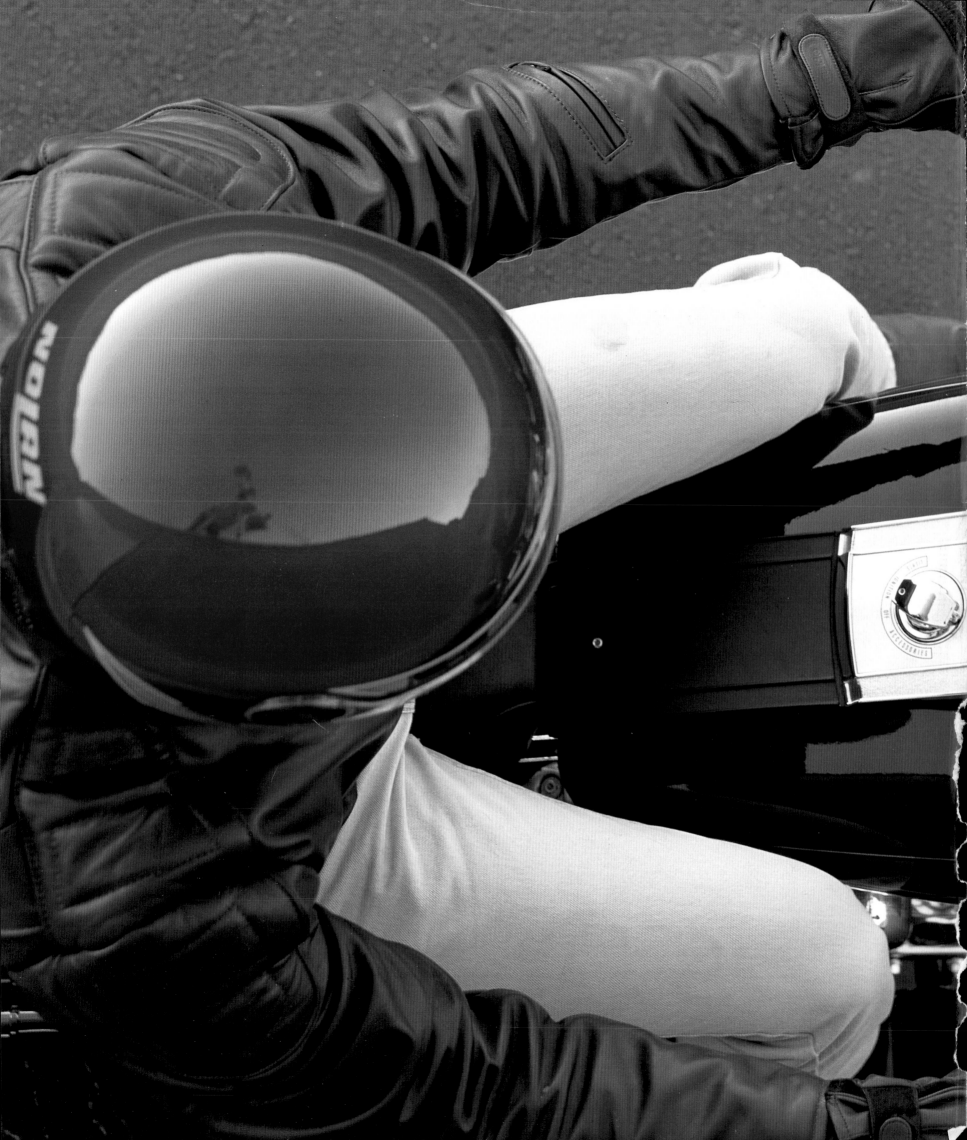